KT-479-093

TANTE MARIE'S FRENCH KITCHEN

TANTE MARIE'S

French Kitchen

TRANSLATED AND ADAPTED

BY CHARLOTTE TURGEON

ENGLISH ADAPTATION

BY ANN ROGERS

Decorated by Julian Brazelton

LONDON
NICHOLAS KAYE

First published by
Nicholas Kaye Ltd
194 Bishopsgate, London, EC2
1950

Reprinted 1950
Reprinted 1951
Reprinted 1952
Reprinted 1954
Reprinted 1955
Reprinted 1956
Reprinted 1957

Printed in England by
ADLARD AND SON LIMITED
London and Dorking

Contents

Introduction

La Véritable Cuisine de Famille par Tante Marie, more commonly known as *Tante Marie,* has been used by generations of French families. The fact that few changes have been made in the many editions that have been published bears witness to the fundamental secrets of French cooking—timelessness and simplicity. The French cuisine, despite its reputation for quality and artistry, is basically simple. It is true than an able French chef can produce culinary wonders of *haute cuisine* that seem extremely complicated, but these complexities are usually matters of decoration and presentation, not of cooking.

French home cooking includes a wide variety of foods. This volume contains recipes for everything from hors-d'œuvre to home-made liqueurs, but there is nothing in it too difficult for an ordinary housewife. Admirers of French cuisine often despair of trying to reproduce it in their own kitchens, fearing that the herbs and ingredients cannot be found in this country. Actually, in spite of the wonderful meals a French hostess invariably provides, there is no ingredient that cannot be found in a good grocer's shop or grown in a kitchen garden.

The French housewife of many generations ago was aware of the importance of time and money in cooking, as the modern woman is nowadays. She knew nothing of frozen or frosted foods or even modern vitamin theories, but the French have instinctively known for centuries how to get the most in flavour and nutrition from every food. The economical and high-in-vitamin parts of animals, such as liver, brains, and sweetbreads, have long been common in everyday diet; vegetables have always been cooked in as little water as possible and the vegetable water used in a variety of ways.

This book is written for homes where one is obliged to consider time and money. All the recipes are given in the clearest and simplest terms possible, so that even those entirely unaccustomed to cooking may readily understand.

Liberties of addition and omission have been taken in preparing this book for use outside France. Measurements and methods have been adapted according to modern standards. For those who know certain dishes by their French name only, or who enjoy presenting their culinary efforts under a French title, we have given both English and French recipe names. Most of the recipes are designed for 4 people. Some of the dinner-party recipes are obviously planned for 8 to 10 guests.

The French proverbs scattered throughout were added in the designing of the book and do not appear in the original *Tante Marie*.

Tante Marie presents her cookery book with the following words:

AVIS

Ce livre de cuisine s'adresse aux intérieurs modestes où l'on est obligé de compter avec le temps et l'argent.

Toutes nos recettes sont formulées en termes simples et compréhensibles pour les personnes les plus étrangères à la cuisine. De plus, ces recettes sont peu coûteuses et donnent les quantités pour trois ou quatre personnes.

Quelle est aussi la maîtresse de maison qui n'adresse pas, quinze fois par mois, cette question à son mari: 'Dis-moi donc ce que je pourrais faire aujourd'hui pour dîner?' Et le mari de répondre invariablement: 'Fais ce que tu voudras.'

*   *   *

NOTA BENE. *Afin d'être absolument clair dans nos recettes, nous n'avons pas craint de répéter plusieurs fois un même mot dans une phrase. Nos lecteurs nous sauront gré d'avoir évité les recherches de style dans un ouvrage qui n'en comporte pas.*

OVEN TEMPERATURE CHART

For kitchens equipped with the various well-known makes of gas cookers with thermostat regulators, the following chart shows the appropriate settings for the Fahrenheit temperatures used in the 'Tante Marie' recipes.

CENTRE OVEN TEMP. °F	THERMO- STAT SETTING
240°	¼
260°	½
280°	1
300°	
320°	2
340°	3
360°	4
380°	5
400°	6
420°	7
440°	8
460°	9
480°	

The Publishers are indebted to the North Thames Gas Board for the information in this chart.

Sauces

Good sauces are an indispensable part of good cooking. The more one knows about their preparation, the greater the variety in one's cooking. This does not mean that the sauces need be complicated or expensive. We shall show our readers how to master this art and thereby discover the secret of French cooking.

TANTE MARIE

TO BIND SAUCES: The purpose of binding sauces is to make them thicker or richer. One must take care that the eggs and flour used do not spoil rather than improve the sauces. This means careful preparation. Soups are thickened in the same manner.

BINDING WITH EGGS: Take one or more eggs according to the amount of sauce. One egg is enough for a pint of sauce. Separate the yolks from the whites. Beat the yolks slightly, adding 1 tablespoon of water per yolk. Stir in a little of the hot sauce that is to be thickened, mix well, and pour the egg mixture into the rest of the sauce, which has been removed from the fire. Blend the mixture thoroughly. Stir over a very low flame or in the top of a double boiler until the sauce has reached the desired thickness. The sauce must not boil or the eggs will curdle.

BINDING WITH EGGS AND CREAM: Follow directions for BINDING WITH EGGS, but substitute cream for the water.

BINDING WITH BUTTER AND FLOUR: Mix 1 tablespoon of flour with 1 oz. of softened butter. Form tiny balls of the mixture and gradually drop them into the hot sauce. Let the sauce simmer for several minutes but do not let it boil.

BINDING WITH BUTTER AND CORNFLOUR: Substitute 1 dessertspoon of cornflour for the flour and follow directions in the preceding paragraph. Do not let the sauce simmer more than 2 minutes.

BINDING WITH FLOUR: Take 1 dessertspoon of flour per pint of sauce. Blend with a little water until perfectly smooth. Stir into the sauce. Continue stirring a moment over a low heat, and serve immediately.

BINDING WITH CORNFLOUR: Mix 1 teaspoon of cornflour with 2 tablespoons of water. Add a little of the hot sauce. When it is thoroughly blended, add to the rest of the sauce. Stir over a low heat until the sauce is very hot. Serve immediately.

BINDING WITH BLOOD: This form of thickening is used in sauces served with wild game. Add the blood of the animal to the liver, which has been crushed to a paste. Add gradually to the sauce, stirring constantly. Reheat the sauce but do not let it boil. Serve immediately.

1. Béchamel Sauce. *Sauce béchamel*

2 ozs. butter	salt
2 tablespoons flour	pepper
½ pint warm milk	

Melt the butter. Add the flour and stir over medium heat until very light brown. Add the warm milk and stir until sauce is thick. Season with salt and pepper.

2. Cream Sauce *Sauce à la crème*

2 ozs. butter	salt
1 tablespoon flour	white pepper
1 gill cream	chopped chives or spring onion
Chopped parsley	

Melt the butter. Stir in flour and, when thoroughly blended, add cream, spring onion, salt, pepper, and parsley. Stir over low heat until the sauce is very thick.

3. White Sauce *Sauce blanche*

2 ozs. butter	1 egg yolk beaten with
1 tablespoon flour	½ teaspoon vinegar
½ pint hot water	salt
	white pepper

Melt the butter and stir in the flour. Add the water and, when the sauce is smooth, add the egg yolk little by little, stirring constantly and taking care that the sauce does not boil. Season with salt and pepper.

4. Caper Sauce *Sauce blanche aux câpres*

Make a White Sauce (3) but do not use the vinegar. Add capers just before serving.

5. Brown Sauce I   *Roux brun*

2 ozs. butter	salt
1 tablespoon flour	dash of freshly ground black
½ pint hot stock or water	pepper

Melt the butter and stir in flour. Continue stirring until mixture is light brown. Add the liquid and seasonings. Cook until the sauce is thick. If this sauce is too thick for the particular recipe calling for it, add more liquid.

6. Brown Sauce II   *Roux blanc*

This sauce is made in the same way as Brown Sauce I except that the heated liquid is added as soon as the flour and butter are blended. It is, therefore, lighter in colour.

7. Blanquette Sauce   *Sauce blanquette*

Follow directions for Cream Sauce (2), but substitute water for the cream.

8. Poulette Sauce   *Sauce poulette*

Follow directions for Cream Sauce (2), but substitute water for the cream and thicken with an egg (page 3). Add chopped parsley.

9. Maître d'hôtel Sauce   *Sauce maître d'hôtel*

3 ozs. butter	black pepper
chopped parsley	Juice of half a lemon, or a dash of
chopped spring onion	wine vinegar
salt	

Heat all the ingredients together but do not let them boil.
Serve very hot.

10. Hollandaise Sauce   *Sauce hollandaise aux œufs*

4 ozs. butter	1 dessertspoon wine vinegar
2 egg yolks	salt

Melt the butter in the top of a double boiler. Add the other
ingredients, stirring constantly until the sauce thickens.

11. Butter Sauce   *Sauce hollandaise au beurre*

4 ozs. butter	1 teaspoon salt

Melt the butter over a low flame. Add the salt and beat vigorously
with a wire whisk. The butter should be almost boiling. Serve
in a heated sauce-boat. This sauce is served with boiled fish.

12. Piquant Sauce   *Sauce piquante*

3 tablespoons wine vinegar	1 oz. butter
black pepper	2 tablespoons chopped gherkin
1 chopped shallot (or grated onion)	½ pint Brown Sauce 1 (5)
chopped parsley	

Mix the vinegar, pepper, shallot, parsley, and butter. Heat until
the butter is melted. Add to the Brown Sauce, and just before
serving add the gherkin. This sauce is used with various pork
and beef dishes.

B

13. Madeira Sauce   *Sauce Madère*

Brown Sauce 1 (5)   salt and pepper
bouquet garni (42)   3 tablespoons Madeira wine

Prepare the Brown Sauce using stock instead of water. Tinned
consommé or beef cubes dissolved in water may be used. Allow
the *bouquet garni* to simmer in the sauce for 20 to 30 minutes.
Just before serving remove the *bouquet garni* and add the wine.
This sauce is excellent with roast beef, steak, and beef kidneys.

14. Black Butter Sauce   *Beurre noir*

4 ozs. butter   2 or 3 sprigs of parsley
2 tablespoons wine vinegar

Melt the butter and heat until dark brown. Take care that it does
not burn. Throw in the parsley and let it fry for a moment or
two. Pour this over the food that is to be served. Return the
pan to the flame and put in the vinegar. As soon as the vinegar
is hot—which is a matter of seconds—pour over the same food.
This sauce is used for fish, brains, and egg dishes.

15. Poor Man's Sauce   *Sauce au pauvre homme*

5 shallots (or tiny onions), finely   chopped parsley
   chopped   salt and pepper
1 pint stock or water

Mix the ingredients and let them simmer until the shallots are
tender. This sauce is good with left-overs.

16. Robert Sauce *Sauce Robert*

2 ozs. butter
2 onions, finely chopped
1 tablespoon made mustard
1 tablespoon flour

½ pint stock
1 teaspoon wine vinegar
salt and pepper

Fry the onions in the butter until they are pale yellow. Add the flour and stir in well. Stir in the liquid and let the sauce simmer for 5 minutes or longer. Just before serving add mustard and vinegar and season with salt and pepper. This sauce is excellent with left-over meat and poultry and with lamb or mutton chops.

17. Mayonnaise *Sauce mayonnaise*

1 egg yolk
salt
white pepper

1 teaspoon wine vinegar (or lemon
   juice)
½ pint olive oil

Combine egg yolk, salt, pepper, and vinegar or lemon juice in a deep bowl. Add the olive oil drop by drop, beating constantly until the sauce is thick and all the oil has been used. If the sauce tastes too oily, add more vinegar or lemon juice. Tante Marie recommends the use of a silver fork or spoon. It is more easily and quickly made, however, with a rotary (hand or electric) beater. The secret is in adding the oil very slowly.

18 Green Mayonnaise *Sauce mayonnaise verte*

Prepare Mayonnaise (17). Add chopped chervil, and chopped chives.

19. Pepper Sauce   *Sauce poivrade*

Brown Sauce 1 (5)
2 teaspoons wine vinegar   *bouquet garni* (42)
1 chopped shallot (or small onion)   a little salt
chopped parsley   a large pinch of freshly ground
chopped chives   black pepper

Combine all the ingredients and simmer 20 minutes. Strain and serve. This sauce is excellent with cold meats, especially pork.

20. Tartar Sauce   *Sauce tartare*

1 egg yolk   1 teaspoon wine vinegar
3 shallots (or very small onions),   ½ teaspoon prepared mustard
   finely chopped   ½ pint olive oil
chopped chervil   salt
chopped tarragon   pepper

Beat the egg yolk slightly. Add the shallots, herbs, vinegar and mustard, salt and pepper. Add the oil, drop by drop, beating constantly until the sauce is thick. See directions for making Mayonnaise (17). Another way to achieve almost the same result is to combine the various herbs and mustard with half a pint of previously prepared or bought mayonnaise. Home-made mayonnaise is always better.

21. Tomato Sauce   *Sauce tomate*

8 large tomatoes   1 clove garlic
1 onion, thinly sliced   1 oz. butter
a sprig of thyme (or dried thyme)   1 teaspoon cornflour
bay leaf   salt and pepper

Crush the tomatoes in a heavy saucepan. Add onion, thyme, bay leaf, and garlic and simmer until the tomatoes are soft. Take care that they do not burn. Force the tomatoes through a strainer or food mill. Work the cornflour into the butter and add to the tomato purée. Season with salt and pepper and simmer 15 or 20 minutes more.

22. Italian Tomato Sauce   *Sauce tomate à l'italienne*

2 ozs. butter (or 2 tablespoons olive oil)	1 small tin of tomato paste
1 onion, finely chopped	4 fresh tomatoes (or 1 tin of tomatoes)
1 clove garlic, chopped	$\frac{1}{2}$ pint red wine
salt and pepper	1 teaspoon sugar

Fry the onion and garlic in the butter or olive oil until the onion is transparent. Add the rest of the ingredients and let the sauce simmer 2 to 3 hours over a very low flame. The sauce should be quite thick. Variations of this sauce are made by adding lean meat, prawns, shrimps, or lobster meat. The meat, veal or beef, can be chopped or minced and fried with the onions. The prawns, shrimps, or pieces of lobster meat are added 15 minutes before the sauce is served.

23. Rémoulade Sauce   *Sauce rémoulade*

Several tarragon leaves	1 small clove of garlic
The leaves of half a bunch of watercress	chopped parsley
	$\frac{1}{2}$ teaspoon made mustard
chopped chives	$\frac{1}{2}$ pint Mayonnaise (17)

Pound the tarragon, watercress, chives, garlic, and parsley to a smooth paste. Combine the paste with the mustard and mayonnaise.

24. Ravigote Sauce   *Sauce ravigote*

Several tarragon leaves
The leaves of half a bunch of
    watercress
chopped chives
1 small clove of garlic

chopped chervil or parsley
salt and pepper
½ teaspoon made mustard
2 tablespoons wine vinegar
1 gill olive oil

Pound the tarragon, watercress, chives, garlic, and parsley to
a smooth paste. Mix thoroughly with mustard, oil, and vinegar
and season with salt and pepper. This is an excellent sauce for
cold meats.

25. Curry Sauce   *Sauce au kari*

2 ozs. butter
1 tablespoon flour

1 teaspoon curry powder
½ pint stock

Melt the butter. Add flour and curry powder. Mix well but do
not allow it to brown. Add the stock. Simmer 2 to 3 minutes.
Strain and serve. This sauce is good for wild game.

26. Italian Herb Sauce   *Sauce italienne*

chopped parsley
chopped shallots (or tiny onions)
1 clove of garlic, finely chopped
2 chopped mushrooms
¼ pint white wine (dry)

1 teaspoon olive oil
1 teaspoon cornflour
knob of butter
salt
black pepper

Simmer the parsley, shallots, garlic, and mushrooms in the wine
for 20 minutes. Add oil, salt, and pepper. Mix the butter and
cornstarch and gradually stir into the sauce. Simmer for a
moment longer.

27. Truffle Sauce   *Sauce Périgueux*

2 truffles	1 tablespoon flour
6 large mushrooms	1 gill hot water
½ clove of garlic	1 gill white wine (dry)
chopped parsley	salt
chopped chives	freshly ground black pepper
1 teaspoon olive oil	

Chop the truffles, mushrooms, garlic, parsley, and chives together until they make a smooth paste. Add oil and heat over a slow flame. Add the flour and, when it is well blended, add the water, wine, salt, and pepper. Simmer 20 minutes. Skim off the fat and serve.

28. Anchovy Butter   *Beurre d'anchois*

6 anchovy fillets (or 1 tablespoon anchovy paste)
    2 ozs. butter

Pound the fillets to a paste or use the prepared paste. Mix with the butter, which has been softened but not melted, using a fork or a mortar and pestle.

29. Financière Sauce   *Sauce financière*

2 lamb's kidneys   *bouquet garni* (42)
2 chicken livers   2 mushrooms
2 cockscombs (if possible)   2 truffles
½ pint stock   6 *quenelles* (38)
1 oz. butter   salt
1 tablespoon lemon juice   freshly ground black pepper
Brown Sauce II (6)

Split kidneys and remove the hard core of fat. Cut kidneys, livers, cockscombs, into small pieces. Soak in cold water for 3 hours. Drain well and cook slowly in stock, lemon juice and butter for 30 minutes. Drain and use the liquor to make Brown Sauce II. Add the meats, *bouquet garni*, mushrooms, and truffles, thinly sliced, and *quenelles* (these may be omitted). Season with salt and pepper and cook slowly for 1 hour. This sauce is used with vol-au-vents, chicken fricassee, and macaroni rings.

30. Béarnaise Sauce   *Sauce Béarnaise*

3 tablespoons wine vinegar   3 egg yolks
2 tablespoons water   4 ozs. butter
1 spring onion, chopped   salt
1 teaspoon chopped chervil or   1 teaspoon chopped parsley
    parsley,   1 teaspoon chopped tarragon
black pepper   leaves

Combine the vinegar, water, spring onion, parsley, and pepper. Simmer 5 minutes. Meanwhile melt the butter in the top of a double boiler. Add the egg yolks and stir until the mixture thickens. Gradually add the hot vinegar, which has been strained stirring constantly so that the eggs will not curdle. Season with salt. Just before serving, add chopped parsley and tarragon leaves. This is delicious with steak.

31. French Dressing   *Sauce vinaigrette*

1 teaspoon chopped onion	$\frac{1}{4}$ teaspoon freshly ground black
1 teaspoon chopped chives	pepper
1 teaspoon chopped parsley	2 tablespoons wine vinegar
1 teaspoon salt	4 tablespoons olive oil

Mix all the seasonings with the vinegar and allow them to stand several minutes before combining with the oil. Mix thoroughly before serving.

32. Marinating Dressing   *Marinade*

3 tablespoons olive oil	a sprig of thyme
1 tablespoon wine vinegar	bay leaf
1 clove of garlic, finely chopped	chopped parsley

Place the ingredients in a shallow dish in which the food is to be marinated. The thyme and bay leaf should be crushed. Place the meat to be marinated in the dish and spoon the sauce over the meat several times a day. The meat should be turned from time to time. Some meats are marinated as long as 6 days before cooking.

33. Garlic Sauce   *Sauce méridionale*

2 cloves of garlic	1 gill milk
1 slice dry bread	$\frac{1}{2}$ pint Mayonnaise (17)

Pound the garlic to a smooth paste. Remove the crusts from the bread and soak in milk. Squeeze out the milk and mix the bread with the garlic. Add this mixture to the mayonnaise. This sauce is excellent with cold beef, lamb, or poultry.

34. Onion Sauce   *Sauce Soubise*

8 large onions   ½ pint hot water
3 ozs. butter   salt
2 tablespoons flour   pepper

Slice the onions as thinly as possible. Fry the onions in butter
over a low flame until they are yellow. Sprinkle the flour over
the onions and stir in gently. Add water, salt, and pepper and
simmer for 15 to 20 minutes. Serve with pork or lamb chops.

35. Spanish Pimento Sauce   *Sauce rouge au piment*

4 cloves of garlic   salt
2 red peppers   freshly ground black pepper
½ pint olive oil

After having removed all the seeds, parboil the peppers until
they are soft, or use tinned peppers. Pound the garlic and peppers
together until they form a smooth paste. Heat the oil and stir
into the garlic and pepper mixture. Season with salt and pepper.
This sauce is used with large fish.

36. Meat Essence   *Jus*

Jus is indispensable in real French cooking. It is made and
used to be sold commercially in France. It adds greatly to the
richness of sauces. Tinned consommé or meat cubes may be
used as a substitute, but they do not give the same quality to
a sauce that *jus* does. It can be made and kept in the refrigerator
for a very long time.

½ pound stewing beef   1 calf's foot (or 1 beef knuckle,
½ pound stewing veal   sawn in 4 pieces)

2 onions   salt
2 carrots   pepper
bouquet garni (42)   water
2 cloves

Place the beef, veal, onions, carrots, cloves, *bouquet garni*, salt, and pepper in a heavy saucepan that has a cover. Add ½ pint of water and cook until the meat juices begin to stick to the pan and the vegetables begin to brown. Add 1 pint of water and put in the calf's foot or knuckle. Any meat or poultry trimmings may also be added. Cook over a very low flame for 3 hours. Strain the liquid into a shallow pan and skim off the fat as it cools. A hard jelly will form. A small square of this will do wonders for a sauce.

37. Aspic

Many beautiful and delicious dishes may be prepared *en aspic*. 1 pint of Meat Essence (36) makes a perfect aspic. Rich meat, poultry, or fish stock combined with granulated gelatine (1 tablespoon gelatine to 1 pint liquid) is very satisfactory.

TO CLARIFY STOCK: It is the clarity of the jelly that gives aspic its particular splendour. When the stock that is to be used has been properly seasoned and the gelatine has been added, the following method is used to clarify it: Beat 2 egg whites until foamy. Add ½ teaspoon salt, 1 teaspoon wine vinegar, and 1 teaspoon cooking brandy. Stir this mixture into the stock and heat to boiling point. Remove from the fire quickly and pour the stock through a double thickness of cheesecloth or a clean kitchen towel. If the jelly is pale, add a little colouring.

TO LINE MOULDS: Enough jelly should be prepared so that the mould may be filled. Fill a chilled mould with the liquid, which should be lukewarm. Place in the refrigerator for a few moments. When a thin layer of jelly has adhered to the bottom and sides of the mould, pour off the rest of the liquid. Place on this first layer of jelly the decorations called for or the first layer of food. The liquid should now be cool enough so that the first layer of jelly will not melt when the second is added. Pour in the second layer and let it jell. The rest of the food is then placed in the mould. Pour the rest of the jelly over the food. Care should be taken that there is a layer of jelly between the food and the mould. Let the mould stand in a cold place until the jelly is firm. When the time comes to serve the mould, place it on a serving dish. Cover with a hot towel and the mould will slip off easily.

38. Forcemeat   *Quenelles*

½ pound lean veal or uncooked chicken	¼ lb. softened butter
	2 eggs
6 ozs. bread crumbs soaked in milk	salt and pepper

Put the meat through a mincer, using the finest blade. Drain the bread crumbs and mix with the butter and meat. Pound the mixture to a smooth paste. Separate the yolks and whites of the eggs. Stir the yolks into the paste. Season with salt and pepper. Fold in egg whites, beaten stiff. The traditional shape of *quenelles* is that of a small link sausage. Form by making little balls of the mixture and rolling them on a floured bread board. Drop into boiling salted water and cook 15 minutes.

39. Fish Forcemeat   *Quenelles maigres*

Substitute fish for meat in the preceding recipe.

40. Frying Batter   *Pâte à frire*

4 ozs. flour	1 teacup water
½ teaspoon salt	1 egg
1 teaspoon salad oil	1 tablespoon brandy (optional)

Beat the egg well and combine with the other ingredients. The batter should be smooth and quite thick. If a lighter batter is preferrred, beat the yolk and the white separately. Fold in the stiffly beaten egg white after the other ingredients have been well blended.

41. Deep Fat Frying

It is advisable to have a special pan reserved for deep fat frying. A deep iron or aluminium one is excellent. It is convenient to have a fat thermometer and frying basket. Lard, vegetable fats, and oil are all suitable for frying. The same fat may be used several times, although it should be poured out of the pan and stored in a cool place between times. To clean the fat, drop several slices of raw potato into the hot fat. The potato will absorb the odours, and extraneous matter will stick to it. It is poor economy not to use enough fat. The temperature should be kept as near constant as possible; otherwise the food will absorb the fat. The proper temperature will be indicated in each recipe. Fried food should be drained on absorbent paper and served immediately.

42. *Bouquet garni*

Bouquet garni is used very commonly in French cooking. It consists of 3 or 4 sprigs of parsley, a sprig of thyme, and a small bay leaf. The thyme should be surrounded by the parsley so that the little leaves will not float into the sauce. Tie the herbs together with string so that they may be removed before the dish which they are flavouring is served. A pinch of dried thyme and 1 teaspoon of dried parsley may be substituted, but in that case the sauce must be carefully strained before serving.

Mieux vaut bon repas que bel habit.

Hors-d'œuvre

HORS-D'ŒUVRE are not to be confused with the canapés served with cocktails. In France, the hors-d'œuvre are served at table in place of soup. They consist chiefly of meat, fish and vegetables served in the form of salad, and an occasional hot spicy cheese dish. The hors-d'œuvre should be decorative as well as delicious. At a family meal, one or two kinds are served; at dinner parties, a greater variety. French or Continental bread should be served with the hors-d'œuvre.

43. Radishes   *Radis*

Wash the radishes carefully. Cut the red peel into petals, leaving it attached to the base, so that the radish resembles a rosebud. Arrange in a silver or glass dish. Serve with butter.

44. Butter   *Beurre*

Although butter is not served with an ordinary meal in France, it is usually served with the hors-d'œuvre. Make butter balls or curls and sprinkle with chopped parsley.

45. Anchovies   *Anchois*

Alternate fillets of anchovies with slices of hard-boiled egg.
Sprinkle with finely chopped parsley.

46. Sardines

Arrange the sardines on a small dish. Decorate with slices of
lemon and sprigs of parsley.

47. Russian Caviar   *Caviar*

Season the caviar with a little finely chopped onion or shallot
and a dash of lemon juice. Arrange on a small, round serving
dish. Boil 2 eggs 10 minutes. When they are cool, separate the
yolks from the whites. Force the yolks through a fine strainer
and sprinkle over the caviar. Chop the egg whites fairly coarsely
and place around the caviar. Cover it all with a little chopped
parsley. Serve with triangles of hot buttered toast.

48. Red Caviar

Place the caviar in a strainer and let cold water run over it for
several moments. This will remove the excess salt and will
improve the flavour. Season and serve in the same way as Russian
Caviar (47).

49 Tunny Fish   *Thon*

Put the contents of a tin of tunny fish and 2 hard-boiled eggs
through a mincer. Add 2 ozs. of softened butter and some
chopped herbs (parsley, chives, and tarragon). Mix well and
shape into a small pyramid. Place on small serving dish and
decorate with sprigs of parsley and a little mayonnaise.

50. Salmon Salad   *Saumon*

Use either smoked, tinned, or cold boiled fresh salmon. Cut
into small pieces. Cut 2 cold boiled potatoes into pieces of the
same size. Blend with Mayonnaise (17). Place in a shallow dish
and surround with thin slices of cold beetroot or tomato.

51. Shrimp Butter   *Beurre de crevettes*

Pound tinned, potted, or boiled shelled shrimps to a smooth
paste. Mix with $\frac{1}{3}$ the amount of butter. Place on small dish.
Sprinkle with chopped parsley and serve with triangles of hot
buttered toast.

52. Lobster Butter   *Beurre de langoustes*

Substitute lobster meat for shrimp in the preceding recipe.

53. Shrimp Salad   *Crevettes*

Arrange fresh or tinned shrimps (see 51) on a thin layer of
Mayonnaise (17). Decorate with sprigs of parsley.

54. Cucumber Salad   *Concombres en salade*

Peel firm green cucumbers. Cut into paper-thin slices. Sprinkle
generously with salt and allow them to stand 45 minutes. Drain
the cucumbers dry. Cover with French Dressing (32).

c

55. Celeriac Salad   *Céleri-rave rémoulade*

Celeriac is a variety of celery grown for its turnip-like root. It is
not very common, but well worth growing.

Slice raw celeriac root very thinly. Marinate at least 8 hours
in 2 tablespoons oil, 1 tablespoon wine vinegar, ½ teaspoon salt,
and a dash of white pepper. Drain and mix with a Rémoulade
Sauce (23).

56. Red Cabbage Salad   *Chou rouge*

Shred a firm red cabbage. Cover with salt and let it stand 45
minutes. This will draw the water from the cabbage. Drain, and
mix with Mayonnaise (17) or French Dressing (31).

57. Lobster and Vegetable Salad   *Macédoine de langouste*

Combine 2 cups of mixed cooked vegetables, diced, with 2 cups
of lobster meat. Add 1 cup of Mayonnaise (17). Arrange the
salad on a dish in the form of a pyramid. Decorate with the
claws of the lobster and with sprigs of parsley.

58. Tongue Salad   *Langue de bœuf en salade*

Cut cold boiled beef tongue in very thin strips. Cover with
French Dressing (31) and sprinkle with chopped parsley.

59. Russian Salad   *Salade russe*

Combine cold boiled potatoes, cold beef, fresh tomatoes, and
boiled beetroot, all cut into small pieces, with Mayonnaise (17).

Add 1 teaspoon chopped parsley, 1 teaspoon chopped chives, and ¾ teaspoon chopped tarragon. Mound on a dish and frost with a thin layer of mayonnaise. Powder with chopped herbs (tarragon, parsley, and chives).

60. Tomato Salad   *Salade de tomates*

Choose small ripe tomatoes. Peel them or not as you wish. To peel easily, drop the tomatoes into boiling water for a moment, plunge into cold water, and then peel. Cut the tomatoes in thin slices, taking care not to cut through completely. Each person will be served a whole tomato. Cover with salt and let the tomatoes stand 45 minutes. Drain thoroughly and cover with French Dressing (31). Powder with chopped herbs (tarragon, parsley, and chives).

61. Fried Anchovies   *Anchois frits*

Dip anchovy fillets into beaten egg. Roll in flour and fry 2 minutes in deep fat (375°F.). Sprinkle with chopped parsley and serve on a heated dish.

62. Stuffed Artichoke Bottoms
Fonds d'artichauts aux champignons

Remove all the leaves from boiled artichokes, being careful not to break the artichoke bottom. Except in regions where artichokes are grown, it is more economical to buy the tinned artichoke bottoms. Fry the bottoms in butter and keep in warm place while frying ½ lb. chopped mushrooms in the same butter. Fill the bottoms with the mushrooms. Cover with grated gruyère and put under the grill until the cheese melts.

63. Leek Salad   *Poireaux à la vinaigrette*

Remove most of the green leaves from medium-sized leeks. Boil
25 minutes in salted water. Drain and cool. Cover with French
Dressing (31).

64. Lentil Salad   *Lentilles à la vinaigrette*

Soak ½ lb. lentils overnight. Drain and boil in salted water until
soft but not squashy. Drain, cool, and cover with French Dressing
(31).

65. Cheese Soufflé   *Soufflé au fromage*

¼ lb. butter	salt
2 ozs. flour	4 eggs
1 pint milk	¼ lb. freshly grated cheese

Melt butter and stir in flour. When it is blended, add milk and
salt. Stir until sauce thickens. Remove from the flame and cool.
Separate the egg yolks from the whites. Beat the yolks for 1
minute and add to the mixture. Add cheese. Beat egg whites
stiff and fold in carefully. Bake in buttered ramekins or baking
dish 20 minutes in 350°F. oven.

66. Cheese Sticks   *Allumettes au fromage*

See recipe 590.

67. Garlic Eggs   *Œufs à l'ail*

See recipe 143.

THE most delicious soups are made from the simplest ingredients. France is justly famous for the subtle art of soup making. In most French country homes the soup pot is constantly simmering on the back of the stove, and anything in the way of left-overs, spare morsels of meat and poultry and vegetables, are thrown into the soup pot. The result is a soup worthy of the finest chef. In so many modern homes constant cooking heat is no longer available and soup must be made according to definite recipes, such as these offered by Tante Marie to capture the subtle flavour and rich goodness of French soup.

NECESSARY UTENSILS: Chopping knife, chopping board or bowl, food mill, large stock pot, or saucepan.

BREAD AND CROUTONS: Most French soups call for bread or croutons. Stale or toasted bread cut into rounds with a biscuit cutter is very presentable. If croutons are called for, cut stale bread into cubes or 3-inch sticks and fry in melted butter. Turn the croutons frequently so that they will brown on all sides.

27

SUBSTITUTION FOR STOCK OR BOUILLON: Since many recipes pre-
suppose the stock pot with a constant source of stock, it is well
to have meat cubes, tinned consommé, or bouillon on the pantry
shelf. These make satisfactory substitutes.

68. Pot-au-feu

The famous French *pot-au-feu* provides the basis of a whole
week of good meals. Many kitchens start their weekly routine
by making this soup. If the dish is to be prepared for the sake
of the soup only, any of the cheapest cuts of beef may be used.
However, if a slightly better cut is used, the meat can be served
hot or cold or in a casserole dish.

3 pounds beef (shin, leg, top rump, or flank)*	2 carrots
	½ parsnip
6 quarts cold water	1 turnip
2 tablespoons salt	*bouquet garni* (42)
1 teaspoon black pepper	3 cloves
3 leeks	1 onion

Place the meat in a large pot. Add water, salt, and pepper. Bring
to the boil over a moderate heat. A white scum will form on the
water. Keep skimming this off until it has all disappeared. Slice
the leeks lengthwise and tie them together with string so that
they may easily be removed. Add the leeks, carrots, parsnip,
turnip, *bouquet garni*, and the onion stuck with the cloves. Let
this simmer for at least 4 hours. Pour the broth through a strainer
and skim off as much fat as possible before serving.

* A delicious chicken soup may be made by substituting a 4- to
5-pound dressed fowl for the meat.

To serve: Place several rounds of stale or toasted bread in the bottom of the soup tureen or individual soup plates. Pour the bouillon over the bread. If top rump has been used, place on a dish, surround with the vegetables and serve with gravy made of some of the bouillon thickened with cornflour (page 4). The rest of the bouillon should be kept in a cool place for future use.

A large variety of soups may be made with the broth of the *pot-au-feu*. The following six recipes (69-74) are recommended. For little children or invalids scalded milk may be used in place of the stock. In this case more salt should be added.

69. Broth with Rice   *Riz au gras*

2 pints bouillon   3 tablespoons rice

When the bouillon boils, add the rice, which has been washed in warm water. Simmer 30 minutes. If any carrots are left from the *pot-au-feu*, crush them and add to the soup. This will add flavour and colour and is known as *Potage Crécy au riz*.

70. Broth with Vermicelli   *Vermicelle au gras*

2 pints bouillon   3 tablespoons vermicelli

Boil the bouillon. Break the vermicelli into small pieces and add gradually, so that the broth will not cease boiling. Stir occasionally to keep vermicelli from sticking to saucepan. Cook 15 minutes and skim off the froth before serving.

71. Broth with Noodles or Macaroni

Pâtes d'Italie au gras

Follow directions for Broth with Vermicelli (70), using noodles or macaroni instead of vermicelli.

72. Broth with Semolina   *Potage à la semoule*

2 pints bouillon   4 tablespoons semolina

Add semolina to boiling bouillon, taking care that the semolina does not stick to the pan. Cook ½ hour.

73. Broth with Tapioca   *Potage au tapioca*

2 pints bouillon   2 tablespoons pearl tapioca

Add tapioca gradually to the boiling bouillon. Stir constantly so that the tapioca will not stick or lump. Cook 10 minutes only so that the broth will not be too thick.

74. Thickened Broth   *Potage à la fécule*

2 pints bouillon   1½ teaspoons cornflour

Mix the cornflour with a little cold bouillon. Add to the boiling bouillon. Cook 2 minutes, stirring constantly. Remove from the heat and the soup will clear.

75. Milk Soup   *Bouillie*

3 pints milk
3 tablespoons flour
croutons, or several slices buttered toast
salt and pepper

Scald the milk. Mix flour with a little cold milk and add slowly to the milk, stirring constantly. Salt and pepper to taste. Simmer 20 minutes and pour over toast.

76. Cabbage Soup   *Soupe aux choux*

6 pints water	3 leeks
½ lb. shoulder* or breast of lamb	1 turnip
½ lb. lean bacon	1 tablespoon chicken fat (optional)
2 carrots	1 cabbage
1 onion, stuck with 3 cloves	6 potatoes
½ parsnip	salt and pepper

Add lamb, bacon, salt, and pepper to the water and bring to boiling point over a moderate flame. A foam will form on the top and must be carefully skimmed off. Add the carrots, onion stuck with cloves, parsnip, leeks sliced lengthwise and tied together, turnip, and, if possible, the chicken fat. Let this cook 2 hours. Wash and take off the outer leaves of the cabbage. Cut in 4 parts. Peel the potatoes and add both cabbage and potatoes to the soup. Cook until the potatoes are soft. Fresh peas or string beans may be added with the cabbage. Season to taste.

* If the shoulder is used, remove and serve grilled the next day See recipe 258.

77. Leek and Potato Soup
Soupe aux poireaux et aux pommes de terre

5 or 6 leeks
2 ozs. butter
3 pints water
salt

5 or 6 potatoes
croutons (page 27)
freshly ground black pepper

Peel the leeks and cut into small pieces. Melt butter and fry the
leeks until they are brown. Add water and salt. Peel, wash, and
cut potatoes into small pieces and add to the soup pot. Cook
1 hour. Force the soup through a food mill, or crush the leeks
and potatoes with a potato masher. The soup should be thick.
Pour over the croutons and season with freshly ground black
pepper.

78. Sorrel Soup   *Soupe à l'oseille*

½ lb. sorrel leaves*
2 ozs. butter
3 pints water or stock
1 egg yolk

several pieces of stale or toasted
    bread
salt

Chop the sorrel leaves and place them in a heavy pot over a
low flame until the leaves are wilted and some of the water is
drawn off. Add the butter and when it is melted add liquid and
salt. Simmer 10 minutes. Beat the egg yolk slightly. Add a little
soup to the yolk, stirring constantly, and then add the egg
mixture to the soup. Do not let the soup boil after the egg has
been added. Pour over the bread and serve.

* Watercress leaves make an excellent substitute for the sorrel leaves.

79. Sorrel Soup with Rice   *Potage au riz à l'oseille*

Follow the preceding recipe for Sorrel Soup. When the soup boils, add 3 tablespoons of well-washed rice and cook 30 minutes. Finish by thickening with egg.

80. Sorrel Soup with Vermicelli   *Vermicelle à l'oseille*

Follow recipe for Sorrel Soup (78). Add 4 tablespoons of broken vermicelli and cook 15 minutes. Finish by thickening with egg.

81. Bread and Butter Soup   *Panade*

3 pints water or stock	3 ozs. butter
salt	1 egg yolk
½ lb. of French bread thinly sliced	1 teaspoon sugar

Place the bread in the salted water or stock. Bring to the boil and simmer for 10 minutes, stirring often. Add butter and thicken with egg (page 3). This soup is used especially for children, and the sugar is added for their benefit.

82. Pea Soup   *Potage Saint-Germain*

½ pint dried peas	salt and pepper
3 pints water or chicken stock	croutons

Cook peas in water or stock for 1½ hours. Force them through a food mill or sieve. Reheat, season with salt and pepper, and pour over fried croutons. The soup should be thick, but if it is too thick add more liquid. Rice or vermicelli may be cooked with the peas. In this case another pint of liquid should be added, and the soup should not be strained.

83. Lentil Soup   *Potage à la conti*

Follow directions for Pea Soup (82), substituting lentils for peas.
Serve with croutons.

84. Potato Soup   *Potage Parmentier*

5 or 6 potatoes	2 ozs. butter
3 pints water or chicken stock (or half water and half milk)	salt and black pepper croutons

Boil potatoes in liquid until they are very soft. Force through
a food mill or sieve. Reheat with the liquid. Add butter. Season
with salt and pepper and pour over croutons.

85. Dried Bean Soup   *Potage à la purée de haricots blancs*

1 pint dried haricot beans (any of the dried white beans are suitable)	2 ozs. butter salt and pepper croutons
3 pints stock or water	

Boil the beans in the liquid for 2 hours. Force through a food
mill or sieve. Reheat, adding more liquid if the soup is too thick.
Add butter, salt, and pepper and pour over croutons.

86. Kidney Bean Soup   *Potage Condé*

Follow the preceding recipe, using red kidney beans. Serve with
croutons.

87. Melon Soup   *Potage au potiron*

1 cooked melon	salt and pepper
2 pints milk	½ teaspoon sugar
2 ozs. butter	croutons

Crush the melon to a paste or force through a food mill. Add
to the hot milk and season with butter, salt, pepper, and sugar
(optional).   Reheat, stirring constantly. Pour over fried croutons
and serve immediately.

88. Onion Soup   *Soupe à l'oignon*

2 ozs. butter	freshly grated gruyère cheese
2 large onions	salt and freshly ground black
2 pints stock or water	pepper
rounds of dried French bread	

Slice onions as thinly as possible. Fry gently in melted butter
until yellow. Add water or stock and simmer until reduced by
one-quarter. Season with salt and pepper. Pour into bowls, add
bread that has been generously sprinkled with cheese and brown
under hot grill or in quick oven. This is another basic French
soup and has the following variations (89–93).

89. Onion Milk Soup   *Soupe à l'oignon et au lait*

Substitute milk for the stock or water in Onion Soup and omit
the cheese.

90. Onion Soup with Vermicelli   *Vermicelle à l'oignon*

Follow recipe for Onion Soup. Add 4 tablespoons of broken
vermicelli to the soup when it begins to simmer. Stir occasionally
so that the vermicelli will not stick.

91. Onion Soup with Semolina   *Semoule à l'oignon*

Follow the recipe for Onion Soup. When the soup reaches boiling point add 2 tablespoons of semolina and simmer 30 minutes.

92. Onion Soup with Rice   *Riz à l'oignon*

Follow directions for Onion Soup. When the soup reaches boiling point, add 2 tablespoons of rice and simmer 30 minutes.

93. Onion Soup with Tapioca   *Tapioca à l'oignon*

Follow directions for Onion Soup. When the soup has simmered 10 minutes, add 2 tablespoons of pearl tapioca and simmer 10 minutes more. Stir to prevent lumping of the tapioca.

94. Julienne Soup   *Julienne*

2 carrots	2 ozs. butter
2 small turnips	3 pints rich stock
2 potatoes	$\frac{1}{4}$ lb. peas (or $\frac{1}{4}$ lb. string beans)
2 leeks	salt and pepper
3 or 4 cabbage leaves	

Slice carrots, turnips, potatoes, leeks, and cabbage leaves into uniformly thin strips about $1\frac{1}{2}$ inches long. Fry vegetables in melted butter until they are brown. Add the stock and, when it boils, add peas or beans or both. Boil until all the vegetables are cooked (about 30 minutes). Season with salt and pepper.

95. Vegetable Purée   *Potage purée de légumes*

Follow the recipe for Julienne Soup (94). Use only 2 pints of stock or water. When the vegetables are cooked, force them through a food mill. The soup should not be very thick and can be thinned by adding more liquid.

96. Peasant Soup   *Potage paysanne*

2 carrots	3 pints stock
2 potatoes	salt and pepper
1 turnip	several rounds of stale bread

Dice carrots, potatoes, and turnip. Cook in 1 pint of stock until they are soft. Add the rest of the stock and boil for 5 minutes. Season with salt and pepper and pour over bread.

97. Crayfish Soup   *Potage à la bisque d'écrevisses*

This soup is expensive and will probably be served only when you have guests. Therefore we are giving you larger proportions than usual.

TANTE MARIE

The *écrevisse* (crayfish or crawdab) is a small fresh-water shell fish usually 3 to 5 inches long.
Lobster or shrimps make excellent substitutes (2 lobsters or 2 pints of shrimps).

2 pints water	20 crayfish
salt	8 slices stale bread
black pepper	3 pints rich stock
1 onion	1 gill of Madeira (or white wine)
1 carrot	3 ozs. butter
bouquet garni (42)	

Dice carrot and onion and add to the water with salt, pepper, and *bouquet garni*. Bring to a full rolling boil and put in fresh crayfish. Reduce heat and cook gently 15 minutes. Strain off liquid but do not throw it away. When the fish is cool enough to handle, extract the meat from the tails. Force the shells through a meat chopper, using the finest blade. Pound to a paste. Add the paste to 1 pint of the broth and simmer 5 minutes. Strain and return to the heat. Add the stock and stale bread. Stir until the bread has blended with the stock. Add the wine and the rest of the broth and bring to boiling point, stirring constantly with a wooden spoon. Just before serving, put in the meat and add the butter. This soup must be served immediately.

98. *Bouillabaisse*

This famous southern dish may be classified as a soup or fish dish. See recipe 188.

99. Tomato Soup   *Potage aux tomates*

4 or 5 large tomatoes, quartered	3 pints water
bay leaf	1 teaspoon salt
1 sprig of thyme (or ¼ teaspoon dried thyme)	2 ozs. butter
	croutons
1 onion, thinly sliced	

Crush the tomatoes slightly in the bottom of a heavy saucepan. Cook very slowly with bay leaf, thyme, and onion for 30 minutes. Take care that the tomatoes do not stick to the pan. Force the tomatoes through a food mill or sieve. Add water, salt, and butter. Bring to boiling point. Pour over croutons. Serve immediately. If the tomatoes are acid, add ½ teaspoon sugar.

100. Tomato Tapioca Soup

Potage au tapioca à la tomate

Follow the preceding recipe for making tomato purée. Add 2 tablespoons of tapioca to 3 pints of boiling salted water. Stir so that the tapioca will not lump. Cook 5 minutes. Combine the mixtures and bring to the boil. Add 2 ozs. of butter and more salt if necessary. Do not use croutons.

D

101. Barley Soup   *Potage à la crème d'orge*

2 ozs. butter
1 tablespoon flour
1 pint hot water
¼ lb. pearl barley
2 pints rich stock, preferably chicken

1 egg yolk
salt and pepper
croutons

Melt the butter and stir in flour. When well blended, add water.
When the surface of the water begins to whiten, add the barley.
As the barley absorbs the water, add a little more from time to
time until the barley is very soft (30 to 40 minutes). Force the
barley through a fine sieve and add to stock. Return to the heat
for 10 minutes. Bind with the egg yolk (page 3). Season with
salt and pepper and serve with croutons.

102. *Julienne languedocienne*

Prepare vegetables as for Julienne Soup (94). Cook them in
¼ pint of olive oil 10 minutes. Drain and add to Pea Soup (82).
Add 1 pint of water, salt and pepper, and simmer 1 to 2 hours.
The vegetables will be thoroughly cooked at the end of 1 hour,
but the longer cooking heightens the flavour. Pour over rounds
of bread.

103. Russian Soup   *Potage livonien*

2 carrots
2 turnips
2 leeks
3 or 4 cabbage leaves
2 onions
4 celery stalks
chopped parsley
2 ozs. butter

2 tablespoons cooked rice
3 pints water or stock
1 cup thick cream
1 teaspoon salt
1 teaspoon sugar
2 egg yolks
fried croutons

Slice the vegetables into narrow 2-inch strips. Boil 30 minutes in salted water. Melt butter. Add the vegetables, which have been well drained, parsley, and cooked rice. Stir the vegetables carefully so that the butter will coat everything. Add liquid and cook 5 minutes. Force through a food mill or sieve. Reheat in the top of a double boiler. Add cream, salt, and sugar. Bind with 2 egg yolks (page 3). Serve with fried croutons. Sprinkle with chopped parsley.

104. Mushroom Julienne   *Julienne aux champignons*

Prepare Julienne Soup (94). 30 minutes before serving add ½ lb. of mushrooms, washed and thinly sliced. Use both caps and stems. Serve with croutons.

105. Finnish Soup   *Potage finlandais*

8 eggs	rounds of stale bread
salt	2 ozs. grated Parmesan cheese
white pepper	2 ozs. melted butter
chopped parsley	2 quarts well-seasoned rich con-
2 tablespoons cream	sommé

Beat eggs and add salt, pepper, a little of the cheese, parsley, and cream. Follow directions for making omelette (125). When the omelette is thoroughly cooked so that it is quite dry, turn upside down on a floured bread board. Cut the omelette with the same biscuit cutter that is used for the bread. Place the rounds of omelette on the rounds of bread. Brush with melted butter, cover with the remaining Parmesan cheese, and place in hot oven for 3 minutes. Serve on heated dish and send to the table with a tureen of good consommé.

106. Mushroom Consommé   *Bouillon de champignons*

¼ lb. dried mushrooms (or 1 lb   *bouquet garni* (42)
    fresh mushrooms)   salt and pepper
2 carrots   3 pints water
2 leeks

Soak the dried mushrooms 3 hours in warm water. Drain and
wash well. If fresh mushrooms are used, wash well and use
without soaking. Dice carrots and leeks and cook with mushrooms
and the *bouquet garni* in water over a low flame for 1 hour. Season
with salt and pepper. Strain before using. This is a delicious
consommé and may be used in place of a meat stock. The mushrooms may be extracted from the other vegetables, cut into strips
and served with the consommé.

107. Italian Cabbage Soup   *Potage aux choux à l'italienne*

3 pints water   1 onion, finely chopped
¼ lb. rice   salt and pepper
1 small cabbage   3 pints stock
2 ozs. butter (or chicken fat)   2 ozs. grated Parmesan cheese

Bring water to the boil. Add the rice and small cabbage. Salt and
cook 45 minutes. Drain well. Melt fat, add onion, cabbage, rice,
salt, pepper, and stock. Simmer 30 minutes, stirring occasionally.
Just before serving, sprinkle with cheese.

108. Milanaise Rice Soup   *Potage au riz à la milanaise*

1 onion, finely chopped   1 oz. butter
3 ozs. butter   2 ozs. Parmesan cheese
3 pints chicken or meat stock   grated nutmeg
¼ lb. rice   salt and pepper
a pinch of saffron

Fry onion gently in melted butter until yellow. Add stock and bring to the boil. Wash the rice thoroughly. Add rice and saffron and simmer 45 minutes. Add more stock if necessary. The rice should keep its shape and the soup should be thicker than most soups, but still liquid. Remove from the fire. Add butter, cheese, nutmeg, salt, and pepper. Serve very hot.

A bon appétit il ne faut pas de sauce.

*One **must** be most careful that the eggs that are being prepared are fresh, for there is nothing as bad as an egg which is not perfectly fresh. It can ruin the most exquisitely prepared dish.*

TANTE MARIE

109. Boiled Eggs in the Shell   *Œufs à la coque*

Place eggs in boiling water and cover the pan. Leave on the heat for 3 minutes. Remove from the water and serve in individual egg cups.

110. Baked Eggs   *Œufs sur le plat*

Put 2 ozs. of butter in a shallow oven-proof dish and place in a moderate oven (350°F.). When the butter is bubbling, break the eggs into the dish, counting 2 eggs per person. Sprinkle with salt and freshly ground black pepper and return to the oven for 10 minutes or until the whites are thoroughly cooked. Serve immediately. A pleasant variation to this dish is made by placing

44

slices of boiled ham or salami in the butter and breaking the
eggs over them.

111. Soft-Boiled Luncheon Eggs   *Œufs mollets*

Boil eggs 5 minutes and plunge into cold water. Remove the shells,
leaving the eggs whole. Serve them on Purée of Peas (455),
Garden Sorrel (486), or French Spinach (487), or in ramekins
with a Robert Sauce (16), Piquant Sauce (12), or Cream Sauce (2).

112. Hard-Boiled Eggs   *Œufs durs*

Boil the eggs 10 minutes. Plunge into cold water and remove the
shell immediately.

113. Eggs in Béchamel Sauce   *Œufs à la béchamel*

Follow the preceding recipe for boiling eggs. Serve them whole
in a Béchamel Sauce (1).

114. Salad Eggs   *Œufs durs en salade*

Slice hard-boiled eggs (112). Cover with French Dressing (31).

115. Poached Eggs   *Œufs pochés*

Fill a frying pan ¾ full of water and add 1 teaspoon salt. When
the water begins to simmer, break the eggs into it very carefully.
Special forms may be bought to keep the eggs in perfect shape,
but these are not necessary. Do not poach more than 3 eggs at a
time. They should not touch each other. Never let the water
actually boil. After 5 minutes, remove the eggs with an egg
slice.

116. Eggs in Black Butter Sauce   *Œufs au beurre noir*

Heat 2 ozs. butter and let it brown without burning. When it is
quite dark in colour, break 4 eggs into the pan and fry until the
whites are thoroughly cooked. Remove the eggs to a heated dish.
Add 1 teaspoon wine vinegar to the butter, stir a moment, and
pour over the eggs quickly. Serve at once.

117. Eggs en Matelote   *Œufs en matelote*

¾ pint red wine	pepper
¾ pint water	2 eggs per person
1 onion, thinly sliced	2 tablespoons butter
1 clove garlic	1 tablespoon flour
bouquet garni (42)	croutons
salt	

Put the wine, water, onion, garlic, *bouquet garni*, salt, and pepper
in a large frying pan. Boil gently 15 minutes. Remove the onion,
garlic, and *bouquet garni* with a skimmer. Poach the eggs in the
liquid (115). When the whites are thoroughly cooked, place the
eggs on a heated dish and keep them warm. Increase the heat
under the frying pan and reduce the liquid to half its amount.
Bind the sauce with butter and flour (page 4). Pour the sauce
over the eggs and serve with croutons.

118. Scrambled Eggs   *Œufs brouillés*

6 eggs	salt
1 oz. butter	freshly ground black pepper
1 tablespoon chopped parsley	

Break the eggs into a bowl and beat until the yolks and whites
are blended. Melt butter in a frying pan. When the butter is

sizzling, add parsley, salt, and pepper. Pour in the eggs and stir constantly with a fork until the eggs are cooked. Do not let the eggs overcook or become dry. If large lumps form, break them with the fork.

119. Scrambled Eggs with Cheese

Œufs brouillés au fromage

Follow the preceding recipe, but add 2 ozs. grated gruyère or Parmesan to the beaten eggs before scrambling.

120. Scrambled Eggs with Truffles

Œufs brouillés aux truffes

Slice one truffle very thinly. Fry gently in butter, cool, and add to beaten eggs before scrambling (118).

121. Scrambled Eggs with Pickled Herring

Œufs brouillés aux harengs saurs

Chop 2 fillets of pickled herring very finely. Mix with beaten eggs before scrambling (118).

122. Scrambled Eggs with Asparagus

Œufs brouillés aux pointes d'asperges

Cut cold cooked asparagus into small pieces and mix with beaten eggs before scrambling (118).

123. Scrambled Eggs with Mushrooms

Œufs brouillés aux champignons

Wash and slice ¼ lb. musrooms. Fry gently in butter. Cool and add to beaten eggs before scrambling (118).

124. Stuffed Eggs   *Œufs farcis*

6 hard-boiled eggs (112)   1 tablespoon fine bread crumbs
1 oz. butter   1 small clove garlic, finely chopped
chopped parsley   salt and pepper

Cut the eggs lengthwise. Remove the yolk and crush with a fork.
Work in butter, bread crumbs, parsley, garlic, salt, and pepper
until they are blended to a smooth paste. Put the mixture into
the white halves. Place in a buttered oven-proof dish and brown
in hot oven.

125. Plain Omelette   *Omelette au naturel*

6 eggs   1 teaspoon water
salt   1 oz. butter
pepper

Beat the eggs thoroughly. Add salt, pepper, and water. Melt the
butter in a light frying pan. When the butter is sizzling hot, but
not brown, pour in the eggs. As the egg mixture begins to set
on the bottom, prick it with a fork and raise a little, thus allowing
the uncooked egg to seep through. Continue the pricking and
and raising process until almost all the liquid has disappeared.
Remove from the heat, loosen the edge of half the omelette from
the pan with a spatula, and fold one half over the other. Turn
upside down on a heated dish. A French omelette should
never be overcooked and the centre should be slightly runny.
This requires practice, but it is an art well worth mastering.
An omelette may be made with any number of eggs, but it is
better to practice on a small quantity.

126. Omelette with Herbs   *Omelette aux fines herbes*

6 eggs   1 tablespoon chopped parsley
salt   1 tablespoon chopped chives
pepper   1 oz. butter
1 teaspoon water

Mix the finely chopped herbs into the beaten eggs, and add the
salt, pepper, and water. Follow the preceding recipe for making
omelette.

127. Mushroom Omelette   *Omelette aux champignons*

Wash and peel $\frac{1}{4}$ lb. of mushrooms. Slice thinly. Fry in butter
10 minutes. Season with salt and pepper and cool. Mix with
the beaten eggs and proceed as in Plain Omelette (125).

128. Truffle Omelette   *Omelette aux truffes*

Substitute 1 or 2 small truffles for the mushrooms in the
preceding recipe.

129. Kidney Omelette   *Omelette au rognon*

Cut 1 veal kidney in small pieces. A beef kidney or 4 lamb kidneys
will do as well. Fry the kidney in 1 oz. butter until brown on all
sides. Season with salt and pepper. Make a Plain Omelette
(125) in a separate frying pan. Just before folding the omelette
spread the kidneys on it so that they will be in the centre of the
finished omelette.

130. Cheese Omelette   *Omelette au fromage*

Add 2 ozs. grated Swiss or Parmesan cheese to the eggs and
follow directions for making Plain Omelette (125).

131. Bread Omelette   *Omelette au pain*

2 slices stale white bread	salt
¼ pint milk	pepper
4 eggs, well beaten	

Remove the crusts from the bread. Soak in milk. When the
bread has absorbed the milk, add the eggs. Follow recipe 125
for making omelette. (The only advantage to this recipe is one
of economy.)

132. Foamy Omelette   *Omelette mousseuse*

Beat separately the yolks and whites of 4 eggs. Fold the whites
into the yolks. Season with salt and pepper and proceed as in
Plain Omelette (125).

133. Macaroni Omelette   *Omelette au macaroni*

4 eggs	1 cup cold, cooked macaroni
4 ozs. grated Swiss or Parmesan cheese	salt and pepper
	2 ozs. butter

Beat the eggs thoroughly. Add the macaroni, cut in small pieces,
cheese, salt, and pepper. Cook the same as Plain Omelette (125).
Take care that it does not stick to the frying pan.

134. Salt Pork or Bacon Omelette   *Omelette au lard*

6 eggs   white pepper
¼ lb. salt pork or bacon, diced

Fry the bacon or salt pork. Pour off the excess fat, leaving not more than 2 tablespoons in the frying pan. Pour in the well-beaten eggs, seasoned with pepper, and proceed as in Plain Omelette (125).

135. Ham Omelette   *Omelette au jambon*

¼ lb. boiled ham   6 eggs
1 oz. butter   white pepper

Trim the fat off the ham. Dice ham and fry in butter. Add to well-beaten eggs and proceed as in Plain Omelette (125).

136. Onion Omelette   *Omelette à l'oignon*

2 ozs. butter   6 eggs
1 large onion, thinly sliced   salt and pepper

Fry the onions in butter until they are a golden brown. Pour well-beaten eggs over the onion and proceed as in Plain Omelette (125).

137. Asparagus Omelette   *Omelette aux pointes d'asperges*

1 cup cold cooked asparagus   6 eggs
2 ozs. butter   salt and pepper

Cut the asparagus in small pieces. Heat in the melted butter in the omelette pan. Pour the well-beaten eggs over the asparagus and proceed as in Plain Omelette (125).

138. Potato Omelette   *Omelette aux pommes de terre*

2 diced boiled potatoes	6 eggs
2 ozs. butter	salt and pepper

Fry the potatoes in butter until they are golden. Mix with well-beaten eggs and proceed as in Plain Omelette (125).

139. Tomato Omelette   *Omelette aux tomates*

4 tomatoes	6 eggs
2 tablespoons olive oil	salt and pepper

Peel the tomatoes and remove the seeds. Cut the tomato flesh into eighths and fry gently in olive oil for 5 minutes. Cool. Mix with well-beaten eggs and proceed as in Plain Omelette (125).

140. Cheese Fondue I   *Fondue I*

3 ozs. butter	6 ozs. freshly grated Gruyère
1 oz. flour	cheese
3 egg yolks	1 egg white
1 gill milk	salt and pepper

Melt the butter in the top of a double boiler and stir in flour. Add milk and egg yolks and simmer over hot but not boiling water until the mixture begins to thicken. Stir constantly with a wooden spoon so that the eggs will not curdle. Remove from the heat. Add cheese, salt, and pepper, and egg white beaten stiff. Bake in a buttered baking dish for 25 minutes in a 350°F. oven. The fondue should not be too thick.

141. Cheese Fondue II   *Fondue* II

2 ozs. butter
4 eggs, well beaten

2 ozs. freshly grated **Gruyère** cheese
salt and pepper

Combine butter, eggs, cheese, salt, and pepper in the top of a double boiler. Do not let the water boil. Stir constantly until the mixture is smooth. Serve immediately with fresh French bread or crisp toast. If Parmesan cheese is used, use 3 ozs. butter and 3 ozs. cheese.

142. Cheese Soufflé   *Soufflé au fromage*

See recipe 65.

143. Garlic Eggs   *Œufs à l'ail*

4 cloves garlic
2 fillets of anchovy
capers
3 tablespoons olive oil

a dash of wine vinegar
salt
freshly ground pepper
6 hard-boiled eggs

Chop and crush the garlic. Add anchovies and capers and mash them all together to make a paste. Stir in oil, vinegar, salt, and pepper. Quarter the shelled hard-boiled eggs and cover with the sauce.

A l'œuvre on connaît l'artisan.

FISH is more appreciated and generally better prepared in France than anywhere else in the world. The variety of commonly used fish is greater and the methods of preparing it are more imaginative. Actually almost every fish caught for the French market can be found in almost every other country, under one name or another. When necessary the substitution of one fish for another of the same type will make little difference to the excellence of Tante Marie's recipes.

FRESHNESS OF FISH: Fish must be absolutely fresh to be good. One can determine freshness by the appearance of the eyes and gills. The eyes should be bright and the gills should be red. Tante Marie warns: *Beware the merchant who colours the gills with lamb's blood.*

TO CLEAN FISH: Usually the fishmonger will clean and prepare the fish for cooking. Some people prefer to do it themselves. Small fish may be cleaned by inserting the finger in the opening of the gills and withdrawing the intestines. The larger fish are cleaned by making a short incision in the belly of the fish and removing the blood and intestines. The gills should be removed but the roe may be left.

TO SCALE FISH: Hold the fish by the tail and scrape the scales off with a sharp knife, running from tail to head. Hold the knife flat against the fish so that the skin will not be broken.

TO SKIN THE FISH: Rub your hands with salt to keep them from slipping. Loosen the skin at either the head or tail with the sharp point of of a knife. Holding the fish with one hand, grasp the loosened skin with a dish cloth or, if possible, a pair of pliers. Jerk the skin off with a quick pull.

TO KEEP FISH: If fish is not to be used immediately, clean it and wipe it with a damp kitchen towel. Wrap it in greaseproof paper and store in the cold part of the refrigerator.

144. *Court-bouillon*

The most common method of preparing fish in France is by simmering it in a *court-bouillon*. The following basic recipe will be called for in many of the recipes:

Into a pan large enough to cook the fish, pour equal amounts of white wine or wine vinegar, and water. There should be enough to cover the fish, which will be put in later. Add salt, white pepper, *bouquet garni* (42), 2 cloves, 1 thinly sliced onion and a sliced carrot. Cover the pan and simmer 45 minutes. Put in the fish and let it simmer until cooked. The *court-bouillon* should never boil. This keeps the flesh from breaking. When the fish is cooked, remove from the fire but keep in the *court-bouillon* until it is to be served.

E

145. Salt-Water Cooking   *A la bonne eau*

When the recipe calls for cooking *à la bonne eau*, put enough water in the saucepan to cover the fish, which will be put in later. Add a large amount of salt—1 tablespoon to a quart of water —and bring the water to boiling point. Place the fish in the water carefully and let it simmer—not boil—until the fish is cooked. It will then be removed and served with the appropriate sauce.

146. Boiled Salmon   *Saumon au court-bouillon*

1½ to 2 lbs. fresh salmon
court-bouillon (144)
parsley

choice of:
   Hollandaise Sauce (10)
   Cream Sauce (2)
   Italian Sauce (26)

Prepare the *court-bouillon*. Wipe the fish and tie it in a piece of cheese cloth. When the *court-bouillon* is ready, lower the fish into it carefully. Let the fish simmer 30 minutes. Do not let it boil. Lift the cloth from the kettle. Drain off all the water and place fish on a dish. Decorate with sprigs of parsley. Serve the sauce separately.

147. Cold Salmon with Green Mayonnaise
                    Saumon froid à la mayonnaise verte

A small salmon or large pink-fleshed trout is perfect for this attractive dish. If a whole fish is used, leave the head and tail on and remove the eyes only. A slice of salmon is equally delicious although not so decorative.

    Prepare the salmon as in the preceding recipe. Let the fish cool in the *court-bouillon*. Drain thoroughly and place on a long dish. Remove the skin carefully. Decorate with sprigs of parsley and thin slices of lemon. A realistic eye may be made with the white end of a hard-boiled egg and a round of truffle or black olive. Serve with a bowl of Green Mayonnaise (18).

148. Trout with Herb Sauce

Truites de rivière à la genevoise

4 trout	chopped parsley
court-bouillon (144)	1 chopped shallot
2 ozs. butter	2 pieces stale bread
¼ lb. chopped mushrooms	salt and pepper

Prepare a *court-bouillon*. Clean the trout. When the *court-bouillon* is ready, let the trout simmer in it 15 to 20 minutes, depending on the size of the trout. Meanwhile, lightly fry the mushrooms, parsley, and shallot in the melted butter. Soak the bread in a little of the *court-bouillon*. Squeeze the liquid from the bread and add the bread and ¼ cup of the *court-bouillon* to the herbs. Blend thoroughly. Season and spread the sauce on a heated dish. Place the trout on the sauce and serve very hot.

149. Fried Trout   *Truites frites*

8 small trout	flour
2 tablespoons salad oil or 2 ozs.	salt
butter	slices of lemon

Heat the oil or butter in the frying pan. Roll each cleaned fish in flour. When the fat is sizzling hot, fry the fish 5 minutes on each side. Salt them and serve on a heated dish with slices of lemon.

150. Tunny Fish   *Thon*

Fresh tunny straight from the sea is prepared in the same way
as salmon. Follow recipes 146 and 147. Tinned tunny is served as
an hors-d'œuvre (48).

151. Bass   *Bar au court-bouillon*

Prepare either the *court-bouillon* (144) or the salted water (145).
Simmer the bass, allowing 15 minutes per pound. Drain and
place on heated dish. Cover with White Sauce (3) and decorate
with sprigs of parsley.

152. Grilled Perch   *Les petits bars grillés*

6 perch   Maître d'hôtel Sauce (9)

Clean and scale the fish (page 54). Brush the grill rack with
oil; this will keep the fish from sticking. Grill the fish 20 minutes,
turning them only once. Place the fish on a hot dish and cover
with Maître d'hôtel Sauce.

153. Mullet with Cream Sauce   *Mulet à la sauce blanche*

1 mullet   Cream Sauce (2)
court-bouillon (144)

Clean the fish (page 54), leaving the head and tail on. Prepare
the *court-bouillon* and, when it is ready, allow the fish to simmer
45 minutes. Remove from the *court-bouillon*, drain, place on
a warm dish. Serve the Cream Sauce separately.

154. Grilled Mullet   *Mulet grillé*

2 mullets   Cream Sauce (2)
mullet liver

When the fish is cleaned, preserve the liver carefully. Brush the grill rack with oil, so that the fish will not stick. Grill the fish under a moderate flame, turning only once. Crush the liver and add to the sauce. This will give it a good colour. Place the fish on a heated dish. Cover with Cream Sauce and garnish with sprigs of parsley.

155. Turbot with Caper Sauce

Turbot, sauce aux câpres

Turbot   parsley
court-bouillon (144)   Caper Sauce (4)
½ lemon

Clean the turbot by cutting off the head and withdrawing the intestines from that end. Tante Marie suggests sewing the head back on. This may seem a little excessive. Prepare the *court-bouillon*. Rub the white side of the fish with the lemon, and when the *court-bouillon* is ready, place the fish white side up in the kettle. Simmer the fish 30 minutes. Remove from the *court-bouillon*, drain, and place on a heated dish. Serve with Caper Sauce.

156. Baked Turbot   *Turbot au gratin*

Turbot	black pepper
3 ozs. butter	fine bread crumbs
1 finely chopped shallot	¼ pint dry white wine
chopped parsley	sprigs of parsley and slices of
salt	lemon

Clean and scale the fish (page 54). Dot the bottom of an oven-proof dish with half the butter and spread half the chopped shallot and parsley over it. Sprinkle generously with salt and pepper. Place the fish, white side up on this mixture. Cover with the remaining butter, shallot, and parsley. Salt and pepper. Add the white wine and bake 30 minutes in 350°F. oven. Cover with bread crumbs and moisten with melted butter. Place under the grill until the crumbs are golden brown. Garnish with the parsley and lemon slices.

157. Skate in Black Butter Sauce   *Raie au beurre noir*

1½ lbs. skate	½ lb. butter
bouquet garni (42)	parsley
salt	1 tablespoon wine vinegar
pepper	

Clean the fish (page 54). Put enough water in a saucepan so that the fish will be completely covered. Add a *bouquet garni*, salt, and pepper. Boil 5 minutes. Reduce the heat and put in the fish. Simmer 25 minutes. Meanwhile, melt butter over a moderate flame, letting it brown but not burn. When the butter is very hot, throw in several sprigs of parsley and fry them. As soon as the fish is done, remove from the water, drain, and take off the black skin. Place on a very hot dish. Pour the butter and parsley over the fish and return the frying pan to the flame. Put in the vinegar. This will boil in a matter of seconds. Pour it over the fish and serve immediately with boiled potatoes.

158. Skate with White Butter Sauce   *Raie au beurre blanc*

Follow the preceding recipe but, instead of browning the butter, simply melt it. When it is very hot, add 2 tablespoons chopped parsley, salt, and freshly ground black pepper. Pour over the cooked skate and serve very hot.

159. Fried Skate   *Raie frite*

1½ lbs. skate	parsley
flour	salt
¼ pint salad oil	

Cut the skate into strips. Roll each strip in flour and fry in a little very hot oil. Fry sprigs of parsley at the same time. Drain on absorbent paper, salt, and serve immediately.

160. Salt Cod   *Morue*

To freshen: Good salt cod may be prepared in many delicious ways. It must be properly freshened before using. Soak in cool water 8 to 10 hours, changing the water twice. If there is no time for freshening, bring the cod to the boil, starting from cold water. Throw the water away and wash the cod in cool water before using. Take care to taste before salting.

161. Salt Cod with Parsley Creamed Potatoes
Morue aux pommes de terre

1¼ lbs. salt cod, in one piece
2 ozs. butter
2 tablespoons flour
½ pint milk
salt

freshly ground black pepper
chopped parsley
5 or 6 medium-sized boiled potatoes

Freshen the cod (160). Start the cod in cold water and bring
to boiling point. Remove from the heat. Skim the water and let
the cod stand in the covered saucepan on the back of the stove
for at least 15 minutes before using. Melt the butter and stir
in flour. Add the milk and stir until smooth. If the sauce is too
thick, add more milk. Season with not too much salt, pepper,
and parsley. Add the potatoes, which have been previously
boiled. Place the cod in the centre of a warm dish and surround
with creamed potatoes.

162. Salt Cod au Gratin   *Morue au fromage*

Follow the preceding recipe, but instead of leaving the cooked
cod in one piece, cut it in small pieces, and add it with the
potatoes to the sauce. Put in an oven-proof dish, cover with
grated cheese and fine bread crumbs. Place under the grill until
the top is golden brown. Serve in the same dish and decorate
with sprigs of parsley.

163. Salt Cod in Black Butter Sauce   *Morue au beurre noir*

1½ lbs. salt cod, in one piece   Black Butter Sauce (14)

Freshen the salt cod (160). Start the freshened cod in cold
water and bring to boiling point. Skim the water and remove

the pan from the heat. Cover and place on the back of the stove for 15 minutes. Place the fish on a very hot dish and cover with Black Butter Sauce. Serve immediately.

164. Burgundian Cod   *Morue à la bourguignonne*

1½ lbs. salt cod, in one piece	*bouquet garni* (42)
3 ozs. butter	salt
1 tablespoon flour	freshly ground black pepper
½ pint hot water	dash of mace
12 small onions	

Freshen the cod (160). Start the freshened cod in cold water and bring to boiling point. Skim the water, cover and set the pan on the back of the stove. Melt butter and stir in flour. When the flour is blended with the butter, stir in water. The sauce should be thin. Add more water if necessary. Cook the onions in the sauce along with the *bouquet garni*, salt, pepper, and mace. When the onions are tender (approximately 20 minutes), remove the *bouquet garni*. Reheat the cod, drain well, and serve on a warm dish with the sauce poured over the fish.

165. Fresh Cod, Hollandaise Sauce

Cabillaud, sauce hollandaise

2 lbs. cod	Hollandaise Sauce (10)
8 to 10 small potatoes	

Fill a saucepan with enough water to cover the fish. Add a generous amount of salt. Bring to the boil. Tie the fish, which has been wiped clean, in a piece of cheesecloth, and place in the water. Add the peeled potatoes at the same time. Simmer 30 to 40 minutes. Drain the fish. Place on heated dish. Surround with the potatoes and serve with a bowl of Hollandaise Sauce

166. Salt Cod Mousse   *Brandade de morue*

.1lb. salt cod
2 tablespoons olive oil
¼ pint warm milk
2 truffles

¼ pint olive oil
salt
freshly ground black pepper

Freshen the cod (160). Bring the fish to boiling point, starting it in cold water. Skim the water and set the fish aside to cool in the covered pan. When the cod is cool, remove the skin and bones.

Heat 2 tablespoons of olive oil in the top of a double boiler. Break the cod into small pieces and add to the oil. Stir until the mixture is smooth. Continue cooking 30 minutes and stir frequently. The cod must become a soft mass, but it must not be too thick. To prevent this, add the warm milk a little at a time. It may be necessary to add more than ¼ pint. Chop the truffles very finely and add to the fish. At the end of 30 minutes, remove from the fire and add the rest of the olive oil, drop by drop, beating constantly as in the making of Mayonnaise (17). An electric beater is a great help. Season highly with salt and pepper. Contrary to other authorities, Tante Marie says, 'Do not add garlic or parsley.'

167. Grilled Mackerel, Maître d'hôtel
Maquereau à la maître d'hôtel

1 large or 2 medium-sized
    mackerel
3 ozs. butter

chopped parsley
salt and pepper
½ lemon

Remove the head and split the fish down the back. Wash and wipe dry. Brush the grill rack with oil, so that the fish will not stick. Grill the fish under a low flame 25 to 30 minutes. Heat the serving dish. Spread the butter on the dish. Sprinkle with

parsley, salt and pepper, and lemon juice. Place the fish over this
mixture and serve immediately.

168. Mackerel with Black Butter Sauce

Maquereau au beurre noir

2 large mackerel   boiled potatoes
Black Butter Sauce (14)

Cook the whole mackerel in salted water (145). The head and
tail should be kept on, but the fish should be cleaned (page
54). Simmer the fish 30 to 40 minutes, depending on the size
of the mackerel. Remove from the water, drain thoroughly,
split open, and remove the backbone. Place the fish on a very
hot dish. Serve with the Black Butter Sauce poured over the
fish, surrounded by small new potatoes, which have been boiled
in their jackets and peeled.

169. Flemish Mackerel   *Maquereau à la flamande*

2 large mackerel   chopped shallot
2 ozs. butter   juice of $\frac{1}{2}$ lemon
chopped parsley   salt and pepper
chopped chives

Clean the fresh mackerel carefully, taking care not to remove
the heads or tails. Make an incision along the belly of the fish.
Soften (not melt) the butter and work into it the parsley, chives,
shallot, salt, pepper, and 1 teaspoon lemon juice. When the
mixture is well blended, place it in the fish. Roll the fish in
oiled paper and tie at both ends. Cook 45 minutes in 350°F.
oven. Remove the fish carefully from the paper onto a warm
dish, and pour the butter that will be in the paper over the fish.
Sprinkle with remaining lemon juice. Garnish with sprigs of
fresh parsley.

170. Italian Mackerel   *Maquereau à l'italienne*

2 large mackerel   Italian Herb Sauce (26)
court-bouillon (144)

Prepare the *court-bouillon*. When it is ready, simmer the mackerel
30 minutes. Drain the fish well and serve with Italian Herb
Sauce.

171. Grilled Fresh Herring   *Harengs frais sur le gril*

3 fresh herrings   1 tablespoon made mustard
Cream Sauce (2)   salt

Clean and scale the herring. Make 3 incisions on each side of
the fish. Preheat the grill so that the fish will not stick. Grill
3 to 4 minutes on each side. Salt and serve with Cream Sauce,
highly seasoned with mustard.

172. Fresh Herring, Maître d'hôtel
                        Harengs frais à la maître d'hôtel

3 herrings   lemon juice
4 ozs. butter   salt
chopped parsley   freshly ground black pepper

Prepare and cook the herring as in the preceding recipe. Arrange on an oven-proof dish. Garnish each herring with butter,
parsley, salt, and pepper. Place under grill 2 minutes, sprinkle
with lemon juice, and serve very hot.

173. Marinated Herring   *Harengs de Dieppe marinés*

12 small herrings	2 small carrots, cut in rounds
1 pint water	2 cloves garlic
1 pint dry white wine	5 peppercorns
½ pint wine vinegar	*bouquet garni* (42)
1 large onion, finely chopped	

Combine water, wine, vinegar, onion, carrots, garlic, peppercorns, and *bouquet garni*. Boil 15 minutes. Scale and clean the herrings. Cook in the liquid for 6 minutes. Remove from the fire and let the fish cool in the liquor. Serve cold. This makes an excellent hors d'œuvre.

174. Sole   *Soles*

To prepare Sole: The black skin of the sole is removed before cooking. To do this, follow directions on page 55 for skinning fish. The white underskin may be removed in the same way, but usually it is sufficient just to scrape off the scales with a blunt knife. If the fish is to be filleted, remove both the black and the white skins. Cut off the head and tail and lift the fillets from each side of the backbone. The fish should be rinsed and wiped dry before cooking. A little lemon juice in the water helps to whiten the flesh.

175. Fried Sole   *Soles frites*

4 soles   salt
flour   several sprigs of parsley
oil

Prepare the soles, removing the black skin only (174). Roll
each fish in flour and fry in hot oil (375°F.). Turn the fish once
only; 3 minutes on each side should be enough. Prick the fish
with a sharp knife. If the flesh falls apart readily it is cooked.
Drain on absorbent paper and serve with fried parsley.

176. Sole in White Wine and Herbs
                          Soles aux fines herbes et au vin blanc

4 small soles   salt
3 ozs. butter   freshly ground black pepper
chopped parsley   ¼ pint dry white wine
chopped shallots or onion   fine bread crumbs

Prepare the soles (174). Put half the butter, parsley, and shallots
in the bottom of a large, shallow oven-proof dish. Sprinkle with
salt and pepper. Place the soles on the mixture and cover with
the rest of the butter and herbs. Salt and pepper generously.
Pour the white wine over the fish, cover with bread crumbs,
and dot with butter. Cook 30 minutes in a 350°F. oven. Just
before serving, place under the grill until the crumbs are golden
brown. Serve in the same dish. Garnish with parsley.

177. Baked Sole   *Soles au gratin*

4 small soles	freshly ground black pepper
2 ozs. butter	¼ pint dry white wine
chopped shallots or onion	¼ lb. small mushrooms
chopped parsley	fine bread crumbs
salt	slices of lemon

Prepare the soles, removing the black skin only (174). Put the butter in a large shallow oven-proof dish. Place the soles in the dish and spread with shallots and parsley. Sprinkle with salt and pepper. Add the wine and place the mushroom caps, which have been thoroughly washed, on the fish. Cover with bread crumbs, dot with butter, and cook in a moderate oven (350°F.) for 30 minutes. Serve with slices of lemon.

178. Baked Fillets of Sole   *Filets de soles au gratin*

Follow the preceding recipe, substituting 6 to 8 fillets for the whole fish. This is an excellent way to prepare fish when only frosted or frozen fillets are available.

179. Fried Fillets of Sole   *Filets de soles à la Colbert*

6 fillets of sole	Maître d'hôtel Sauce (9) or
flour	Mayonnaise (17)
salt	

Split each fillet in two. Roll each piece up and place on a skewer. Four pieces to each skewer does very well. Dredge with flour and fry in hot (375°F.) deep fat (41) for 4 to 5 minutes. Serve with Maître d'hôtel Sauce or Mayonnaise.

180. Sole Filling for Vol-au-vent

Filets de soles pour garniture

6 fillets of sole	salt
2 ozs. butter	pepper
3 tablespoons dry white wine	Béchamel Sauce (1)
¼ pint water	

Put into a saucepan the water, wine, butter, salt, and pepper. Bring to the boil and simmer the fillets in it for 20 minutes. Drain well and mix with a fairly thick Béchamel Sauce. This is used to fill a large Vol-au-vent (372) or individual pastry cases.

181. Normandy Sole   *Soles normandes*

2 soles	10 shrimps
2 ozs. butter	2 ozs. butter
½ pint water	2 tablespoons flour
½ pint dry white wine	1 egg yolk
12 mussels	fried croutons
12 mushroom caps	several sprigs of parsley
10 oysters	

Prepare the soles, removing both skins (174). Put the water, wine, and butter into a large pan. Bring to boiling point and add the sole, mushrooms, mussels, and oysters. Simmer 20 minutes. Remove the sole carefully and place in an oven-proof dish. Drain the rest, but save the liquor. In another pan, melt the butter and stir in flour, allowing it to cook until light brown in colour. Stir constantly with a wooden spoon to prevent burning. Add ½ pint of the liquor in which the fish has been cooked. If the sauce is too thick, add more liquor. Thicken with egg yolk (page 3), and pour the sauce over the fish. Place the mushrooms, oysters, and mussels on the fish and bake 15 minutes in a 350°F. oven. Meanwhile fry shrimps and croutons in butter and use as garnish. Decorate with sprigs of parsley.

182. Fried Whiting   *Merlans frits*

4 small whiting	salad oil
flour	salt

Clean and scale the whiting (page 54). Leave the heads on.
Roll in flour and fry in ½ inch hot oil (375°F.). Sprinkle with
salt and serve.

183. Baked Whiting.   *Merlans au gratin*

Follow the recipe for Baked Sole (177), substituting 4 whiting
for sole.

184. Whiting in White Wine and Herbs
Merlans aux fines herbes et au vin blanc

Follow recipe 176, substituting 4 whiting for the sole.

185. Fillets of Whiting in Tomato Sauce
Filets de merlans à l'Orly

8 fillets of whiting	chopped parsley
juice of ½ lemon	flour
salt	Tomato Sauce (21)
freshly ground black pepper	

Place the fillets in a shallow dish. Sprinkle with lemon juice,
salt, pepper, and parsley. Let them stand for at least 1 hour.
Put a generous amount of flour in a kitchen towel. Drain and
wipe the fillets and roll them in the towel. Each fillet should be
well coated. Fry 4 to 5 minutes in 375°F. fat or oil (41). There
should be enough fat to cover the fish. Serve with Tomato
Sauce, which has been prepared during the marinating of the
fish.

F

186. Fried Smelts   *Eperlans frits*

8 smelts   flour
milk   lemon wedges

Clean the fish through the gills, if possible (page 54). Otherwise, make as small a slit as possible in the belly and remove the intestines. Do not remove heads or tails. It is important to keep the fish whole. Place smelts on skewers, allowing 2 to each skewer. Dip in milk and then in flour. Plunge into deep fat (375°F.) and fry 4 minutes. Drain on absorbent paper, salt, and serve immediately. Garnish with lemon wedges.

187. Mixed Fish in Red Wine   *Matelote bourgeoise*

2 lbs. mixed fish (fresh haddock,   salt and pepper
      whiting, eel, fresh cod, perch, 2 cloves garlic
      carp)   3 ozs. butter
1 bottle red wine   2 tablespoons flour
several sprigs of parsley   20 small onions
1 large onion, finely chopped   ½ lb. mushrooms
1 carrot, cut in rounds   10 shrimps
1 sprig thyme   croutons

Combine red wine, parsley, carrot, onion, thyme, garlic, salt, and pepper and simmer 1 hour. Cut the fish in 3-inch strips and simmer in this *court-bouillon* for 15 minutes. Melt butter in a large saucepan and stir in flour. Add gradually 2 cups of the strained *court-bouillon* and stir with a wooden spoon until the sauce is smooth. If the sauce is thick, add more *court-bouillon*. Add the fish strips, the mushrooms, which have been thoroughly washed, and the onions, which have been peeled and fried lightly in butter. Continue cooking the sauce over a low flame until the onions are tender—approximately 20 minutes. Meanwhile fry the croutons and shrimps. Serve in a deep dish, using the shrimps and croutons as a garnish.

188. Bouillabaisse   *Bouillabaisse*

This is a home version of the famous Marseillaise bouillabaisse.

2 lbs. mixed fish (fresh haddock, carp, eel, whiting, sole)	pepper
	generous pinch of saffron
1 cup lobster meat (optional)	1 pint white wine
6 onions, cut in quarters	2 pints water
1 bay leaf	chopped parsley
3 cloves	4 tablespoons olive oil
2 cloves garlic	several slices of stale bread
salt	

Tie the fish, lobster meat, onions, bay leaf, cloves, and garlic in a piece of cheesecloth. Suspend this in a *court-bouillon* made of white wine, water, parsley, olive oil, salt, pepper, and saffron. Cook gently 45 minutes. Drain the fish. Remove the onions, bay leaf, cloves and garlic and place the fish in the *court-bouillon*. Add the stale bread and serve in a large tureen.

189. Fried Carp   *Carpe frite*

1 carp	chopped parsley
1 large onion, finely chopped	1 tablespoon wine vinegar
bay leaf	flour
dried thyme	salad oil

Clean, scale, and wash the carp (page 54). Split open. If there is roe, save it carefully. Put the fish in a shallow dish (not metal). Cover with chopped onion, herbs, and vinegar. Let the fish marinate 1 to 2 hours. Drain and roll in flour. Heat oil in a large frying pan and fry the fish 6 minutes, or until tender, at 390°F. During the last 3 minutes of cooking, add the roe, which has been rolled in flour. Salt the fish and serve on a heated dish with a garnish of lemon slices and sprigs of parsley.

190. Grilled Carp   *Carpe grillée*

1 large carp	slices of lemon
¼ pint salad oil	sprigs of parsley

Clean, scale and wash the carp (page 54). Split open and marinate in oil 15 minutes. Brush the grill rack with oil to prevent sticking. Grill 20 minutes, turning once only. Salt and serve with lemon slices and sprigs of parsley.

191. Carp in Mushroom Herb Sauce   *Carpe à la provençale*

1 large carp	chopped parsley
½ bottle red wine (burgundy)	1 small shallot, finely chopped
2 tablespoons oil	1 clove garlic, finely chopped
1 oz. butter, creamed with 1 table-	¼ lb. mushrooms, finely chopped
spoon flour	salt and pepper

Heat wine, oil, butter and flour. Add parsley, shallot, garlic, mushrooms, salt, and pepper. Cook 5 minutes. Add the carp and cook slowly 1 hour in the sauce. Place the carp on a hot dish and pour the sauce over it. If it is too liquid, reduce by quick boiling.

192. Eel with Tartar Sauce   *Anguille tartare*

Eel is apt to have a very strong fishy flavour. The French method of cooking eel in a *court-bouillon* reduces this. If the fish merchant

will not skin the eel, do it yourself. Rub your hands in salt.
Loosen the skin around the neck with the sharp point of a knife.
Hold the head with the left hand and strip off the skin with a
pair of pliers. Cut off the head. Clean the eel by making a split
in the belly and removing the entrails. Wipe well before cooking.

1 eel

½ bottle dry white wine

1 pint stock or water

3 small onions

2 carrots, sliced

bouquet garni (42)

2 cloves

2 cloves garlic

salt and pepper

2 ozs. butter

2 tablespoons flour

1 egg yolk

fine bread crumbs

chopped   parsley,   shallot,   and
    chives, mixed

1 whole egg beaten with 2 table-
    spoons oil

¼ pint salad oil

Tartar Sauce (20)

Prepare a *court-bouillon* of the water or stock, wine, onions,
carrots, *bouquet garni*, cloves, garlic, salt, and pepper. Simmer
30 minutes. Roll the cleaned and skinned eel into a circle, placing
the tail in the slit in the belly. Tie securely so that the eel will
keep its shape. Place the eel in the *court-bouillon* and simmer
30 minutes. Remove it carefully and place on a dish to cool.
Melt butter and stir in flour. Keep stirring with a wooden spoon
until the flour is pale brown. Add ½ pint of the *court-bouillon*,
which has been carefully strained. Continue stirring until the
sauce is smooth. Remove from the flame and add the egg yolk.
Cool the sauce and smear the eel with it. Roll the eel in bread
crumbs and then in the chopped herbs. Dip in the oil and egg
mixture and then again in the bread crumbs. Heat ¼ pint of
salad oil in a large frying pan. Fry at 390°F. until the eel is
golden brown. Place on a hot dish and fill the centre with Tartar
Sauce.

193. Eel with Wine and Mushroom Sauce

Anguille à la poulette

1 eel	2 tablespoons flour
½ bottle dry white wine	12 very small onions
2 bay leaves	¼ lb. mushrooms
several sprigs of parsley	1 egg yolk
1 onion, finely chopped	12 shrimps
salt and pepper	fried croutons
2 ozs. butter	

Clean and skin the eel according to the preceding recipe. Cut in 3-inch pieces and place in a pan with wine, bay leaves, parsley, onion, salt, and pepper. Boil briskly 30 minutes. In another saucepan, melt the butter and stir in flour. Moisten with 1 cup of the *court-bouillon* in which the eel has been cooked. Season with salt and pepper according to taste, and stir until the sauce is smooth. Add the onions and mushrooms. Cook until the onions are tender. Add more of the *court-bouillon* if sauce is too thick. Just before serving, bind the sauce with the egg yolk (page 3). Place the eel on a warm dish, cover with the sauce, and garnish with shrimps and croutons, which have been lightly fried in butter.

194. Fried Eel   *Anguille frite*

1 eel	fine bread crumbs
2 beaten eggs	Tomato Sauce (21)

Follow recipe 192 for skinning and cleaning the eel. Cut the eel in 3-inch pieces and cook in *court-bouillon* as in the preceding recipe. When the eel is cooked, drain and dry the pieces. Dip in egg and roll in bread crumbs. Heat some salad oil to 390°F. and fry until the pieces are golden brown. Serve with Tomato Sauce.

195. Crayfish *Ecrevisses*

The *écrevisse* (crayfish) is perhaps better known and more appreciated in France than anywhere else. It has a very delicate flavour. Although it is not very often sold by fishmongers, it abounds in some lakes, rivers and streams. The average crayfish does not measure more than 4 or 5 inches long and looks like a small lobster. It takes a great many crayfish to make a respectable meal.

196. Crayfish in *Court-bouillon*

Ecrevisses au court-bouillon

20 crayfish	1 bay leaf
½ bottle white wine	2 small cloves garlic
1 pint water	several small sprigs of parsley
1 onion, finely chopped	salt
1 carrot, sliced in rounds	freshly ground black pepper

Prepare the *court-bouillon* of wine, water, onion, carrot, bay leaf, garlic, parsley, salt, and a generous amount of black pepper. Simmer 30 minutes. Wash the crayfish in several waters. Add to the *court-bouillon* and simmer (not boil) 12 minutes. Serve very hot, piled in a pyramid shape on a hot dish. Garnish with sprigs of fresh parsley. The crayfish are eaten like lobsters. Most of the meat is in the tail. Take care to remove the black strip in the centre of the tail.

L'hôte et le poisson en trois jours sont poison.

197. Crayfish in Paprika Butter Sauce
Ecrevisses à la marinière

20 crayfish   ¼ lb. butter
court-bouillon (196)   ¼ teaspoon paprika

Prepare the crayfish as in the preceding recipe. Melt butter in
the top of a double boiler. Add paprika, and salt. When the butter
is piping hot it is ready to be served with the crayfish.

198. Crayfish in Herb Sauce   *Ecrevisses à la bordelaise*

20 crayfish   1 clove garlic
court-bouillon (196)   4 ozs. butter
6 shallots   3 tablespoons dry white wine
finely chopped parsley   salt and pepper

Follow recipe 196 for cooking crayfish. Melt the butter. Add
finely chopped shallots, parsley, garlic, and white wine. Season
highly with salt and pepper. Pour the sauce over the crayfish,
which have been piled in a pyramid shape on a heated dish.

199. Frog Legs in White Wine Sauce
Grenouilles à la poulette

12 pairs frog legs	salt
2 ozs. butter	black pepper
2 tablespoons flour	chopped parsley
¼ pint dry white wine	small chopped onion
	1 egg yolk

Wash the frog legs and soak in cold water 3 hours. Drain them and wipe very dry. Melt butter in heavy saucepan. Fry the legs 2 minutes on each side. Sprinkle with flour and stir carefully so that the flour and butter are blended. Add wine, parsley, onion, and season with salt and pepper. Cook 15 minutes over a moderate flame. Put the legs on a heated dish. Thicken the sauce with the egg yolk (page 3) and pour over the legs. Serve immediately. 3 pairs of legs per person is usually enough.

200. Fried Frog Legs   *Cuisses de grenouilles frites*

12 pairs frog legs	1 small onion, finely chopped
2 tablespoons wine vinegar	salt
1 bay leaf, broken into small pieces	freshly ground black pepper
chopped parsley	flour
	4 ozs. butter

Wash and dry the frog legs. Marinate in vinegar, bay leaf, parsley, onion, salt, and pepper for 1 hour. Spoon the liquid over the legs several times. Drain and wipe dry. Roll in flour and fry in butter until brown on both sides. Salt and serve very hot.

201. Snails   *Escargots à la bourguignonne*

50 snails	1 clove garlic
1½ pints water	½ lb. butter
1 onion, finely chopped	chopped parsley
1 carrot, sliced	2 cloves garlic finely chopped
bouquet garni (42)	salt and pepper

To clean the snails, cook them in heavily salted water for 20 minutes, stirring often. Meanwhile prepare a *court-bouillon* with water, onion, carrot, *bouquet garni*, and garlic. Let this simmer 15 minutes. Change the snails from the salt water to the *court-bouillon* and cook 15 minutes. While the snails are cooling, soften the butter and work into it the chopped parsley and garlic. Season highly with salt and pepper. When the snails are cool, remove each from its shell and run water over the shells to be sure they are clean. Place a bit of the butter mixture at the bottom of each shell, replace the snail, and fill to the top with the butter mixture. Divide the snails into lots of at least 12 and bake in individual baking dishes in a hot (400°F.) oven until they are bubbling. Serve very hot.

202. Snails in White Wine Sauce   *Escargots à la poulette*

50 snails	2 tablespoons flour
court-bouillon (201)	1 glass dry white wine
2 ozs. butter	salt and pepper

Follow the preceding recipe for cleaning and cooking the snails. Melt butter and stir in flour. As soon as the butter and flour are well blended, stir in the wine and ¼ pint of strained *court-bouillon*. Stir until the sauce is smooth. Put the snails in the sauce and simmer 5 minutes. If the sauce is too thick add more *court-bouillon*. Serve in individual ramekins.

203. Mussels in White Sauce   *Moules à la béchamel*

Mussels should be very fresh and not too large. If they are open they are not fit for use. Before they are cooked they should be well scrubbed and washed in several waters.

4 pints mussels	1 cup liquor from the mussels
2 ozs. butter	chopped parsley
2 tablespoons flour	1 clove garlic, finely chopped
½ pint milk	salt and black pepper

Place the mussels in a fish kettle with half a teacup of water. As soon as the mussels open, remove them from the kettle and take off the top shell. Melt butter in a large saucepan. Stir in flour. Add the milk and the liquor from the mussels which has been allowed to settle a few moments. Stir the sauce with a wooden spoon until it is smooth. The sauce should be thin. Add parsley garlic, salt, and pepper and cook 5 minutes. Reheat the mussels in the sauce and serve.

204. Mussels Marinière   *Moules à la marinière*

4 pints mussels	1 bay leaf
¼ pint white wine	a sprig of thyme or dried thyme
1 carrot, sliced	1 clove garlic
1 onion, finely chopped	salt and pepper
chopped parsley	3 ozs. butter

Scrub the mussels and wash in several waters. Place them in a large pan with wine, carrot, onion, parsley, bay leaf, thyme, garlic, salt, pepper, and butter. Cover the pan and place over a high flame. When all the mussels are open they are cooked. Remove the mussels from the pan, take the top shell off each one, and place them in a deep heated dish, or tureen. Strain the *court-bouillon* and pour over the mussels.

205. Mussels in Scallop Shells   *Moules en coquilles*

Follow recipe 203. Remove both shells and mix the mussels
with the sauce, which should be quite thick. Place 5 or 6 mussels
in each scallop shell or ramekin. Cover with bread crumbs, dot
with butter, and brown in a hot oven. Garnish with fresh parsley
finely chopped.

206. Mussels with Spanish Rice   *Paella*

4 ozs. rice	3 tomatoes, cut in eighths
¼ pint olive oil	½ green pepper, cut in strips
2 large onions, chopped	salt and pepper
chopped parsley	3 pints mussels
1 large clove garlic	

Wash rice and mix with oil, onions, parsley, garlic, tomatoes,
green pepper, salt, and pepper. Cook in a covered pan over a
slow fire until the rice is tender but not too soft. Stir the rice
from time to time to prevent crusting; 30 minutes should be
enough to cook the rice. Open the mussels, after they have
been thoroughly washed, by steaming them with ¼ cup water
over a high flame. As soon as they are open, remove the top shell
and put the mussels in a deep dish. Cover with rice and pour
the liquor of the mussels, which has been allowed to settle, over
the rice. Serve very hot.

207. Oysters   *Huîtres*

Open fresh oysters with special oyster knife. Serve the oyster in
the bottom shell. Place the oysters on a bed of chopped ice.
Serve with lemon wedges. Allow 6 to 9 oysters per person.

208. Oysters in Scallop Shells   *Huîtres en coquilles*

2 dozen oysters	¼ pint dry white wine
2 ozs. butter	2 tablespoons water
2 tablespoons flour	fine bread crumbs
¼ lb. small mushrooms	salt and pepper
chopped parsley	

Open the oysters over a saucepan in order to catch the juice. Set the shells aside and simmer (not boil) the oysters in the juice for 3 minutes. Remove from the fire. Wash and stem the mushrooms. Fry lightly with the parsley for 3 minutes. Stir in the flour and add wine, water, and the oyster liquor. Stir until the sauce is smooth. Reheat the oysters in the sauce. Put 4 or 5 oysters in each scallop shell, cover with bread crumbs, dot with butter, and place in hot oven for 5 minutes.

209. Lobster Mayonnaise   *Homard à la mayonnaise*

2 lobsters	Mayonnaise (17)
court-bouillon	

Follow the recipe for Crayfish in *court-bouillon* (196), substituting lobsters for the crayfish. Let the lobsters cool in the *court-bouillon*. Split each lobster down the middle and crack the claws. Serve with a bowl of Mayonnaise.

210. Lobster à l'Américaine   *Homard à l'américaine*

4 lobsters	2 tablespoons cooking brandy
2 tablespoons olive oil	2 tablespoons tomato sauce
salt	A little beef jelly
black pepper	*bouquet garni* (42)
4 small onions, finely chopped	2 ozs. butter
1 clove garlic, finely chopped	juice of ½ lemon
¼ pint dry white wine	dash of cayenne pepper

Kill the lobsters by putting a knife through the head. Take
off the claws and crack them. Take off the tail and cut into 3
or 4 pieces. Heat olive oil in a pan large enough to hold all the
lobsters. Put in the lobster. Sprinkle with salt and pepper and
cook 5 minutes. Meanwhile, fry the chopped onion and garlic
in 1 oz. butter until transparent. Add to the lobster. Then add
the white wine and brandy. Touch with a lighted match. It will
flame for a moment. When it has died down, add tomato sauce,
beef jelly, and *bouquet garni*, and cook 10 minutes more over a
moderate flame. Put the lobster on a deep, heated dish. Arrange
the other pieces on top. Add 1 oz. butter, lemon juice, and
cayenne to the sauce and when it is boiling pour over the lobsters.
There is no way to eat this dish delicately, but it is wonderfully
delicious to taste and to smell.

211. Shrimps   *Crevettes*

The French shrimps are very tiny and high in flavour. The same
shrimps are found on the British Coast. They are usually boiled
10 minutes in salted water and served cold as an hors-d'œuvre.
They are also delicious hot.

212. Shrimps Béchamel   *Crevettes à la béchamel*

1 pint small shrimps   Bechamel Sauce (1)

Shell one pint of freshly cooked shrimps. Reheat in a Béchamel
Sauce and serve either in pastry or scallop shells. This makes
a good filling for Vol-au-vent (372).

213. Scallops in the Shell   *Coquilles Saint-Jacques*

In France, scallops are always sold in the shell. They are opened
by placing them in a hot oven and then detaching the white
muscle and yellow part which are the edible portions. In other
countries scallops are often sold out of the shell. The shells in
which they are served can be bought or gathered at the sea shore.
If one has not any shells, individual ramekins may be used.

4 or 8 scallops   1 tablespoon water
¼ pint dry white wine   3 ozs. butter
½ pint water   2 tablespoons flour
bouquet garni (42)   1 egg yolk
¼ lb. mushrooms   2 tablespoons cream
1 small onion, finely chopped   salt and pepper
1 teaspoon lemon juice   bread crumbs

Bring scallops to the boil in water, wine, and *bouquet garni*.
Simmer 10 minutes or until tender. The scallops should not
be overcooked. Remove the *bouquet garni*, strain the scallops,
but reserve the liquor. Wash and chop mushrooms. Mix with
onion, 1 tablespoon butter, lemon juice, and water. Cook in a
covered saucepan for 10 minutes. Strain and reserve the liquor.
Melt 2 ozs. butter and stir in flour. Add the liquors saved from
the mushrooms and scallops and stir with a wooden spoon until

the sauce is smooth. Thicken with egg yolk and cream (page 4). Cut the scallops into small pieces and add with the mushrooms to the sauce. Put this mixture into the scallop shells or ramekins, cover with bread crumbs, dot with butter, and brown in hot oven. Garnish each shell with fresh sprigs of parsley. One of these per person makes an excellent hors-d'œuvre; two make a good main course.

La caque sent toujours le hareng.

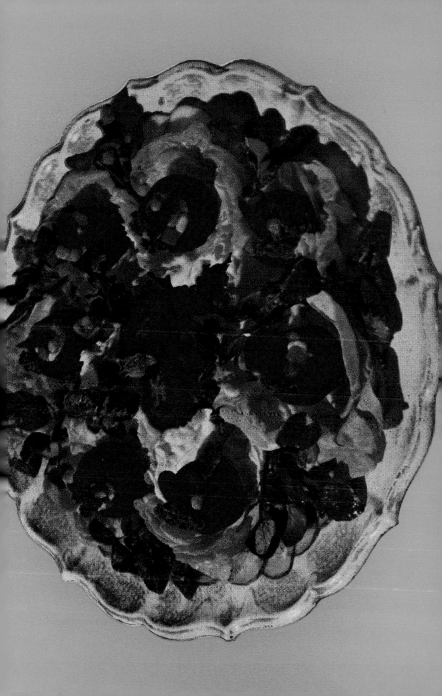

IN FRANCE, meat is cut in a very different manner from the way it is cut in other countries. It is unreasonable to expect your own butcher to cut meat in the French way. For the best cuts, the French butcher makes no attempt to economise. The best one can usually do is to approximate the cut called for in the French recipe. Each recipe will indicate the most suitable cut.

Unless meat is to be used immediately, it should be stored in the coldest part of the refrigerator. Remove the meat from the paper and place in a covered dish. Do not wash the meat, but wipe it with a damp cloth so that any bits of bone will be removed.

LARDING: Many recipes call for larding the meat. This consists of inserting strips of salt pork, $\frac{1}{4}$ inch square and 3 to 4 inches long, in the meat. To do this, insert the pork in the eye end of a larding needle and pierce the meat with the sharp end. These insertions can be made in the thick part of the meat or small stitches can be taken on the top. The pork will remain

G

in the meat. The 'stitches' should be ½ inch deep and 1 inch long
and should be spaced 2 inches apart in parallel lines.

COOKING MEAT: There are many ways of cooking meat—roasting,
boiling, grilling, frying, stewing, and in casseroles. In general
it is best to cook at a moderate temperature. Each recipe will
indicate the best temperature for the particular meat. It is best
to have a thermometer for both oven and frying purposes.

BEEF   *BŒUF*

214. Boiled Beef   *Bœuf bouilli*

*This is only to be served in the bosom of the family, but it is ex-
tremely good and is not to be despised for its simplicity.*

TANTE MARIE

Bœuf bouilli is the 3 lbs. of top rump used in *Pot-au-feu* (68).
Remove the string. Place on a dish and surround with the
vegetables cooked with the meat. Serve with Robert Sauce (16),
Piquant Sauce (12), Tomato Sauce (21), or Onion Sauce (34).

215. Beef Stew   *Bœuf en miroton*

2 ozs. butter	8 small onions
2 tablespoons flour	6 potatoes
1 pint stock or water	*bouquet garni* (42)
salt	1½ lbs. cold boiled beef, cut in
black pepper	pieces

Melt butter and stir in flour. Continue stirring until flour is
brown. Add liquid, salt, and pepper and stir until the sauce is

smooth. Peel onions and leave them whole; peel and quarter
the potatoes. Add these and the *bouquet garni* to the sauce and
simmer 45 minutes. Cut the beef into small pieces and add
to the sauce. Simmer 15 minutes more. Remove the *bouquet
garni* before serving.

216. Cold Beef Salad   *Bœuf en vinaigrette*

Cold boiled beef, thinly sliced   French Dressing (31)
3 hard-boiled eggs

Place the thin slices of cold beef on a deep dish. Cover with slices
of hard-boiled egg and pour French Dressing over it all. This
makes a delicious luncheon dish.

217. Beef Balls   *Boulettes de hachis de bœuf frites*

1 lb. lean minced beef, raw	pepper
¼ lb. sausage meat	1 egg
2 onions, finely chopped	flour
chopped parsley	1 egg, well beaten
2 slices dry bread soaked in	fine bread crumbs
1 gill milk	parsley
salt	

Combine the raw minced beef, sausage meat, onion, and parsley.
Add the bread, egg, salt, and pepper and mix thoroughly. Chill
the mixture and form into small balls or into ovals. Roll in
flour, dip in beaten egg and roll in bread crumbs. Fry in deep
fat (375°F.). Turn the balls often so that they will brown on all
sides. Serve on a dish with fried parsley (see under recipe 240).

218. Minced Beef   *Bœuf en hachis*

1 lb. lean minced beef	2 tablespoons flour
¼ lb. sausage meat	¼ pint stock
2 onions, finely chopped	salt and pepper
chopped parsley	croutons
2 slices dry bread, soaked in	3 hard-boiled eggs
1 gill milk	sprigs of parsley
2 ozs. butter	

Combine and mix thoroughly the raw minced beef, sausage
meat, onion, parsley, and bread. Melt butter in large frying
pan and cook the mixture 10 minutes, stirring frequently.
Sprinkle with flour and add stock, salt, and pepper. Cook 5
minutes longer. Place the meat in the centre of a heated dish.
Surround with croutons and garnish with slices of hard-boiled
egg and sprigs of parsley.

219. Beef Casserole   *Bœuf bouilli au gratin*

¼ lb. salt pork	salt
¼ lb. mushrooms	black pepper
2 onions, finely chopped	2 tablespoons fine bread crumbs
chopped parsley	¼ pint white wine
1 clove garlic, chopped	8 slices of boiled beef (214)

Dice the pork and fry gently until most of the fat has been
drawn. Place the pieces in the bottom of a casserole. Wash
mushrooms and chop with onions, parsley, and garlic. Add
bread crumbs, wine, salt, and pepper and mix well. Put a layer
of this mixture on the bottom of the casserole, add the slices
of meat and cover with the rest of the mixture. Bake 20 minutes
in 375°F. oven.

Ce qui nuit à l'un sert à l'autre.

220. Beef Balls in Sauce   *Boulettes de bœuf à la sauce*

Beef Balls (217)   1 pint stock
2 ozs. butter   *bouquet garni* (42)
2 tablespoons flour   salt and pepper

Make the beef balls but instead of frying them, cook them in
the following sauce: melt butter and stir in flour, allowing it
to brown but taking care that it does not burn. Add stock,
bouquet garni, salt and pepper to taste. Stir until the sauce begins
to thicken, and simmer 20 minutes. Place the balls in the sauce
and cook 15 minutes.

221. Minced Beef, Potato Purée
                    Hachis de bœuf à la purée de pommes de terre

Minced Beef (218)   2 ozs. butter
6 or 8 potatoes   salt and pepper

Follow directions for Minced Beef. At the same time, boil
potatoes until soft. Force through a food mill or potato masher,
or whip with an electric beater. Season with butter, salt, and
pepper. Alternate layers of beef and potato purée in a buttered
baking dish, beginning with beef and finishing with potato. Dot
with butter and bake in 400°F. oven until the potatoes are golden
brown (approximately 10 minutes). Decorate with sprigs of fresh
parsley.

222. Roast Fillet of Beef   *Filet de bœuf*

Ask the butcher for a fillet of beef. This should weigh 2 to
3 lbs. and should be about 4 inches in diameter. This is an
expensive cut but it is very delicious and commonly used in
France. Wrap in a paper-thin layer of salt pork and roast in
300°F. oven. 15 minutes per pound is enough.

223. Roast Fillet of Beef with Madeira Sauce

Filet de bœuf au Madère

Follow the preceding recipe and serve with a Madeira Sauce (13).

224. Roast Beef   *Aloyau rôti ou Rosbif*

Ask the butcher for a joint of sirloin or top-side. A rib roast is not used in France. Rub the surface with salt and black pepper. Roast in 300°F. oven. allowing 15 minutes per pound. For those who do not like underdone beef, 17–20 minutes per pound should be allowed. Prolonged cooking lessens the flavour. Serve on a heated dish. Garnish with parsley, watercress, or with Stuffed Mushrooms (445).

To make gravy: Pour the excess fat from the roasting tin. Put tin on top of the stove. Add ½ pint boiling water and scrape off the juices that have adhered to the tin. Mix well, strain, and serve in a heated gravy jug with the joint.

225. Chuck Roast   *Paleron de bœuf*

Marinate 3- to 4-lbs. chuck roast (part of shoulder, in front of the fore-rib) from 12 to 24 hours (see recipe 32). The meat is thus made tender and may be roasted like Roast Beef (224).

Les folles dépenses refroidissent la cuisine.

226. Burgundy Beef   *Bœuf bourguignon*

1½ lbs. lean stewing beef	¼ pint red wine
2 ozs. butter	¼ pint stock
2 onions	salt and pepper
1 carrot	*bouquet garni* (42)
2 tablespoons flour	

Melt the butter in a heavy saucepan. Dice carrot and onions and fry gently with the beef in the butter. When the meat is seared on all sides, remove the meat and vegetables and stir in flour. Add wine, stock, *bouquet garni*, and stir until the sauce is smooth. Put back the meat and vegetables, cover, and simmer 3 hours.

227. Steak   *Bifteck-grillade*

Order individual steaks cut from the sirloin or fillet or minute steaks cut from the rump. Do not salt until after cooking, because the salt tends to draw out the juices. Grill or quick-fry according to the following directions. Meanwhile cream softened butter with chopped parsley. Season the butter with salt, pepper, and a dash of lemon juice. Spread over the sizzling steaks, garnish with watercress, and serve immediately.

TO GRILL: Place the steaks under the electric or gas grill, or if possible over live charcoal. Grill 4 minutes on each side, or longer if medium or well-done steaks are preferred.

TO QUICK-FRY: Heat frying pan until very hot. Rub the frying pan with a piece of fat or melt a little butter. Fry the steaks 2 to 4 minutes on each side, depending on the thickness of the steaks.

228. Chateaubriand Steak   *Chateaubriand*

A Chateaubriand is a thick steak—1½ to 2 inches thick, or 3 to
4 inches if the occasion is gala and the price not to be considered.
Sirloin, fillet, or rump steaks are all good cuts. Grill or quick-fry
(227), but increase the time allowance to 10 or 12 minutes on
each side according to the thickness of the steak. For medium
or well-done steak allow more time. Season with butter, salt, and
a generous amount of freshly ground black pepper. Garnish with
parsley or fresh watercress.

229. Filets Mignons in Mushroom Sauce
                          Filets sautés aux champignons

4 to 6 individual fillet steaks	½ pint beef stock
(1 inch thick)	½ lb. mushrooms
2 ozs. butter	salt and pepper
2 tablespoons flour	

Melt the butter in a large frying pan. When it is sizzling, put
in the pan as many steaks as there are persons to be served.
Sear the steaks 2 minutes on each side. Remove the steaks. Stir
in flour and stock and continue stirring until the sauce is smooth.
Season with salt and pepper. Add mushrooms which have been
washed thoroughly and sliced. Use both caps and stems. Cook
10 minutes. Put the steaks back into the sauce and simmer 5
minutes longer. Do not let the sauce boil. Place the steaks in the
centre of a heated dish. Surround with the mushrooms and
garnish with watercress.

230. Filets Mignons in Olive Sauce   *Filets sautés aux olives*

Follow the preceding recipe but substitute ½ cup of stoned olives
for the mushrooms.

231. Braised Beef   *Entrecôte braisé*

2 to 3 lbs. rump steak
¼ lb. diced salt pork
2 tablespoons flour
½ pint beef stock or water
salt
5 peppercorns

2 cloves
bouquet garni (42)
2 onions
1 carrot
2 tablespoons cooking brandy

Fry the salt pork in a heavy saucepan. Sear the meat on both
sides. When well browned, take out the salt pork and meat.
Stir in flour and add stock. Stir until the sauce is smooth. Add
onions and carrots, cut in small pieces, salt, peppercorns, cloves,
bouquet garni, and brandy. Put the meat in the sauce and simmer
3 hours with the pan covered. Skim off the fat and strain the
sauce before serving.

232. Beef à la mode   *Bœuf à la mode*

3 to 4 lbs. of beef cut from the
   rump
several larding strips 4 to 5 inches
   long
2 ozs. butter or chicken fat
1½ pints water
¼ pint dry white wine
2 tablespoons cooking brandy

salt
black pepper
½ calf's foot (or ½ beef or pig's
   knuckle)
bouquet garni (42)
2 cloves
2 carrots, cut in small pieces
12 small onions

Lard beef with strips of salt pork (page 87). Melt butter or
chicken fat in a deep pan. Sear the meat on all sides, and place
in a casserole. Add water, wine, brandy, salt, pepper, *bouquet
garni*, cloves, carrots, and onions and the calf's foot or knuckle,
which will add greatly to the richness of the sauce. Place in a
300°F. oven. The dish should be covered. Cook 5 hours. Place
the meat on a heated dish. Remove the *bouquet garni*, skim off
the fat, and surround the meat with the sauce.

233. Beef à la mode in Aspic   *Bœuf à la mode en gelée*

Strain and save some of the sauce from Beef à la mode (232).
Chill and remove the coating of fat. Add 1 teaspoon of gelatine
to 1 pint of the sauce, unless it is already quite stiff, and bring
to the boil. Arrange thin slices of cold beef on a dish. Cover with
rounds of carrot. Let the sauce cool until it is syrupy but not
stiff. Pour over the meat carefully and place the dish in the
refrigerator. When the aspic is stiff the dish is ready. Garnish
with sprigs of parsley and serve with mustard. This makes a
delicious luncheon dish.

234. Beef Kidneys in Madeira Sauce
                                 Rognons de bœuf au Madère

1 beef kidney	$\frac{1}{4}$ pint Madeira wine
2 ozs. butter	$\frac{1}{4}$ pint water
2 tablespoons flour	salt and pepper

Split the kidney in two and cut out the fatty core. Cut the kidney
in small pieces. Melt butter and fry the pieces of kidney, stirring
gently so that the pieces will be browned on all sides. Sprinkle
with flour and moisten with wine and water. Season with salt
and pepper and stir until the flour is well blended. Simmer 10
minutes but do not let the sauce boil. Kidneys become tough
if overcooked, but they should be served very hot.

235. Kidneys and Mushrooms in Madeira Sauce
                                 Rognons de bœuf aux champignons

Add $\frac{1}{2}$ lb. of well-washed mushrooms to the kidneys and follow
directions in the preceding recipe. Add 2 teaspoons of finely
chopped parsley just before serving. Serve with triangles of
buttered toast.

236. Beef Tongue, Piquant or Tomato Sauce
Langue de bœuf, sauce piquante ou sauce tomate

1 fresh tongue*	salt
1 carrot, cut in rounds	pepper
2 leeks	2 cloves
bouquet garni (42)	Piquant Sauce (12) or Tomato
2 quarts of water	Sauce (21)

Cover tongue with cold water. Add carrots, leeks slit length-wise and tied together with kitchen string, *bouquet garni*, cloves, salt, and pepper. Simmer 3 hours. Remove tongue from the water. Take off skin and cut out the hard roots. Split the tongue lengthwise. Arrange in a crown around a dish and fill the centre with Piquant or Tomato Sauce.

237. Beef Tongue Casserole   *Langue de bœuf au gratin*

Cold cooked beef tongue (236)	chopped parsley
4 ozs. butter	salt
2 tablespoons white wine	pepper
6 small gherkins	2 tablespoons fine bread crumbs
3 spring onions or tiny onions	

Slice the cold tongue as thinly as possible. Chop gherkins, spring onions, and parsley. Mix with bread crumbs, wine, salt, and pepper. Dot the bottom of the casserole with butter and spread with half the mixture. Cover with the slices of cold tongue and put the rest of the mixture on the tongue. Bake 30 minutes in 300°F. oven.

* Corned or smoked tongue may be used. These should be soaked in cold water several hours before using.

238. Beef Brains in Black Butter Sauce
Cervelle de bœuf au beurre noir

Beef brains are not as delicate as calf's brains, but if carefully prepared they are very delicious.

TANTE MARIE

3 pairs brains	1 clove garlic
2 tablespoons vinegar	*bouquet garni* (42)
1 teaspoon salt	3 pints water
4 peppercorns	Black Butter Sauce (14)
4 cloves	

Soak brains 2 hours in cold water, changing the water at least twice. Clean them carefully. Remove loose pieces of skin, blood, and fibres. Combine vinegar, salt, peppercorns, cloves, garlic, *bouquet garni*, and water. Add the brains and bring slowly to boiling point. Cook gently 45 minutes. Remove the brains. Cut in two and serve on a heated dish with Black Butter Sauce poured over them.

239. Beef Brains in Mushroom and Onion Sauce
Cervelle de bœuf en matelote

3 pairs cooked beef brains	*bouquet garni* (42)
1 oz. butter	10 small onions
1 tablespoon flour	$\frac{1}{4}$ lb. mushrooms
$\frac{1}{2}$ pint water	salt and pepper
$\frac{1}{4}$ pint red wine	croutons

Follow recipe 238 for cooking brains. Melt butter and add flour, allowing it to brown but taking care that it does not burn. Add water and wine and stir until sauce begins to thicken. Add *bouquet garni*, onions, mushrooms cut in small pieces, and simmer 30 minutes. Remove *bouquet garni*, add brains, salt, and pepper, and simmer 15 minutes longer. Serve on a heated dish and garnish with long croutons.

240. Fried Beef Brains   *Cervelle de bœuf frite*

Soak and clean the brains (238). Boil gently in ½ pint water and ¼ pint vinegar for 20 minutes. Drain and cut in small pieces. Dip in a thick batter (40). Fry in deep fat (360°F.), turning frequently so that the pieces will brown on all sides. Serve on a warm dish and garnish with fried parsley.

To fry parsley: Wash and dry the parsley. Throw into the hot fat and remove almost immediately with a slice.

241. Tripe Lyonnaise   *Tripes à la Lyonnaise*

1 to 1½ lbs. tripe	salt and pepper
2 ozs. butter or oil	nutmeg
4 onions, sliced very thinly	

Wipe tripe very carefully. Cut in squares. Heat oil or butter in heavy saucepan and fry onion slices until they are yellow. Add tripe and brown on both sides. Add salt, pepper, and nutmeg. Cook 5 minutes. Serve very hot, because otherwise this dish is not good.

242. Tripe à la mode de Caen   *Tripes à la mode de Caen*

1 to 1½ lbs. tripe	2 cloves of garlic
1 calf's foot, cut in 3 pieces	2 ozs. salt pork, diced
2 carrots, cut in rounds	6 peppercorns
bouquet garni (42), tied in 2 small	4 slices bacon
bunches	¼ pint water
4 cloves	½ bottle white wine

Wipe the tripe clean and cut into large pieces. At the bottom of an earthenware pot put a layer of carrots, 1 clove garlic, and ½ of the diced salt pork, and three pieces of calf's foot. Over this put a layer of tripe. Repeat the process omitting the calf's foot. Cover the last layer of tripe with slices of bacon. Fill the jar ¾ full with white wine diluted with a little water. Put a tight cover on the pot and cook 5 hours in a 350°F. oven. Just before serving thicken the sauce with a little cornflour (page 4).

243. Left-over Beef with Tomato or Piquant Sauce
                        Restes de bœuf, sauce tomate ou sauce piquante

Slice cold roast or boiled beef very thinly and heat in Tomato Sauce (21) or Piquant Sauce (12).

244. Left-over Beef in Cream Sauce
                        Restes de bœuf, sauce poulette

Dice cold boiled or roast beef and heat in a Poulette Sauce (8). Garnish with sprigs of fresh parsley.

245. Beef and Cabbage   *Restes de bœuf aux choux*

¼ lb. diced salt pork
2 tablespoons flour
1 pint water
1 onion, finely chopped
salt

pepper
bouquet garni (42)
1 cabbage, cut in eighths
1 to 2 lbs. of cold roast or boiled
    beef, in one piece

Fry the salt pork in deep saucepan. When most of the fat has been rendered, take out the pork and keep warm. Stir in the flour and let it brown. Add water, onion, *bouquet garni*, salt, and pepper. Stir until the sauce is smooth. Add cabbage and beef. Simmer 45 minutes. Place beef in centre of deep dish. Surround with cabbage dotted with the salt pork. Strain the liquid and thicken with cornflour (page 4). Pour the sauce over the beef.

246. Croquettes   *Croquettes*

2 cups cooked meat (beef, veal,
    lamb, chicken, rabbit, sweet-
    breads, or fish)
chopped parsley
salt
pepper
2 ozs. butter

2 tablespoons flour
¼ pint stock or water
¼ lb. chopped mushrooms
1 egg yolk
1 egg, beaten with
    2 tablespoons oil
fine bread crumbs

Chop the meat or put it through a mincer. Add parsley, salt, and pepper. Melt butter in a heavy saucepan. Stir in flour and add water, stirring until well blended. Add the meat and mushrooms. Simmer 20 minutes without a cover so that the mixture will be very thick. Taste for seasoning and add more salt and pepper, if necessary. Chill the mixture and add unbeaten egg yolk. Form the croquettes in balls or long ovals, using 1 tablespoon of the mixture for each. Dip in the egg beaten with oil and roll in bread crumbs. Fry in deep fat (375°F.) until golden brown (3 to 5 minutes) and serve with fried parsley.

LAMB   *AGNEAU*

Mutton is very commonly used in France and any of the recipes given below for lamb may be used for mutton, provided it is of good quality. Meat described as 'Lamb' is commonly taken from young sheep. 'Spring lamb' applies to the meat taken from 3- to 5-month-old lambs and is preferable to ordinary lamb or mutton. The flesh of lamb should be pink and the fat should be hard and white. The flesh of mutton is dark red and should be well 'aged' to be good.

247. Roast Lamb   *Gigot rôti*

Order a leg of lamb weighing 3 to 5 lbs. Peel 4 small cloves of garlic. Pierce the flesh with the sharp point of a knife in 4 well-separated places and insert the garlic. Place the lamb on a rack in an oven tin. Place ½ pint water, I tablespoon of butter, and I teaspoon of salt in the tin. Roast in 325°F. oven, counting 17 to 20 minutes per pound. French lamb is always served under-done, with the flesh still bright pink.

To make gravy: Add a little water to the pan after the meat has been placed on a heated dish. Scrape the juices from the bottom of the pan. Strain and serve with the roast. Garnish with watercress or sprigs of parsley.

248. Marinated Lamb or Mutton   *Gigot mariné*

Purchase a leg of lamb or mutton. Wipe it carefully. Make several incisions with a sharp knife and insert ¼-inch-by-1-inch pieces of salt pork in the flesh of the meat. Prepare a Marinating

Dressing (32). It is wise to double the recipe for a large piece of meat. Marinate the lamb 3 to 4 days, keeping it in a cool place. Baste the meat with the sauce several times a day. When it is ready to be cooked, place the meat on a rack in an oven tin. Pour 6 tablespoons of the sauce in the bottom of the tin. Roast in a 300°F. oven allowing 30 minutes per pound. The meat should be well done. Serve with Piquant Sauce (12) or Tomato Sauce (21). The meat will have a gamey flavour. It is delicious.

249. Braised Lamb   *Gigot d'agneau braisé*

4 lbs. boned and rolled leg of lamb
several larding strips, 3 inches long
salt
black pepper
2 ozs. butter
1 pint water
2 tablespoons cooking brandy
bouquet garni (42)
5 carrots
½ calf's foot or knuckle (sawn in small pieces)

Wipe the meat carefully. Lard the meat with strips of salt pork (page 87). Rub with salt and pepper. Melt the butter in a deep saucepan that has a cover. Sear the meat on all sides. When it is browned all over, add water, brandy, *bouquet garni*, carrots cut in ½ inch pieces, and calf's foot. Cook slowly 4 hours with cover on. Remove the *bouquet garni*. Place meat on dish, surround with carrots, and pour over it all the liquid in which the meat has cooked.

Selon ta bourse gouverne ta bouche.

250. Shoulder of Lamb with Turnips

Epaule d'agneau aux navets

3- to 4-lb. shoulder of lamb, boned and rolled	salt
2 ozs. butter	pepper
2 tablespoons flour	*bouquet garni* (42)
2 pints water	2 cloves
	3 cups diced turnips

Melt the butter in a saucepan that has a cover. Brown meat on all sides in the butter. Remove the meat and add flour, allowing it to brown but taking care that it does not burn. Stir in water, and when it is well blended add salt, pepper, *bouquet garni*, and cloves. Place the meat back in the pan and simmer gently for 2½ hours. Meanwhile, peel and dice the turnips. Fry the pieces in butter or chicken fat until they are dark yellow in colour. Add the turnips to the meat 1 hour before the meat is to be served. Place meat in the centre of a warm dish. Surround with a ring of turnip. Strain the sauce and pour over the meat. Garnish with parsley.

251. Stuffed Shoulder of Lamb

Epaule de mouton farcie

4 lbs. boned shoulder	chopped parsley
½ lb. sausage meat	salt and pepper
1 small chopped onion	2 ozs. butter

Ask the butcher to bone but not roll a shoulder. Fill the centre with a stuffing made by combining sausage meat, onion, parsley, salt, and pepper. Roll and tie securely. Brown the meat in melted butter. Add ½ pint of water, cover, and place in 300°F. oven. Cook for 2½ hours, adding a little water from time to time so that the meat will not be too dry.

252. Lamb Chops   *Côtelettes d'agneau*

Order loin chops or cutlets. Wipe the chops and cut off excess
fat. Roll the chops in fine bread crumbs (optional). Place the
chops on a rack 3 inches below the grill. Sear chops on both
sides with a hot flame. Lower the flame or finish cooking the
chops in a moderate (350°F.) oven. Chops ¾ to 1 inch thick
require 10 to 12 minutes; thicker chops require more time. Season
with salt and pepper and serve with plenty of melted butter,
Piquant Sauce (12), Tomato Sauce (21), or Onion Sauce (34).

253. Lamb Ragout   *Ragoût de mouton (navarin)*

1½ lbs. stewing lamb, middle neck or breast	6 potatoes salt
2 ozs. butter or fat	pepper
2 tablespoons flour	4 or 5 carrots
2 pints water	6 small onions
bouquet garni (42)	chopped parsley

Cut the lamb in small pieces and fry in melted butter. When
the meat is browned, stir in flour, allowing it to brown. Add
water and when it is blended add salt, pepper, carrots, *bouquet
garni*, and onions. Cook slowly for 1 hour. Add the potatoes,
which have been peeled and quartered, and cook another hour.
Remove the *bouquet garni* and place in a deep dish. Sprinkle
with bright green chopped parsley.

Sans pain, sans vin, amour n'est rien.

254. Skewered Lamb Kidneys

Rognons d'agneau à la brochette

8 lamb kidneys	lemon juice
4 ozs. butter	salt and pepper
chopped parsley	

Wash the kidneys, remove the filmy skin, and split open. Cut out the hard core of fat. Thread 4 halves on a skewer and place the skewers on a rack under a hot grill. Grill for 8 minutes, turning the skewers every 2 minutes. Soften the butter and add parsley, a dash of lemon juice, and season with salt and pepper. Spread the mixture on a small serving dish and place the piping hot kidneys on it. Serve immediately.

255. Lamb Kidneys with Tartar Sauce

Rognons de mouton à la tartare

8 lamb kidneys	black pepper
2 tablespoons oil	2 ozs. melted butter
chopped parsley	fine bread crumbs
salt	Tartar Sauce (20)

Wash, skin, and split the kidneys. Marinate 2 hours in combined oil, parsley, salt, and pepper. Drain the kidneys, dip in melted butter, roll in bread crumbs, skewer them, allowing 4 halves to a skewer, and grill for 10 minutes. Serve with Tartar Sauce.

256. Lamb Kidneys, Madeira Sauce

Rognons d'agneau au Madère

Split the kidneys, cut out the hard core of fat, and prepare the same as Beef Kidneys in Madeira Sauce (234).

257. Lamb's Brains   *Cervelles d'agneau*

Lamb's brains have a more delicate flavour than beef brains.
They are prepared in the same manner as recipes 238–40. They
should be served piping hot.

258. Grilled Breast of Lamb   *Poitrine de mouton sur le gril*

When Cabbage Soup (76) has been made with breast of lamb,
the meat can be used for another meal. Extract the meat from
the soup, grill on both sides, and serve with Piquant Sauce (12),
Pepper Sauce (19), or Tomato Sauce (21).

259. Lamb Chops Milanaise   *Côtelettes à la milanaise*

4 to 6 thick loin chops	1 egg, well beaten
4 ozs. melted butter	salt and pepper
4 tablespoons fine bread crumbs	Tomato Sauce (22) (or slices of
2 ozs. Parmesan cheese, grated	lemon)

Wipe the chops carefully. Dip in melted butter, roll in combined bread crumbs and cheese. Dip in egg and then again in
bread crumbs and cheese. Place on grill rack. Brush with melted
butter, sprinkle with salt and pepper, and grill under a low
flame, turning once. 10 minutes on each side should be enough.
Serve with Tomato Sauce or lemon slices.

260. Left-over Lamb or Mutton   *Restes de mouton ou d'agneau*

Slice cold roast lamb very thinly and serve with Mayonnaise
(17). Follow recipes 243–6, substituting lamb or mutton for
beef.

261. Left-over Lamb in White Wine Sauce
Restes de gigot à la Brissac

Cold roast lamb, sliced ¼ inch thick
2 ozs. butter
2 tablespoons flour
chopped parsley

1 small chopped onion
¼ pint water
¼ pint white wine
2 tablespoons olive oil
salt and pepper

Brown the slices of lamb in melted butter, turning each slice once. Add parsley and onion and cook 5 minutes more. Stir in flour. Moisten with wine and water and cook 1 hour. Ten minutes before serving add the olive oil. Season with salt and pepper. Serve with boiled potatoes or boiled rice.

262. Kid   *Chevreau*

Kid and lamb are very similar in taste and recipes given for lamb serve equally well for kid.

VEAL   *Veau*

Veal is more commonly used on the Continent than in other countries. Most recipes for veal have a Continental origin. Veal should be greyish pink in colour. The cuts used in France differ from the cuts used elsewhere, but each recipe will indicate the cut most adaptable to the French recipe.

Où la chèvre est attachée il faut qu'elle broute.

263. Veal Casserole   *Veau à la bourgeoise*

3 lbs. of shoulder or breast of veal	pepper
3 ozs. butter	2 cloves
3 tablespoons flour	*bouquet garni* (42)
2 pints water	7 or 8 carrots
salt	6 small onions

Melt butter in a heavy saucepan. Brown the meat on all sides
and remove from the butter. Stir in flour and water. When well
blended, add salt, pepper, *bouquet garni*, cloves, carrots cut in
small pieces, and onions left whole. Bring to boiling point and
pour over the meat in a casserole. Cover and bake in 300°F.
oven for 2½ hours. Place the meat on heated dish and surround
with carrots and onions. Strain the sauce, thicken with cornflour
(page 4), and pour over the meat. Garnish with sprigs of parsley.

264. Roast Veal   *Veau rôti*

Ask the butcher for a loin of veal weighing 2 to 3 lbs. Persuade
him to lard it with pork back fat or to tie strips of salt pork
around it. Veal is lean and needs extra fat in cooking. The roast
should be well tied. Place the roast on a rack in an oven tin.
Put 1 oz. of butter, salt, and ½ pint of water in the bottom of the
tin. Veal requires long cooking. 30 minutes per pound should
be allowed.

To make gravy: Place the roast on a heated dish and keep in
a warm place. Pour off excess fat, add 1 cup of boiling water,
and scrape off all the juices adhering to the tin. Keep over a hot
flame during this process. When the water and juices are well
blended, strain and pour into a gravy jug. If the gravy is too
pale add a few drops of gravy colouring.

265. Veal Ragout   *Ragoût de veau*

1½ to 2 lbs. neck or breast of veal	salt
2 ozs. butter	pepper
2 tablespoons flour	*bouquet garni* (42)
2 pints hot water	6 small onions
	¼ lb. mushrooms

Cut the veal into small pieces. Brown it in butter in a heavy
saucepan. Add flour and let it brown. Stir in water and when
well blended add salt, pepper, *bouquet garni*, onions, and mushrooms which have been well washed. Use both caps and stems.
Cover and cook 1 hour over a low flame. Skim off the fat floating
on the top, remove the *bouquet garni*, and serve.

266. Veal Ragout with Peas   *Ragoût de veau aux pois*

Follow the preceding recipe, but substitute 1 lb. of green peas for
the mushrooms and use only 3 onions. If frozen or tinned peas
are used, add 15 minutes before serving.

267. Veal in Red Wine   *Veau en matelote*

1½ lbs. breast or neck of veal, cut in small pieces	salt
	pepper
2 ozs. butter	2 cloves
2 tablespoons flour	*bouquet garni* (42)
½ pint hot water	8 small onions
½ pint red wine	¼ lb. mushrooms

Melt butter in heavy saucepan. Brown the pieces of meat on
all sides. Remove the meat, add flour, and moisten with water
and wine. Stir until well blended. Add salt, pepper, cloves,
bouquet garni, onions, and mushrooms. Use both caps and stems.
Add meat, and cover and simmer 1½ hours. Remove *bouquet garni*,
skim off fat, and serve.

268. Grilled Veal Chops   *Côtelettes de veau sur le gril*

8 thin cutlets or loin chops
salt and pepper
3 ozs. butter

1 teaspoon lemon juice
chopped parsley

Wipe the chops clean. Sprinkle with salt and pepper. Grill under slow flame, allowing 8 to 10 minutes on each side. Melt butter, add lemon juice and parsley. Pour this sauce over the chops, which are served on a heated dish.

269. Veal Chops with Herbs   *Côtelettes de veau aux fines herbes*

8 veal chops
salt and pepper
3 ozs. butter
1 gill white wine
1 gill water

2 teaspoons chopped chives (or onion tops)
2 teaspoons chopped parsley
1 teaspoon lemon juice

Melt the butter in a heavy saucepan. Brown chops on both sides. Sprinkle with salt and pepper. Add water and wine. Cover and simmer over a very low flame 30 minutes. Add the herbs and simmer 5 minutes longer. Just before serving, sprinkle with lemon juice.

270. Veal Chops in Buttered Paper

Côtelettes de veau en papillotes

8 thin veal chops
2 tablespoons olive oil
2 teaspoons chopped parsley
2 teaspoons chopped onion
2 teaspoons chopped chives

4 tablespoons chopped mushrooms
salt and pepper
unglazed paper
butter

Marinate the veal chops in the olive oil for 12 hours. Combine parsley, onion, chives, and mushrooms. Cut 8 pieces of unglazed paper—your best stationery is not too good for this—large enough to envelop the chop and have a margin for overlapping. Spread the papers with butter and sprinkle with a layer of the herb mixture. Place a chop on each paper, cover with another layer of the herb mixture. Sprinkle generously with salt and freshly ground black pepper. Fold the paper over the chop so that no steam or juice will escape. Cook 30 minutes in 300°F. oven. Serve with the paper on.

This recipe is one of the oldest known French recipes. It has been passed down through the ages and is honoured by both historians and gourmets.

271. Larded Veal   *Fricandeau*

2lbs. veal cut from the leg	2 cloves
12 ¼-inch by 3-inch strips of salt pork	¼ pint of stock or water
2 carrots	salt
6 small onions	pepper
bouquet garni (42)	

This cut of veal, from the leg, is lean and needs extra fat to be good. Lard with salt pork (page 87). Place in a casserole with carrots cut in small pieces, onions, *bouquet garni*, cloves, stock, salt, and pepper. Cover and cook in 300°F. oven for 2½ hours. Just before serving, strain off the liquid into a small saucepan and boil down the sauce to half its amount. Place the meat on a layer of cooked spinach or chicory (recipe 429 or 487) and pour the sauce over the meat.

272. Escallopes of Veal   *Escalopes de veau*

6 or 8 veal slices	chopped parsley
3 ozs. butter	chopped onion
½ pint stock	salt and pepper

Order individual, well-trimmed slices of veal from the leg, cut ½ inch thick. Ask the butcher to pound them. Heat the butter in frying pan until it is sizzling hot. Sear escallopes 3 minutes on each side. Add stock, parsley, onion, sprinkle with salt and pepper, and cover. Simmer 20 minutes. Arrange the escallopes in a crown around a heated dish. Fill the centre with the sauce left in the frying pan or with Tomato Sauce (21).

Morceau avalé n'a plus de goût.

273. French Veal Stew   *Blanquette de veau*

1½ lbs. breast or neck of veal
salt and pepper
1 carrot
1 onion cut in half
bouquet garni (42)
2 pints water or stock
2 ozs. butter

2 tablespoons flour
6 small onions
½ lb. mushrooms
1 oz. butter
2 egg yolks
½ teaspoon lemon juice (or ½ tea-
    spoon vinegar)

Combine veal, carrot cut in pieces, onion, *bouquet garni*, and water. Season with salt and pepper. Bring to the boil and simmer 20 minutes. Extract the pieces of veal and keep in a warm place. Melt butter and stir in flour. Add gradually the strained liquid in which the veal was cooked. When the sauce is smooth, add onions and mushrooms which have been well washed. Use both stems and caps. Cook until the onions are tender. Add the meat and cook 15 minutes longer. Thicken with egg yolks (page 3), add butter, and just before serving add lemon juice or vinegar. Do not let the sauce boil after the eggs have been added. Taste for seasoning. Garnish with chopped parsley.

274. Baked Calf's Liver   *Foie de veau à la broche*

1 to 1½ lbs. calf's liver in 1 piece
12 small pieces of salt pork
several paper-thin slices of salt pork

½ pint water
1 oz. butter

With a sharp, pointed knife insert small pieces of salt pork into the liver. Cover the whole piece of liver with a thin layer of salt pork. Place on a rack in an oven tin into which the water and butter has been put. Bake 45 minutes in 350°F. oven.

To make gravy: Pour ½ pint of boiling water into the bottom of the tin. Scrape the juices with a fork, mix well, strain, and serve in a gravy jug.

275. Calf's Liver, Family Style   *Foie de veau à la bourgeoise*

2 lbs. of calf's liver in one piece	*bouquet garni* (42)
12 small pieces of salt pork	2 cloves
2 ozs. butter	salt
2 tablespoons flour	pepper
¼ pint white wine	8 carrots, cut in small pieces
¼ pint water	6 small onions

With a sharp pointed knife insert small pieces of salt pork in the liver. Heat butter in a heavy oven-proof dish. Sear liver on both sides and remove the meat from the pan. Add flour and stir in water and wine. When the sauce is smooth add *bouquet garni*, cloves, salt, and pepper. Parboil onions and carrots 10 minutes. Add liver and vegetables to the sauce. Cover the dish and place in 300°F. oven. Bake 1 hour. Place the liver on a heated dish. Surround with onions and carrots. Strain the sauce and thicken with cornflour (page 4). Pour the sauce over the liver and garnish with green parsley sprigs.

276. Calf's Liver, Maître d'hôtel   *Foie de veau à la poêle*

1½ lbs. calf's liver, sliced   Maître d'hôtel Sauce (9)
2 ozs. butter

Melt butter in frying pan. When butter is sizzling hot, brown
liver on both sides. Reduce the heat and continue cooking 10
minutes, turning the slices once or twice. It should remain
slightly pink in the centre. Place meat on hot dish and cover
with Maître d'hôtel Sauce.

277. Calf's Liver en Papillotes   *Foie de veau en papillotes*

6 slices calf's liver   12 thin slices salt pork
2 ozs. butter   chopped parsley
6 pieces unglazed paper   chopped chives or onions
salad oil   salt and pepper

Brown the liver in sizzling hot butter; 2 minutes on each side
should be enough. Cut pieces of unglazed paper a little more
than twice the size of the pieces of liver. Oil the paper and
place a paper-thin layer of salt pork on each piece. Sprinkle each
piece with half the combined herbs, salt, and pepper. Place a
slice of liver on each paper, sprinkle again with herbs, salt, and
pepper. Cover with a slice of salt pork. Wrap each piece of
paper around the liver and fold the edges carefully so that none
of the juices will escape. Bake 20 minutes in 350°F. oven. Serve
with the paper still on.

278. Veal Kidneys   *Rognons de veau*

Veal kidney has a finer flavour than beef kidney. It is prepared
in the same way as Beef Kidneys in Madeira Sauce (234) or as
Kidneys and Mushrooms in Madeira Sauce (235). It is also
delicious served in an omelette (129).

279. Larded Sweetbreads   *Ris de veau en fricandeau*

2 large sweetbreads	2 cloves
12 small strips salt pork	½ pint stock
2 carrots	salt and pepper
6 small onions	Tomato Sauce (21)
bouquet garni (42)	

Soak the sweetbreads in warm water for 1 hour. Drain and plunge into boiling salted water. Boil 10 minutes. Drain and plunge into cold water. Drain and wipe dry. With a sharp pointed knife make little incisions in the sweetbreads and insert the salt pork. Place the sweetbreads in a casserole. Cover with carrots and onions sliced thinly, *bouquet garni*, cloves, and stock. Sprinkle with salt and pepper. Bake 1 hour in 300°F. oven. Spread the bottom of a hot dish with French Spinach (487), Garden Sorrel (486), or Tomato Sauce (21) and place the sweetbreads on top.

280. Sweetbreads à la Financière   *Ris de veau à la financière*

1 large or 2 small sweetbreads	1 gill Madeira wine
3 small onions, sliced thinly	salt and pepper
2 ozs. butter	¼ lb. mushrooms
2 tablespoons flour	1 teaspoon lemon juice
½ pint chicken stock	croutons
1 gill white wine	parsley

Follow the directions in the preceding recipe for preparing and parboiling the sweetbreads. Fry the onions and sweetbreads in the melted butter. When they are yellow, stir in the flour. Moisten with stock and wine. Add mushrooms, which have been washed, stemmed, and fried in butter 10 minutes. Season with salt and pepper and simmer 15 minutes. Just before serving, add lemon juice. Garnish with croutons and sprigs of parsley.

281. Calf's Brains, Black Butter Sauce
Cervelles de veau au beurre noir

Calf's brains are considered the best for flavour and delicacy. In France, because of their high nutritive value and easy digestibility, brains are frequently given to children. They are prepared in the same manner as Beef Brains in Black Butter Sauce (238).

282. Calf's Brains in Mushroom and Onion Sauce
Cervelles de veau en matelote

Follow directions given in recipe 239.

283. Fried Calf's Brains   *Cervelles de veau frites*

Follow directions given in recipe 240.

284. Calf's Brains a la Poulette   *Cervelles de veau à la poulette*

3 pairs calf's brains	10 small onions
2 ozs. butter	¼ lb. mushrooms
2 tablespoons flour	2 egg yolks
1 pint hot water	1 teaspoon lemon juice
salt and pepper	

Wash brains and soak 1 hour in warm water. Remove arteries and membranes. Parboil in salted water 15 minutes and drain. Melt butter in a heavy saucepan and stir in flour. Add water and when well blended add salt, pepper, onions, and mushrooms, which have been washed and stemmed. Simmer until the onions are tender (30 to 40 minutes). Add brains and simmer 15 minutes more. Place the brains on a heated dish. Bind the sauce with 2 egg yolks (page 3). Do not let the sauce boil again, but when it is piping hot add lemon juice and pour over the brains. Serve immediately.

285. Calf's Head with French Dressing

Tête de veau à la vinaigrette

1 calf's head	*bouquet garni* (42)
2 tablespoons flour	1 onion, stuck with
5 quarts water	2 cloves
1 teaspoon salt	2 tablespoons wine vinegar
10 peppercorns	

The butcher will split the head and remove the tongue and brains. Soak overnight in cold water or, if there is not time, blanch it by bringing it to a boil, starting in cold water, and then plunging it into cold water. Mix the flour and water. Add salt, peppercorns, *bouquet garni*, onion, cloves, and vinegar. Bring to boiling point and add the calf's head, brains, and tongue. The brains and tongue should be extracted after 30 minutes, but the head requires 2 hours of slow cooking. Cut the hot meat from the calf's head. Arrange on a hot dish with slices of tongue and brains which have been reheated. Garnish with a ring of parsley and serve with French Dressing (31).

286. Calf's Feet with French Dressing

Pieds de veau à la vinaigrette

Ask the butcher to split 3 calf's feet lengthwise. Follow the preceding recipe for cooking calf's head. The feet may be left in the broth to cool and be eaten cold, or may be eaten hot. In either case they should be accompanied by French Dressing (32).

I

287. Veal Birds   *Veau roulé*

6 to 8 thin slices of veal
¼ lb. minced left-over beef or chicken
¼ lb. sausage meat
2 ozs. butter
2 tablespoons flour

¾ pint water
¼ pint wine
salt and pepper
2 teaspoons chopped onion
2 teaspoons chopped parsley

The veal slices, from the leg, should be ½ inch thick and uniform in size and shape. Ask the butcher to pound them for you. Pound sausage meat and left-over meat together. Season with salt and pepper. Put a thin layer of this mixture on each cutlet. Roll and tie securely. Melt butter in pan large enough to accommodate all the 'birds'. Brown the meat on all sides in the butter. Remove the 'birds' and add flour to the butter. Add water, wine, salt, pepper, onion, and parsley. When the sauce is well blended, put back the 'birds', cover, and simmer 45 minutes.

288. Cold Veal, Mayonnaise or Rémoulade Sauce
Salade de veau

Cut cold roast or boiled veal in thin slices. Arrange on a dish and serve with Mayonnaise (17) or Rémoulade Sauce (23).

Il n'y a si méchant pot qui ne trouve son couvercle.

289. Tarragon Veal   *Restes de veau à la l'estragon*

2 ozs. butter   salt and pepper
2 tablespoons flour   2 tablespoons chopped tarragon
½ pint water   sliced veal
¼ pint dry white wine

Melt butter and stir in flour. Let the flour brown, taking care
that it does not burn. Add water and wine. Season with salt
and pepper. Stir until sauce is smooth. Add veal and tarragon.
Reduce the heat and simmer 30 minutes.

290. Left-over Veal, Blanquette Sauce
Restes de veau en blanquette

1 lb. diced left-over veal   6 small onions
Blanquette Sauce (7)   *bouquet garni* (42)
½ lb. mushrooms   salt and pepper

Prepare a Blanquette Sauce. Fry washed and stemmed mushrooms in butter or use tinned button mushrooms. Parboil the
onions 15 minutes. Add the veal, mushrooms, onions, *bouquet
garni*, season with salt and pepper, and simmer 30 minutes.
Remove the *bouquet garni* and serve.

291. Left-over Veal à la Poulette   *Veau à la poulette*

Follow the preceding recipe but just before serving thicken the
sauce with egg and cream (page 4).

292. Left-over Veal in Herb Sauce   *Veau en capilotade*

2 lbs. cold roast veal, sliced
1 oz. butter
1 tablespoon flour
1 teaspoon chopped parsley
1 teaspoon chopped chives
1 teaspoon chopped onion

½ pint water
2 tablespoons brandy
salt and pepper
1 tablespoon olive oil
croutons

Melt butter and add flour and herbs. Stir until the flour is light brown. Add water and brandy and simmer gently 15 minutes. Season with salt and pepper. Add veal and cook slowly 15 minutes more. Cover the pan. Just before serving, add olive oil. Serve on a heated dish and garnish with croutons and sprigs of parsley.

293. Sweetbread Balls   *Restes de ris de veau en boulettes*

1 pair cooked sweetbreads
¼ lb. mushrooms
Béchamel Sauce (1)
salt and pepper

1 egg, beaten
fine bread crumbs
parsley

Cut the cooked sweetbreads (279) in small pieces. Wash the mushrooms and cut in equally small pieces. Make a thick Béchamel Sauce and simmer sweetbreads and mushrooms in the sauce 15 minutes. Season with salt and pepper. Remove from the heat and chill. When the mixture is very cold, make small balls. Dip them in egg and then in bread crumbs. Fry in deep fat (375°F.) 2 to 3 minutes. Serve with fried or fresh parsley.

294. Veal Salad   *Restes de veau en salade*

1 lb. left-over veal, thinly sliced	*Sauce:*
3 tablespoons oil	3 tablespoons oil
2 teaspoons wine vinegar	2 teaspoons wine vinegar
salt	1 teaspoon made mustard
black pepper	3 anchovy fillets
2 hard-boiled eggs	6 capers (optional)
6 sweet gherkins	salt and pepper

Marinate the veal in oil, vinegar, salt, and pepper for at least 2 hours. Arrange the slices of veal on a dish. Garnish with slices of hard-boiled egg and gherkin.

To make sauce: Chop the anchovies and add to oil, vinegar, mustard, capers, salt, and pepper. Stir well and serve in a sauce boat.

295. Veal Croquettes   *Croquettes de veau*

See Croquettes (246).

296. Left-over Calf's Liver on Skewers
Restes de foie de veau en brochette

Left-over liver is often given to the family pet, but it is delicious for human consumption when it is prepared this way:

Cut cold, cooked liver in small squares. Cut bacon in same size and shape. Alternate the liver and bacon on the skewers. Dip skewer in oil, roll in bread crumbs, and grill under very hot flame.

PORK   *PORC*

Fresh pork should be very pale pink. It should be firm and free of excess fat, since even the lean cuts have a good deal of fat running through them. Pork should never be served underdone, but should be thoroughly cooked. Long cooking not only heightens the flavour but safeguards the consumer from trichinosis.

297. Roast Pork   *Rôti de porc*

Order a 3 to 4-lb. loin of pork. Wipe clean and place on rack in an open tin. Put ½ pint water and 2 teaspoons salt in the bottom of the pan. Baste the pork with the salted water several times during the roasting. Roast in a moderate oven (325°F.), allowing 30 minutes per pound.

To make gravy: Pour off the excess fat in roasting pan. Place tin over a flame. Add ½ pint boiling water and stir with a fork, scraping off any juices that adhere to the pan. Strain into a gravy jug.

298. Grilled Pork Chops   *Côtelettes de porc grillées*

4 to 6 thick pork loin chops	Tomato Sauce (21), or Robert
salt and freshly ground black pepper	Sauce (16), or Onion Sauce (34)

Wipe the chops carefully and sprinkle with salt and pepper. Grill under hot flame 5 minutes on each side. Finish cooking in 325°F. oven for 30 minutes. Serve with the sauce of your choice.

299. Breaded Pork Fillets

Filets mignons de porc, panés et grillés

6 pork fillets	2 teaspoons chopped parsley
1 egg, beaten	Anchovy Butter (28), or Tartar
bread crumbs	Sauce (20), or Onion Sauce
salt and pepper	(34)

Order fillets of pork cut ½ inch thick. Dip in egg and roll in
bread crumbs. Sprinkle with salt, pepper, and chopped parsley.
Brown under hot flame allowing 5 minutes on each side. Finish
cooking in 325°F. oven for 30 minutes. Spread with the sauce
of your choice.

300. Pork Chops with Chestnuts and Red Cabbage

Côtelettes de porc à la Courlandaise

6 thick loin pork chops	½ pint stock
1 egg, beaten	1 teaspoon lemon juice
2 ozs. butter	2 teaspoons chopped parsley
2 tablespoons flour	1 large red cabbage
salt and pepper	20 chestnuts

Trim the chops and wipe them. Dip in beaten egg and brown
them in melted butter, allowing 5 minutes to each side. Reduce
the heat, cover, and continue cooking 20 minutes longer. Remove
chops and keep in a warm place. Stir the flour into the fat, add
salt and pepper. Moisten with stock and simmer 10 minutes.
While the chops are cooking, combine chestnuts, which have
been previously parboiled 20 minutes and peeled, with coarsely
shredded red cabbage. Boil 15 minutes and drain. Arrange the
chops in the centre of a heated dish. Surround with a ring of
cabbage and chestnuts. Add lemon juice and parsley to the
sauce, strain into a gravy jug and serve with the chops.

301. Head Cheese   *Fromage de cochon*

small pig's head	12 pepperoorns
1 onion, quartered	nutmeg
2 carrots, cut in rounds	cayenne
double *bouquet garni* (42)	1 tablespoon chopped parsley
2 teaspoons salt	salt and pepper

Ask the butcher to split the pig's head. Soak in warm water 15 minutes. Remove any blood that there may be. Place the head in a deep saucepan. Cover with water. Add onion, carrot, *bouquet garni*, cloves, salt, and pepper. Boil gently 5 hours. Cut the flesh from the bones in small strips. Season highly with nutmeg, a little cayenne, parsley, salt, and pepper. Place in a mould. Moisten with ½ pint of the strained liquid. Cover with a board or piece of wax paper and weight it down so that the meat will be firmly pressed. Chill in refrigerator overnight and serve cold.

302. Pork Liver   *Foie de cochon*

Pig's liver is not so delicate in flavour as calf or lamb's liver. It is, however, the most nutritive and can be very delicious. Follow recipes 274-7. Allow a little more time for cooking pig's liver, for it should be well done. Pig's liver is more economical and should be tried by those sceptics who have never dared.

303. Pork Kidneys   *Rognons de cochon*

Follow recipes 234-5, 254-5. Allow a little more time for cooking pork kidneys.

304. Grilled Pig's Feet   *Pieds de cochon grillés*

Order 6 pig's trotters and ask the butcher to split them lengthwise. Wipe them carefully. Dip in oil, roll in bread crumbs,
and grill under a hot flame 15 minutes. Turn from time to time
so that they will brown on all sides. Serve with a Piquant Sauce
(12). If only fresh pig's feet are obtainable, split them lengthwise and wrap each piece in cheese cloth and tie at both ends.
Put in a deep pan. Weight them down and fill the saucepan with
water, salt, pepper, 3 cloves of garlic, a large *bouquet garni* (42),
and 2 tablespoons vinegar. Boil gently 5 hours. Drain, cool and
unwrap each piece. They are then ready to be cooked like pig's
trotters.

305. Boiled Ham   *Jambon au naturel*

Scrub a whole ham, or half a ham if the family is small. Place in
a deep saucepan and cover with water. Add 2 onions and 2 carrots
cut in small pieces, 1 clove of garlic, and a double *bouquet garni*.
Cover and simmer very, very gently allowing 45 minutes per
pound. The slower the cooking the better. When the bone is
loosened from the meat, the ham is done. Let the ham cool in
the liquid. It should be thoroughly chilled before slicing.

306. Ham with Spinach or Chicory

Jambon aux épinards ou à la chicorée

Serve boiled ham—in this case it should be hot—with French
Spinach (487) or braised Chicory (429). Surround with fried
croutons.

307. Ham in White Wine Sauce   *Jambon à la poêle*

6 to 8 thin slices uncooked ham	½ pint dry white wine
2 ozs. butter	salt and pepper
2 tablespoons flour	

Melt butter in frying pan. When the butter is sizzling hot, brown the ham slices on both sides. Allow 5 minutes for cooking the ham. Remove the meat, stir in the flour, moisten with white wine, and stir until the sauce begins to thicken. Season with only a little salt, as the ham is quite salty. Add a dash of freshly ground black pepper. Place the slices of ham on a hot dish. Pour the sauce over the ham and garnish with sprigs of parsley.

308. Roast Sucking Pig   *Cochon de lait au four*

4- or 5-week-old piglet	1 tablespoon chopped shallots
3 ozs. butter	2 ozs. lean salt pork
2 teaspoons chopped parsley	¼ lb. mushrooms
2 onions, stuck with	the pork liver
2 cloves apiece	salt and pepper

Wash the young pig in several waters, taking care that the orifices are thoroughly cleaned. Wipe dry. Soften the butter and work in the parsley. Rub the interior of the piglet with this mixture. Place one of the onions in the cavity. Chop the shallots, salt pork, and mushrooms together. Season with salt and pepper. Fill the cavity with this mixture and put in the remaining onion. Sew up the cavity. Truss the forelegs forward and the hind legs backward, tying the pairs of legs together tightly. Place on a rack in an open pan. Brush with melted butter. Sear the piglet in 450°F. oven 15 minutes. Reduce the temperature to 325° F. and continue cooking, allowing 25 minutes per pound. Baste from time to time with salted boiling water. Five minutes before serving, brush again with melted butter. Place a bright red apple in the mouth of the piglet. Place on a large warm dish. Decorate him with a garland of parsley and serve with a bowl of Ravigote Sauce (24).

309. Sausages and Cabbage   *Saucisses aux choux*

1 lb. chipolata sausages	salt and pepper
1 oz. butter or bacon fat	*bouquet garni* (42)
3 tablespoons flour	1 medium cabbage
1 pint hot water	

Prick the sausages with a fork and fry in sizzling hot fat until they are well browned. Remove the sausages and add the flour. Brown the flour and stir in the water. When the flour and water are blended, add *bouquet garni*, salt, and pepper and bring to a boil. Meanwhile quarter a cabbage and boil 15 minutes. Add the well-drained cabbage and the sausages to the sauce and simmer 30 minutes. Pile the cabbage in the centre of a warm dish. Place the sausages on it. Remove the *bouquet garni* and pour the sauce around the cabbage.

310. Sausages with Pea or Potato Purée

Saucisses à la purée de pois ou de pommes de terre

1 lb. pork sausages	Pea Purée (455) or
1 oz. fat	Potato Purée (471)

Prick the sausages and fry in hot fat. Place in the centre of a heated dish and surround with a crown of Pea Purée or Potato Purée. Garnish with sprigs of fresh parsley.

POULTRY includes fowl, chicken, capon, turkey, goose, pigeon, and domestic duck.

A *fowl* is a hen that has begun to lay eggs. It requires longer cooking—usually boiling.

A *chicken* is a young hen that has been fattened with care and has not begun to lay. It usually weighs 4 to 5 lbs.

A *capon* is a gelded rooster. It is sold weighing 8 to 10 lbs. The meat is particularly sweet and firm.

Small chickens or *poussins* are sold weighing 1½ to 2 lbs.

A *turkey* is sold weighing anywhere from 8 to 30 lbs. For French recipes it is best to try and find a 10- to 12-lb. turkey.

Goose and *duck* are more gamey in flavour. They do not have as much meat per pound. Younger birds are better. Old birds run to fat.

TO TRUSS POULTRY: Order the poultry cleaned and dressed. When it comes from the butcher, wipe the inside and outside with a damp cloth. There are many ways of trussing poultry. Skewers may be used instead of string. If skewers are used, place bird on its back. Press thighs close to the body and hold in place by inserting the skewer in the middle of a thigh, running it through the body and bringing it out in the middle of the other thigh. If string is used, run a trussing needle through the thighs in the same way and tie the string over the back. Draw neck skin out and tuck under a wing. Press the wings close to the body and skewer or tie in the same manner. Tie drumsticks together. If the bird is to be stuffed, both neck and body ends must be filled and the skin skewered or sewn.

311. Roast Chicken   *Poulet rôti*

Order a 4- to 5-lb. chicken. Wipe and truss according to directions in the preceding paragraph. Cover the chicken with a thin layer of salt pork, tied on with twine. Place chicken on rack in an oven tin. Place 1 oz. of butter and ¼ pint water in the pan. Roast in 375°F. oven, allowing 20 minutes to the pound. Baste every 10 minutes with the liquid in the pan. Insert a fork into the breast at the end of the cooking time. If the meat is tender and no red juices come out, the chicken is done. Take off the salt pork, remove the skewers, and place the chicken on a warm dish. Garnish with watercress.

To make gravy: Pour off the excess fat in roasting tin. Place over a flame. Add ½ pint of boiling water and stir with a fork, scraping off any juices that adhere to the pan. Strain into a gravy jug.

La belle cage ne nourrit pas l'oiseau.

312. Chicken and Rice*   *Poule au riz*

5-lb. fowl or chicken	2 cloves garlic (optional)
water	1 carrot, cut in rounds
salt	1 onion, sliced
pepper	¾ lb. rice
bouquet garni (42)	

Wipe and truss the chicken (page 130). Make a *court-bouillon* by putting enough water to cover the chicken in a deep sauce-pan. Add salt, pepper, *bouquet garni*, garlic, carrot, and onion and simmer 30 minutes before adding chicken. Let the chicken simmer—not boil—in the *court-bouillon* 2 to 3 hours or until tender. Do not overcook or the chicken will not keep its shape.

Three quarters of an hour before serving remove the *bouquet garni*, add washed rice, and continue cooking. The rice will absorb most of the liquid. Serve on a deep dish. Remove string or skewers from the chicken and serve on a bed of rice. Garnish with fresh parsley.

313. Chicken Blanquette   *Blanquette de volaille*

1 lb. cooked chicken or fowl (311 or 312)	salt and pepper
	bouquet garni (42)
2 ozs. butter	8 small onions
2 tablespoons flour	½ lb. mushrooms
1½ pints chicken stock or water	1 tablespoon chopped parsley

Melt butter in a saucepan. Stir in flour. Add liquid and when the sauce is blended add *bouquet garni*, salt, pepper, onions,

* The first paragraph of this recipe is the basic method of boiling chicken or fowl. It is the basis for other recipes. If the chicken is not to be eaten hot, allow it to cool in the broth.

and mushrooms which have been washed and stemmed. Use both caps and stems. Simmer 45 minutes. Add the chicken which may be cubed or left in fairly large pieces. Heat the chicken but do not let the sauce boil. Serve very hot. Sprinkle with chopped parsley.

314. Chicken Mayonnaise *Mayonnaise de volaille*

cold cooked chicken (31–112)   Mayonnaise (17)

Slice the chicken and arrange on a dish. Garnish with fresh parsley and serve with a bowl of Mayonnaise.

315. Chicken Casserole *Poulet à la casserole*

3- to 4-lb. chicken   salt and pepper
3 ozs. butter

Wipe and truss the chicken (page 130). Melt butter in a casserole. When the butter is sizzling, brown the chicken on all sides. Sprinkle with salt and pepper. Cover and place in 300°F. oven Cook 1½ hours. Turn the chicken once or twice, letting it rest on one thigh and then the other. Remove from the casserole and place on heated dish. Pour the juice and butter from the casserole over the chicken. Serve with new boiled potatoes and peas. This is a simple but delicious dish.

Pain tant qu'il dure, vin à mesure.

316. Truffled Chicken   *Poulet truffé*

5-lb. roasting chicken (or 2 2½-lb. spring chickens)	salt
	black pepper
2 truffles or 1 small tin truffles	chopped parsley
½ lb. sausage meat	⅛ teaspoon powdered thyme
6 ozs. bread crumbs	paper-thin slices salt pork

Peel truffles. Chop the peelings and mix with the sausage meat, salt, pepper, parsley, and thyme. Cook gently 15 minutes. Remove from the fire, stir in bread crumbs, and chill. Slice the whole truffles very thinly. Lift the skin of the chicken and slide the slices of truffle under the skin. Take care not to break the skin. The round black truffles, placed ½ inch apart, make a very pleasing effect.

When the stuffing is cold, fill the interior of the bird. Sew the skin over the openings. Truss the bird (page 130). Cover the chicken with a layer of salt pork and roast in 350°F. oven, allowing 25 minutes per pound.

317. Chicken Fricassee   *Fricassée de poulet*

4-lb. chicken or fowl, cut in pieces for serving	pepper
	bouquet garni (42)
2 ozs. butter	10 small onions
2 tablespoons flour	½ lb. mushrooms
2 pints water	1 egg yolk
salt	1 teaspoon lemon juice

Ask the butcher to cut the chicken in 8 pieces or, if you are to do it yourself, cut it in the following way. Remove the legs and wings. Split the body in the centre. It is best to place the chicken on a wooden board and to use a sharp knife and a mallet to split the bird. Divide each side in two. Soak the pieces in warm water for 30 minutes.

Melt butter in a heavy saucepan. Mix in flour, stirring well but not allowing it to brown. Add water and stir until the sauce is smooth. Add salt, pepper, *bouquet garni*, chicken, and onions. Cook 1 hour over a moderate flame. 15 minutes before the end of the cooking, add the mushrooms, which have been washed, stemmed, plunged in boiling water, and drained. Strain off the sauce.

Place the chicken in the centre of a heated dish. Surround with onions and mushrooms. Thicken the sauce with the egg yolk (page 3), add lemon juice, and pour over the chicken. Garnish with fresh parsley. See recipe 337 for using left-over fricasseed chicken.

318. Chicken in White Wine   *Poulet sauté au vin blanc*

2 small frying chickens	salt and pepper
2 ozs. butter	8 small onions or
2 tablespoons flour	2 large onions, thinly sliced
¼ pint dry white wine	¼ pint water
¼ pint water	2 ozs. butter

Split or quarter the chickens, depending on size. Cook the onions in ¼ pint water and 2 ozs. butter for 10 minutes. Melt butter in pan large enough for all the chicken. Brown the chicken on all sides. Remove the chicken, stir in flour. Add water and wine and, when the sauce is smooth, put back the chicken and the onions along with the liquid in which they have been cooking. Season with salt and pepper. Cover and cook over a low flame for 45 minutes. Serve on a heated dish. Garnish with parsley.

K

319. Tarragon Chicken   *Poulet à l'estragon*

4- to 5-lb. roasting chicken	2 sprigs of tarragon
4 or 5 tarragon leaves	2 carrots, cut in rounds
3 paper-thin slices salt pork	1 onion, thinly sliced
water	2 teaspoons cornflour
salt	2 or 3 drops yellow colouring
pepper	8 tarragon leaves
bouquet garni (42)	

This is a wonderful summer chicken dish if you have tarragon growing in the garden.

Wipe and truss the chicken as for roasting (page 130). Mince tarragon leaves and place in the interior of the chicken. Sew up the openings. Tie a thin layer of salt pork over the breast of the chicken. Prepare the following *court-bouillon:* Put enough water in the saucepan to cover the bird. Add salt, pepper, *bouquet garni*, tarragon sprigs, carrots, onion, and bring to the boil. Place the chicken in the saucepan and cook until tender. Remove the chicken and drain well so that there is no liquid inside the bird. Strain the *court-bouillon.*

To make sauce: Mix the cornflour in a little cold water and add to ½ pint of the *court-bouillon.* When it is well blended, pour into 2 pints of the broth. Add the yellow colouring to the sauce. Remove the salt pork from the chicken and place 4 tarragon leaves diagonally on each side. Fill a deep dish with the sauce and place the chicken on it. Serve with rice or new potatoes.

320. Chicken with Olives   *Poulet aux olives*

3- to 4-lb. chicken	*bouquet garni* (42)
2 ozs. butter	salt and pepper
2 tablespoons flour	¼ lb. stoned green olives
1½ pints water	

Clean and truss the chicken as for roasting. Melt butter in deep saucepan and brown chicken on both sides. Remove the chicken, add flour and allow it to brown, taking care that it does not burn. Add water, *bouquet garni*, salt, and pepper. Stir until the sauce is smooth. Put back the chicken and cover. Simmer 45 to 60 minutes or until tender. 15 minutes before serving add olives. Place chicken on dish. Remove the strings or skewers. Surround with olives and pour the sauce over it all. Serve with boiled potatoes or rice.

321. Chicken Marengo   *Poulet Marengo*

Tradition has it that during a quiet moment in the battle between the Austrians and Napoleon's army at Marengo in northern Italy, supplies were very low, and the chef was desperately trying to find something to give Napoleon for his dinner. He captured a straying hen, gathered wild mushrooms, and concocted this now famous dish. [C. T.]

4-lb. chicken, cut in pieces for serving	2 tablespoons flour
4 tablespoons olive oil	1 tablespoon tomato paste
salt and pepper	¼ pint stock or water
bouquet garni (42)	¼ pint dry white wine (or ¼ pint Madeira wine)
1 clove garlic, finely chopped	½ lb. mushrooms

Heat the olive oil in a deep saucepan. Brown the chicken in the oil, turning each piece so that all sides are crisp. Remove the chicken. Stir in flour and moisten with stock and wine. When well blended add *bouquet garni*, tomato paste, garlic, and mushrooms, which have been washed and cut in pieces. Season with salt and pepper. Replace the chicken and cover. Simmer 1 hour. Remove the *bouquet garni* and serve.

322. Chicken Galantine   *Galantine de poulet*

Wipe clean a 4-lb. chicken. Remove the wings. Make an incision
the entire length of the back. With a sharp knife loosen the
flesh from each side of the backbone, being careful not to pierce
the skin. Lay the chicken wide open and remove the bones.
The main skeleton will come out in one piece. The thigh bones
have to be eased out carefully. This is not easy and takes practice.
Lay the boned bird as near flat as possible on a double layer of
cheese cloth. It is then ready for stuffing.

Stuffing:
1½ lbs. finely minced veal
1½ lbs. finely minced fresh pork
salt and pepper
1 teaspoon poultry seasoning
1 clove garlic, finely chopped
1 tablespoon chopped onion
2 teaspoons chopped parsley
several strips of boiled ham

Court-bouillon:
water
bouquet garni (42)
½ calf's foot or 2 tablespoons
    gelatine
2 carrots, cut in pieces
1 large onion, sliced
3 drops yellow colouring

Ask the butcher to mince the pork and veal together. Mix well
with the seasonings and spread half of it on the chicken, making
sure that all the cavities where the bones were removed are
filled. Lay thin strips of boiled ham on this, and finish by filling
the chicken with the rest of the stuffing. Sew the chicken up so
that it resumes its original shape. Wrap it up in cheese cloth
and tie securely. Meanwhile prepare the *court-bouillon* and when
it has reached boiling point, place the chicken in the saucepan.
The bird should be completely immersed. Cook over a moderate
flame 5 to 6 hours. Remove carefully from the saucepan and do
not touch until it is cold.

Strain the broth, add a little colouring, and let it cool. If
calf's foot is not obtainable, add the gelatine, softened in cold

water, at this point. The broth will jell. When it is cold, remove
the fat from the top and clarify the jelly (37). This necessitates
boiling the liquid again. When it is cooling for the last time,
watch carefully for the moment when the jelly is thick but not
firm. The process can be hastened by placing the pan in cold
water. When the jelly has the consistency of egg white, pour
1 cupful carefully over the galantine, which has been unwrapped
and placed on a dish. Chill in the refrigerator and allow the rest
of the jelly to become firm. Just before serving, chop up the
remaining jelly and place around the galantine. Forcing it through
a pastry tube is a good way to do this. Chop fresh parsley and
sprinkle on the jelly. This dish can be prepared a day in advance
and kept in the refrigerator.

323. Roast Turkey, Sausage and Chestnut Stuffing

Dinde rôtie

Wipe clean a 12-lb. turkey (page 130). Make the following
stuffing:

1 lb. chestnuts	2 tablespoons flour
½ lb. sausage meat	salt and pepper
3 ozs. butter	¼ pint stock or water

Slash each chestnut twice and throw into boiling water. Boil
20 minutes and peel while hot. Fry sausage and chestnuts in
sizzling butter 5 minutes. Stir in flour and stock. Season with
salt and pepper. Cook 3 minutes longer. When the stuffing is
cool it should be thick—stuff the turkey, sew up the openings,
truss, and place on a rack in an oven tin. Pour ½ pint water
mixed with 1 teaspoon salt in the bottom of the pan and baste
with this mixture from time to time. Roast in a 350°F. oven,
allowing 25 minutes per pound.

324. Truffled Turkey   *Dinde truffée*

Order an 8- to 10-lb. turkey at least 2 days before serving.
Chop 2 small tins of truffle peelings and mix with 1 large tin
of whole truffles. Fry ½ lb. diced fat salt pork. Remove the
pork and add the truffles, salt, pepper, and 1 teaspoon poultry
seasoning. Fry gently 15 minutes. Remove from heat and cool.
Place the truffles inside the turkey, sew up the openings and
truss. Leave the turkey in a cool place for at least 2 days so that
the taste of the truffles will permeate the bird. Cover the breast
with a thin layer of salt pork and roast in 350°F. oven for 2½
to 3 hours. Place on a bed of watercress and serve with a Truffle
Sauce (27). *Haute cuisine* would require slipping slices of truffle
under the skin before cooking, but Tante Marie does not demand
this extra touch.

325. Roast Pigeon   *Pigeon rôti*

Dress and truss pigeons (page 130). Place a thin layer of salt
pork over the breast of the birds and tie in place. Roast in
350°F. oven 30 to 45 minutes, depending upon the size. Unless
pigeons are unusually large it is best to count one per person.
Serve on a bed of watercress and pour over it all a gravy made
as follows: pour ¼ pint boiling water into the baking tin. Scrape
off the juices adhering to the bottom of the tin with a fork. Add a
little salt and strain.

326. Pigeons with Peas   *Pigeons aux pois*

4 pigeons	1 pint water
3 ozs. butter	salt and pepper
¼ lb. diced lean bacon	*bouquet garni* (42)
3 tablespoons flour	2 pints shelled peas

Wipe and truss the birds (page 130). Melt butter in a heavy large saucepan. When butter is sizzling, brown the pigeons on both sides, allowing 5 minutes to each side. Do not have the flame too high. When the birds are well browned, remove them and put in the bacon. Brown this and remove it. Stir in flour and when this has browned add water, salt, pepper, and *bouquet garni*. Stir until smooth. Replace the bacon and add the fresh peas.* Cook ½ hour, add the pigeons, and continue cooking 30 minutes longer or until the pigeons are tender. Place pigeons on heated dish, remove the *bouquet garni* and the pieces of bacon (optional), and pour the peas and sauce around pigeons.

327. Pigeon Casserole   *Pigeons en compote*

2 large pigeons	salt
2 ozs. butter	*bouquet garni* (42)
¼ lb. diced salt pork	10 small onions
2 tablespoons flour	¼ lb. mushrooms
1 pint stock	10 green stoned olives
black pepper	croutons

Split the pigeons in two. Heat the butter until it sizzles. Brown pigeons on both sides and remove. Brown the salt pork in the same butter. Stir in flour. Add stock, salt, pepper, and *bouquet garni*. Stir until the sauce is smooth. Put back the pigeons. Add onions and cook 30 minutes. Add mushrooms, which have been washed and stemmed, and, if desired, olives. Cook 15 minutes longer. One can also add Forcemeat Balls (38). Serve the pigeons on a deep dish. Remove the skewers or strings. Take out the *bouquet garni* and pour the sauce around the birds. Garnish with croutons and parsley. If pigeons weigh at least 1 lb. apiece this recipe will serve 4 people.

* If frozen peas are used, add them when the pigeons are put back into the sauce. If tinned peas are used, add them 15 minutes before serving.

328. Roast Duck   *Canard rôti*

Wipe clean and truss a 5½- to 6-lb. duck (page 130). Place on
rack in oven tin. Rub the breast with salt and roast in 400°F. *(Reg. 6)*
oven, allowing 15 minutes per pound.

To make gravy: Pour ¼ pint boiling water in the pan. Scrape
off the juices with a fork, mix well and pour over duck. See
recipes 332 and 339 for using cold roast duck.

329. Duck with Peas   *Canard aux pois*

1 5- to 6-lb. duck (or 2 ducklings)	1 pint water
3 ozs. butter	salt and pepper
¼ lb. diced lean bacon	*bouquet garni* (42)
3 tablespoons flour	2 pints shelled peas

Follow directions given in recipe 326.

330. Duck with Olives   *Canard aux olives*

1 small duck (or 2 ducklings)	*bouquet garni* (42)
2 ozs. butter	salt and pepper
2 tablespoons flour	¼ lb. stoned olives
1½ pints water	

Follow directions given in recipe 320.

331. Duck with Orange Sauce   *Canard à l'orange*

Fill the cavity of a 5½- to 6-lb. duck with ½ peeled orange. Sew
up the opening and truss (page 130). Roast according to recipe
328. When the duck is cooked, remove the fat from the pan.
Scrape off the juices with ¼ pint boiling water. Put in a small
saucepan. Add the juice of ½ orange, ¼ pint of dry white wine,

and the peel of one orange which has been parboiled 10 minutes and finely chopped. Now add, if desired, the giblet, finely chopped. Thicken with cornflour and butter (page 4). Heat thoroughly and serve in a gravy jug.

332. Duck Salmis   *Salmis de canard*

1 5-lb. cold roast duck (328)	$\frac{1}{4}$ pint red wine
duck liver	1 tablespoon olive oil
1 gill stock	salt and pepper
1 oz. butter	$\frac{1}{2}$ teaspoon grated lemon peel
	croutons

Remove the legs, wings, and breasts of duck. The breasts may be divided in two. Pick off the rest of the meat and pound it with the liver to a smooth paste, moistening it with stock. Put the paste in a saucepan with butter, wine, oil, salt, pepper, and lemon peel. Simmer 1 hour and during last 15 minutes reheat the duck in the sauce. Place the pieces of duck on large fried croutons, thicken the sauce with butter and cornflour (page 4), and pour over the duck. This is a good recipe for left-over duck or wild duck.

333. Roast Goose   *Oie rôtie*

Goose is prepared and stuffed as turkey (323). A 10- to 12-lb. goose is very satisfactory. Roast $2\frac{1}{2}$ to 3 hours in 325°F. oven. Do not let the fat collect in the pan. Remove it from time to time, leaving only the juices. It should not be too tightly stuffed. Baste frequently with salted water. Serve with Boiled Rice (387).

Goose fat should be carefully saved. It makes an excellent seasoning for vegetables and may be used in place of butter. In this case, it should be well-salted.

334. Goose Galantine   *Oie en daube*

Follow directions for Chicken Galantine (322).

335. Poultry Left-overs in Salad   *Restes de volaille en salade*

Slice or dice cold cooked chicken, duck, goose, or turkey. Arrange
on lettuce leaves and serve with Mayonnaise (17), or Rémoulade
Sauce (23).

336. Poultry Left-overs Fricasseed

Restes de volaille en fricassée

1 lb. cooked poultry, diced	8 small onions (or 2 medium onions,
2 ozs. butter	quartered)
2 tablespoons flour	croutons
1 pint poultry stock or water	juice of ½ lemon
¼ lb. mushrooms	1 egg yolk

Melt butter and stir in flour. Add stock and stir until the sauce is
smooth. Wash the mushrooms and cut in small pieces. Add
mushrooms and onions to the sauce and simmer over a low
flame until the onions are tender—approximately 30 minutes.
Add the poultry and simmer 10 minutes more. Thicken with
egg yolk (page 3) and add lemon juice. Serve in a deep dish and
garnish with croutons and parsley.

337. Fried Fricasseed Chicken   *Restes de volaille en fricassée*

If there remain any pieces of fricasseed chicken (317) take each
piece with the cold sauce still on it, dip in bread crumbs, then

in an egg yolk beaten with 1 tablespoon oil, and then again in bread crumbs. Fry in deep fat (390°F.) and serve very hot.

338. Duck in Red Wine   *Canard au vin rouge*

2 ozs. butter	salt and pepper
2 tablespoons flour	1 teaspoon grated orange or lemon
½ pint stock	rind
¼ pint red wine	*bouquet garni* (42)
chopped onion	slices of cold roast duck
chopped parsley	duck liver

Melt butter and stir in flour. Add wine and stock and stir until the sauce is smooth. Add onion, parsley, salt, pepper, grated rind, *bouquet garni*, and duck. Simmer 1 hour. Remove *bouquet garni*, add the liver which has been crushed (raw or cooked), and serve on rounds of toasted bread.

339. Left-over Duck with Olives   *Restes de canard aux olives*

Make a Brown Sauce 1 (5). Add ¼ lb. stoned olives, sliced or whole. Heat slices of left-over duck in this sauce and serve with Boiled Rice (387).

340. Boar   *Sanglier*

Boar is a wild pig, and any of the pork recipes (297–303, 308)
may be used. As with other game, it is best to marinate the
meat 4 or 5 days before cooking (see recipe 32).

341. Roast Leg of Venison   *Gigot de chevreuil mariné*

In France almost all game is marinated before cooking. It makes
the meat tender and heightens the flavour.

With a sharply pointed knife, make 1-inch incisions all over
the leg of venison and insert small pieces of salt pork. Prepare
the following marinating sauce:

¼ pint red wine   *bouquet garni* (42)
¼ pint wine vinegar   2 onions, sliced
1 tablespoon salt   2 carrots, sliced
½ teaspoon black pepper   4 tablespoons oil

146

Marinate the venison in this sauce from 5 to 6 days. Turn the leg over occasionally and baste with the sauce so that the flavour will permeate the whole leg. Roast in 350°F. oven, allowing 18 minutes per pound. Venison should be underdone. Serve with Piquant Sauce (12) or Pepper Sauce (19).

342. Roast Fillet of Venison   *Filet de chevreuil rôti*

This corresponds to a roast fillet of beef and is particularly delicious. Marinate the roast as in the preceding recipe and follow directions in recipe 222 for cooking.

343. Venison Casserole   *Civet de chevreuil*

2 lbs. breast venison	salt
¼ lb. diced salt pork	black pepper
2 ozs. butter	*bouquet garni* (42)
2 tablespoons flour	1 clove garlic
1 pint water	12 small or 3 large onions
¼ pint red wine	¼ lb. mushrooms

Fry the salt pork in butter until brown. Remove the pork and fry the venison, which has been cut in small pieces, in the fat. When the venison is well browned, remove it and add flour. Add water and wine and stir until well blended. Add salt, pepper, garlic, onions, *bouquet garni*, and put back the venison. Cook gently 60 minutes. Add mushrooms, which have been washed and stemmed, and simmer 30 minutes longer. Use both caps and stems. Place the venison in a deep warm dish. Cover with a layer of onions and then with a layer of mushrooms. Strain the sauce and pour it over all. If the sauce is too thin, thicken with cornflour (page 4).

344. Venison Chops   *Côtelettes de chevreuil*

Wipe and trim thin chops cut from the loin. Dip in bread crumbs.
Melt 2 ozs. butter in bottom of grill pan. When the butter is
sizzling, place the chops in the pan. Do not use the grill rack.
Grill 5 minutes on each side. Season with salt and freshly ground
black pepper. Serve with Pepper Sauce (19).

345. Left-over Venison   *Restes de chevreuil*

Heat left-over venison in Pepper Sauce (19) or in Piquant
Sauce (12).

Hare   *Lièvre*

Hare resembles rabbit in flavour but is much gamier. It is a
prized dish in France. When a hare has been cleaned and skinned,
it is divided in the following manner: Cut the hare in two just
below the shoulders. The breast, neck, and shoulders are used
for jugged hare. The back and hind quarters are used for roasting.

346. Roast Hare   *Lièvre rôti*

Prepare the marinating sauce described in recipe 341. Marinate
the part to be roasted 1 or 2 days before cooking. Cover with
a layer of paper-thin slices of salt pork. Roast 1 hour in 350°F.
oven.

347. Jugged Hare   *Lièvre en civet*

forequarters, breast, and neck of hare
¼ lb. diced salt pork
2 ozs. butter
2 tablespoons flour
1 pint water

1 pint red wine
salt and pepper
bouquet garni (42)
2 cloves
10 small onions
½ lb. mushrooms

Melt butter in a deep saucepan. Fry pork in the butter until it is brown. Remove the pork. Cut the forequarters, breast, and neck into small pieces and brown in the butter and pork fat. Stir in flour and when it is slightly browned add water, wine, salt, pepper, *bouquet garni*, cloves, and onions. Put back the pork, cover, and cook slowly 2½ hours. Add mushrooms, which have been washed and stemmed, and cook 30 minutes longer. Use both caps and stems. If the hare has been killed and dressed at home, save the blood carefully and bind the sauce with the blood several minutes before serving (page 4). Remove the *bouquet garni* before serving.

348. Potted Hare   *Lièvre haché en terrine*

1 small hare	½ bay leaf, crushed
1 lb. lean veal	1 teaspoon chopped parsley
1 lb. lean fresh pork	2 teaspoons chopped onion
¼ lb. suet	¼ teaspoon ground cloves
¼ lb. salt pork, sliced paper-thin	salt and pepper
¼ teaspoon powdered thyme	½ cup cooking brandy

Cut the flesh from the bones of the hare. Put the hare, veal, pork,
and suet through a mincer, using the finest blade. Season with
thyme, bay leaf, parsley, onion, clove, salt, and pepper. Blend
well and divide the mixture in 4 parts. Line an earthenware
terrine with 1 layer of salt pork. Put in a layer of the mixture
and cover with a layer of salt pork. Alternate the salt pork and
combined meats until the terrine is full. Over the last layer of
meat mixture pour ½ cup of brandy. Cover with a final layer of
salt pork. Place a cover on the terrine, making sure that it fits
tightly. Seal the top with strips of pastry or a paste made of
flour. Cook 4 hours in 300°F. oven. Remove from the oven and
cool. Weight the cover down while it is cooling, so that the meat
will hold its shape when it is unmoulded. The unmoulded terrine may be garnished with Aspic (37), made of broth from the
bones or of other stock, or it may be served in the terrine. It
makes a delicious entrée or hors-d'œuvre. It can be kept 8 to 10
days in a cool place without spoiling.

349. Hare in White Wine   *Levraut au vin blanc*

1 young hare	1 teaspoon chopped parsley
2 ozs. butter	2 teaspoons chopped onion
salt and pepper	½ pint dry white wine
¼ teaspoon powdered thyme	½ pint stock or water
dash of nutmeg	

Cut a young hare, dressed and cleaned, into pieces for serving.
Melt the butter in a large pan and brown the pieces well on
both sides. This should take at least 20 minutes. Add the seasonings, wine, and stock or water. Cover and simmer 25 minutes.
Taste for seasoning and serve in the sauce.

350. Left-over Hare with Mushrooms
                                    Emincé de lièvre aux champignons

left-over hare cut in thin strips	1 tablespoon flour
2 ozs. butter	¼ pint white wine
¼ lb. mushrooms	salt and pepper
1 teaspoon chopped parsley	juice of ½ lemon
2 teaspoons chopped shallots or onion	croutons parsley

Place the hare, butter, mushrooms, which have been washed
and stemmed, parsley, and shallots in a heavy saucepan. When
the butter is melted, sprinkle with flour and stir in gently. Add
wine, salt, and pepper and cover. Simmer very gently for 30
minutes. Just before serving add lemon juice. Serve on a heated
dish and garnish with parsley and croutons.

Rabbit   *Lapin*

Rabbit, when properly prepared, is very delicious. It is commonly served in France and is gradually becoming more popular
in other countries. The butcher will usually clean and dress the
rabbit. If the rabbit is to be used for roasting, it is cut through
just behind the shoulders. The back and hind quarters are
roasted. If the recipe calls for cutting the rabbit into serving
pieces, the body should be split down the middle and each
side divided into 3 pieces—foreleg, body, and hind leg. Rabbit
and Hare recipes may be used interchangeably.

L

351. Rabbit Fricassee   *Lapin en gibelotte*

rabbit, cut in pieces for serving
3 ozs. butter
2 tablespoons flour
1 pint dry white wine
¼ lb. diced lean salt pork
bouquet garni (42)

4 cloves
12 small onions
salt and pepper
dash of nutmeg
½ lb. mushrooms (or 8 small peeled potatoes)

Melt butter in heavy saucepan and when it is sizzling, brown the pieces of rabbit on both sides. Meanwhile, in another pan, fry the salt pork until it is brown. When the rabbit has been thoroughly browned, sprinkle with flour and stir gently until the flour is blended. Add wine and when that begins to boil, add the fried pork, *bouquet garni*, cloves, onions, salt, pepper, onions, and potatoes. Cover and simmer gently for 60 minutes. If mushrooms are used in place of potatoes, add them 15 minutes before serving. If sauce is too thin, thicken with a little cornflour (page 4), or if by chance the rabbit has been killed and dressed at home save the blood and thicken the sauce with it (page 4). This gives a gamey flavour to the dish.

352. Rabbit à la Marengo   *Lapin à la Marengo*

1 young rabbit, cut in pieces for serving (page 151)
3 tablespoons olive oil
2 teaspoons chopped onion
2 teaspoons chopped parsley
1 tablespoon tomato paste

¼ pint water
¼ lb. small mushrooms
salt and pepper
½ oz. butter
juice of ½ lemon

Heat the olive oil until it is smoking. Fry the rabbit in the oil, turning the pieces often. This takes 20 to 30 minutes, depending on the thickness of the pieces. When the rabbit is tender, remove from the heat but keep in a warm place. Put half of the oil in which the rabbit has been cooked in a saucepan. Add parsley, onion, tomato paste, and water. Cook the mushrooms, which have been washed and stemmed, in this sauce until they are tender (10 to 15 minutes). Add butter and lemon juice, season with salt and pepper, and pour over the rabbit.

353. Papa Douillet's Rabbit   *Lapin au Père Douillet*

rabbit, cut in pieces for serving (page 151)
3 ozs. butter
2 ozs. diced lean salt pork
½ pint dry white wine
½ pint water
1 tablespoon chopped parsley

1 tablespoon chopped onion
1 tablespoon chopped chives
salt and pepper
1 teaspoon cornflour mixed with ½ oz. butter

Brown the rabbit and salt pork in sizzling butter. When the rabbit is well browned on both sides, add wine, water, herbs, salt, and pepper. Cover and simmer gently for 1 hour. Just before serving, thicken with cornflour and butter (page 4).

354. Roast Rabbit   *Lapin rôti*

Rabbit is roasted the same as hare (346). It may or may not be marinated before roasting. The marinating gives a gamey flavour.

355. Roast Partridge   *Perdreaux rôtis*

2 partridges
paper-thin slices of salt pork

watercress
lemon slices

Clean and truss the partridges in the same way as chickens (page 130). Cover each bird with a thin layer of salt pork and tie in place with twine. Place on rack in open baking tin. Pour ¼ pint of water seasoned with ½ teaspoon salt in the tin. Roast in 375°F. oven 30 to 40 minutes. Place the birds on a bed of watercress. Pour the juices and fat from the pan over the birds and garnish the dish with slices of lemon.

356. Truffled Partridge   *Perdreaux truffés*

Procure 2 or 3 partridges and follow recipe for Truffled Chicken
(316).

357. Partridge and Cabbage   *Perdrix aux choux*

This is a good recipe to use when the birds are a little old and
tough.

2 partridges	salt and pepper
¼ lb. lean bacon, thinly sliced	¼ teaspoon powdered thyme
6 pork sausages	4 cloves
2 ozs. butter	1 carrot, thinly sliced
2 tablespoons flour	1 medium-sized cabbage, cut in
½ pint stock or water	eighths

Melt butter in heavy saucepan. Split the partridges and brown
them along with the bacon and sausages. As the various pieces
become brown take them out of the butter. Add flour and stir
until brown. Add stock, thyme, carrot, and cloves and stir until
the sauce is smooth. Meanwhile, remove the outer leaves of
the cabbage, cut it in eighths, and parboil 20 minutes. Drain
thoroughly. Put the cabbage and partridges in the sauce, cover
and simmer very gently for 2 hours. Skim off the fat. Place the
cabbage on a heated dish. Arrange the partridges in the centre
and surround with sausages and bacon. Strain the sauce and
pour carefully around the cabbage.

358. Roast Pheasant   *Faisan rôti*

Rub the cleaned and dressed pheasant with softened sweet
butter. Place on a rack in oven tin. Roast in 375°F. oven for 45

minutes. At the end of the first 15 minutes, add 2 tablespoons
Madeira wine to the melted butter in the pan. Baste with this
mixture every 10 minutes. 15 minutes before serving, place 7
or 8 small rounds of stale bread in the pan. This will absorb the
juices and become brown. Place the pheasant on a bed of watercress. Surround with the rounds of bread and garnish with slices
of lemon.

359. Roast Quail   *Cailles rôties*

Clean, dress, and truss quails as directed for chicken (page
130). Wrap each bird in a fresh vine leaf and in thin slices of
salt pork. Tie in place and place on rack in baking tin. Roast
30 minutes in 375°F. oven.

360. Hunter's Quail   *Cailles au chasseur*

4 quails	¼ teaspoon powdered thyme
3 ozs. butter	2 tablespoons flour
2 teaspoons chopped parsley	½ pint water
2 teaspoons chopped spring onions	¼ pint white wine
½ bay leaf	1 teaspoon lemon juice
salt and pepper	croutons

Dress and truss quails as directed for chicken (page 130). Melt
butter in a heavy oven-proof casserole. Put quails, parsley, spring
onions, salt, pepper, and thyme in the casserole and brown the
birds on both sides. Add flour and stir in gently. Add water
and wine and bring to boiling point. Cover and place in a 350°F.
oven for 30 minutes. Place each quail on a round crouton. Taste
the sauce to be sure it is properly seasoned. Strain and pour
some over each bird. Garnish with watercress and slices of
lemon.

361. Roast Woodcock   *Bécasses rôties*

It is not necessary to dress the woodcock. Remove the head and
wing tips. Place each bird on a skewer. Cover the breast of
each bird with a thin layer of salt pork. Roast on a rack in an
open tin 30 minutes in 375°F. oven. Place rounds of toasted
bread in the bottom of the tin to catch the juices. Remove the
skewers and place each bird on a round of bread. Garnish with
lemon slices and parsley.

362. Wild Duck   *Canard sauvage*

Wild duck may be prepared in the same manner as domestic
duck. Follow recipes 328–32, 338, 339.

Qui court deux lièvres n'en prendra aucun.

Pâtés and Vols-au-vent

PÂTÉS are a combination of meat or fish, carefully prepared and highly spiced, which are cooked in either a round or oval earthenware terrine which has a cover, or in a vol-au-vent. They may be used as hors-d'œuvre, an entrée, a luncheon dish, or as the main attraction at a midnight collation.

363. Chicken Pâté   *Pâté-terrine de volaille*

1 3½- to 4-lb. chicken	1 bay leaf
½ lb. minced veal	1 sprig of thyme
½ lb. minced fresh pork	2 large paper-thin slices salt pork
2 slices stale bread, soaked in	¼ pint water
1 gill milk	½ pint cooking brandy
½ lb. fillet of veal	salt and pepper
½ lb. sliced lean ham	

Make an incision down the back of a properly cleaned chicken. With a sharp knife loosen the flesh from each side of the skeleton, taking care not to pierce the skin. Lay the chicken wide open and remove the skeleton in one piece. Kitchen scissors are very helpful. The thigh bones should be eased out. This is difficult and for the unpractised it is better to leave them in. The wings and legs are left on. Lay the skin and flesh as flat as possible and prepare the following stuffing: Chop the liver and heart rather finely and mix with the minced veal and pork. Squeeze the excess milk from the bread and add to the meat. Season with salt and pepper. Fill the holes left by the bones with stuffing and spread a layer of stuffing over the entire surface. Cut the veal and ham in thin strips and put a layer of each over the stuffing. Continue this until the chicken is full. Make sure that there are no holes left. Sew up the back so that the chicken will resume its original shape.

Place a thin layer of salt pork in the bottom of an oval terrine. On this put ½ bay leaf and half of the sprig of thyme. Add water and brandy. Place the chicken in the terrine and cover with another strip of salt pork, ½ bay leaf, and the other half of the sprig of thyme. Sprinkle with salt and pepper and cover. The terrine should be absolutely filled: if there are any open spaces between the chicken and the terrine, fill them with the stuffing. Cover and seal the rim with a little flour-and-water paste. Cook 2½ hours in a 300°F. oven. Remove from the oven but do not open until it is completely cooled. Serve cold.

A vaincre sans péril, on triomphe sans gloire.

364. Rabbit Pâté   *Pâté-terrine de lapin*

1 small rabbit
½ lb. fillet of veal
½ to ¾ lb. sausage meat
2 small bay leaves
pinch of ground cloves
pinch of nutmeg

sprig of thyme
two wide paper-thin slices salt
    pork
¼ pint water
½ pint cooking brandy

Remove the flesh from the bones of the cleaned and dressed rabbit. Cut the flesh into strips approximately 3 inches long and ¾ inch wide. Cut the veal into strips of the same size. Chop the liver and heart and mix with the sausage meat. Season with salt and pepper, nutmeg, and cloves. Place a layer of salt pork in the bottom of a terrine. Sprinkle with some freshly ground black pepper and place a bay leaf and half of the thyme on the salt pork. Cover this with a layer of sausage meat. Over this place a layer of rabbit meat and a layer of veal. Continue this alternation until the terrine is full. Press down so that the meat is firmly packed. Cover with a layer of salt pork. Sprinkle with pepper and place another bay leaf and half a sprig of thyme on top. Pour water and brandy over it all, piercing the pâté with a fork so that the liquid will seep through. Cover tightly and seal with flour-and-water paste. Cook 3 hours in a 300°F. oven. Cool in the terrine and do not open until it is ready to be served. It is always better to let a pâté stand at least 24 hours before eating.

365. Partridge Pâté   *Pâté-terrine de perdreaux*

Follow directions for Chicken Pâté (363).

366. Ham and Veal Pâté   *Pâté-terrine de veau et jambon*

¾ lb. fillet of veal	2 small bay leaves
½ lb. ham	1 sprig thyme
½ lb. sausage meat	2 paper-thin slices salt pork
3 ozs. bread crumbs, moistened with a little water	¼ pint water
	½ pint brandy
salt and pepper	

Trim the veal and ham so that they are the approximate size and shape of the terrine. Insert small pieces of ham fat in the veal. Chop the trimmings finely and mix with sausage meat and bread crumbs. Season with salt and pepper. Place a piece of salt pork in the bottom of the terrine and on this put a small bay leaf and half a sprig of thyme. Spread a layer of the sausage mixture on this, followed by a layer of ham and a layer of veal. Continue this alternation until the terrine is completely full. Press the meat down and pour the water and brandy over the top, piercing the meat with a fork so that the liquid will seep through. Place a layer of salt pork, a bay leaf, and the other sprig of thyme over this. Cover tightly, seal with a little water-and-flour paste. Cook in 300°F. oven for 3 hours. 15 minutes before the end of the cooking pour ¼ pint of consommé through the hole in the cover. This is not absolutely necessary but does render the pâté a little more moist. Do not remove the cover until the terrine is really cool. It is served cold.

367. Goose Liver Pâté   *Pâté-terrine de foie gras*

This wonderful dish can rarely be reproduced outside France, as it calls for fattened goose livers, which are difficult to obtain. The tinned *foie gras* is too expensive to warrant its use in a pâté. A passable imitation of this dish may be made by using ordinary chicken or goose livers.

1 lb. calf's liver
1 lb. chicken or goose livers
    (instead of 1 lb. *foie gras*)
¼ lb. fresh lean pork
½ lb. lard
salt and black pepper
¼ teaspoon ground cloves
⅛ teaspoon mace

2 tablespoons chopped parsley
1 small tin truffles
½ lb. fine bread crumbs moistened
    with
1 gill water
2 thin slices salt pork
1 bay leaf

Cut the chicken or goose livers in ½-inch pieces. Slice the truffles very thinly. Chop the calf's liver, pork, and lard rather coarsely. Add bread crumbs and any trimmings of truffles. Put ½ inch of this mixture in the bottom of a small round terrine. Place a layer of chicken or goose livers on this and cover with a single layer of truffles. Continue this alternation until the terrine is tightly packed. After each layer of truffles sprinkle with salt, pepper, cloves, and mace. The pâté is not highly spiced but should have a subtle aromatic flavour. Cover with a thin layer of lard. Place a bay leaf on this and seal the cover on with a little water-and-flour paste. Place the terrine in a tin of hot water and cook 3½ hours in 300°F. oven. Cool the pâté in the terrine. When it is thoroughly chilled, it may be unmoulded by plunging it in boiling water and turning upside down on a small dish. To be traditional it should be wrapped and served in tin foil.

368. Calf's Liver Pâté   *Pâté-terrine de foie de veau*

1 lb. calf's liver	salt and black pepper
1 lb. lean fresh pork	¼ teaspoon ground cloves
5 wide paper-thin slices salt pork	⅛ teaspoon mace
	1 bay leaf

Chop the liver and pork together. Season with salt, pepper, cloves, and mace. Mix well. Line the bottom of a round terrine with a layer of salt pork. Divide the mixture in 4 parts and alternate layers of the mixture with layers of salt pork. Finish with a layer of salt pork. Place a bay leaf on this and seal the cover of the terrine with a flour-and-water paste. Place the terrine in a pan of hot water and cook 3½ hours in a 300°F. oven. Do not remove the cover until the terrine is very cold. It may be served in the terrine or unmoulded.

369. Pig's Liver Pâté   *Pâté-terrine de foie de cochon*

Follow the preceding recipe using pig's liver instead of calf's. Do not be afraid to use pig's liver; the prolonged cooking mellows the sharp taste.

370. Fish Pâté   *Pâté-terrine de poisson*

1 lb. salmon, turbot, brill, or halibut	salt and pepper
	1 tablespoon chopped parsley
½ lb. butter	1 lb. fresh haddock, or cod steak
½ lb. fine breadcrumbs, moistened with	mace
	cayenne
1 gill milk	2 ozs. butter
1 egg yolk	

Chop the salmon, or other fat fish, very finely, and mix with softened butter, bread crumbs, egg yolk, and chopped parsley. Mix well and season highly with salt and pepper. Free the fish steaks of skin and bones and cut in narrow strips. Put a

½-inch layer of the fish mixture on the bottom of a small round terrine. Place a layer of fish strips over this. Sprinkle with salt, pepper, a dash of mace, and cayenne. Continue this process until the terrine is tightly packed. Dot the top layer with butter and seal the cover on the terrine with flour-and-water paste. Cook 2½ hours in a 300°F. oven. Do not take the cover off until the terrine is chilled. Unmould and garnish with parsley.

371. Pâtés in Pastry Cases   *Pâtés en croûtes*

These pâtés are prepared in the same way as those described in the preceding recipes. They are, however, served in a pastry case, which makes them more decorative and delicious. Special oval or round metal moulds are used for this. The moulds may be plain or elaborate.

To line moulds: Prepare Pie Pastry (553). Butter the mould carefully, making sure that all the indentations have been covered. Roll the pastry to ½-inch thickness. Cut out a round or oval large enough to form the bottom and sides, with ¾ inch to spare to take care of the shrinkage. Line a baking tray with a buttered piece of wax paper. Place the mould on the baking tray and line the mould with the pastry. Press the pastry in all the indentations. Trim the edge so that there will be an even ¼- to ½-inch border. Moisten the edge with water. Fill the mould with the desired filling. Follow recipes 363–70, but do not add the liquid. This would soften the pastry. Roll out the remaining pastry and cut a cover, allowing for shrinkage. Make a few decorative incisions and a small hole for the steam to escape. It is easy to keep this hole open by inserting the end of a pastry tube. Brush the cover with egg yolk beaten with 1 tablespoon water. Cook 3 hours in 375°F. oven. Just before the end of the cooking pour ¼ pint consommé and 2 tablespoons brandy through the hole, using the pastry tube as a funnel. The pâtés may be eaten hot or cold.

372. Vol-au-vent   *Vol-au-vent*

This large pastry case, filled with Sweetbread Financière (280),
Lamb Ragout (253), Veal Ragout (265), Shrimp Béchamel (212)
or Brains (239), makes a delicious entrée.

Make a double recipe of Puff Paste (555). After the last folding,
roll the pastry to a thickness of $\frac{1}{2}$ inch. Place the cover to a
2-quart saucepan on the pastry and cut out around it. For a large
vol-au-vent make 2. Brush the lower thickness with water and
lay one on top of the other. Roll out the remaining dough $\frac{1}{4}$ inch
thick and cut out 2 more circles of the same size. With a biscuit
cutter cut out the centre of these circles so that a circular band
$1\frac{1}{2}$ inches wide remains. Save one of the centres for a cover.
Brush the outer edge of the top whole layer with water and lay
one of the bands on this, taking care that the edges are even.
Moisten this band and put the remaining band on this. Prick
the bottom with a fork. Let it stand 10 minutes. Scallop the
edges by using a finger and the dull edge of a knife. Place top
in the centre. Mix 2 yolks of egg with 2 tablespoons water and
brush the whole shell with this mixture. Moisten a thick baking
tray with water and place the shell on it. Place in a 500°F. oven.
At the end of 5 minutes reduce the heat to 350°F. and cook
30 minutes. Remove the centre cover, scoop out the interior,
fill with the desired filling, and replace the cover.

373. Individual vol-au-vent   *Petits vol-au-vent*

Follow the preceding recipe but use a large scalloped biscuit
cutter for the base and sides. There should be only a single
layer for the base. Cut out the centres of the remaining 2 or 3
layers with a small smooth biscuit cutter. Follow the same
directions for baking and cooking.

374. Puff Paste Tartlets   *Petits pâtés*

Cut out rounds of Puff Paste (555) with a small biscuit cutter.
Moisten the edges of half of them. Fill the centre with a small
dab of sausage meat, or a shrimp dipped in butter, or smoked
oysters. Cover with the other half of rounds. Press the edges
together. Paint with an egg yolk beaten with 1 tablespoon water
and bake 10 minutes in 500°F. oven. These are delicious with
a salad or as hors-d'œuvre.

375. Filled Pastry Squares   *Rissoles*

Pie Pastry (553).

½ lb. cooked meat, poultry or fish,
    finely chopped

1 small onion, finely chopped

salt and pepper

2 ozs. fine bread crumbs mois-
    tened with a little water

Roll out the pastry as thinly as possible. Divide into 2 long strips.
Brush one half with water. Mix the rest of the ingredients to
form a stuffing. Season highly. Place little dabs of this mixture
2 inches apart on the moistened strip of pastry. Lift the other
strip and place it carefully over the first strip. Press the pastry
together around each dab. Cut out in squares with a pastry
wheel. Fry in deep fat (370°F.) 3 to 5 minutes or until the *rissoles*
are light brown. Sprinkle with salt and serve very hot. For the
unpractised it is easier to handle the pastry in smaller amounts.
Make several small strips instead of 2 large ones.

A moitié fait qui commence bien.

376. Cabbage Pie (Russian)   *Coulibac (koulibiac) aux choux*

½ pint milk	6 eggs
1 oz. yeast	2 ozs. butter
8 ozs. flour	1 large onion, finely chopped
½ lb. butter	2 white cabbages
8 ozs. flour	4 hard-boiled eggs
1 teaspoon salt	salt and pepper

Scald the milk and set aside to cool. When it is lukewarm dissolve the yeast. Stir in 8 ozs. of flour and when it is well blended, cover and set in a warm place until the dough is doubled in size. Wash the butter by placing it in a large bowl of cool water and squeezing it with your hands for 3 minutes to remove most of the salt. (It is not necessary with sweet butter.) Add butter, 8 ozs. flour, eggs, and salt to the dough and beat with your hands until the dough is very smooth. Place on a floured board and knead until the dough no longer sticks to the fingers. Place in a covered bowl and let it stand in a warm place for 45 minutes. It is then ready to be rolled out.

Roll out the dough ¼ inch thick to form a large square. Place in the centre the following filling: Shred 2 white cabbages coarsely and mix with chopped onion. Fry gently in melted butter until the cabbage is tender. Combine with the hard-boiled eggs, chopped coarsely. Season well with salt and pepper. Moisten the edges of the pastry square. Turn the edges toward the centre and lap them over the filling. Turn the pie upside down on a well-floured cooking sheet so that the smooth side is visible. Let it stand 30 minutes and then bake 60 minutes in 350°F. oven. When it is cooked, brush generously with melted butter, cut into 12 squares, and serve.

377. Salmon Pie (Russian)   *Coulibac de saumon*

Coulibac pastry (376)
3 thin salmon steaks
½ lb. semolina, cooked in
1 pint water
1 teaspoon salt

½ lb. mushrooms
melted butter
egg yolk beaten with
1 tablespoon water
salt and pepper

Prepare the pastry as in the preceding recipe. While the dough is rising prepare the following filling: Fry the salmon steaks in butter, allowing 5 minutes to each side. They should not be entirely cooked. Mix the semolina, salt, and water, and when it is cooked, set aside to cool. Wash and stem the mushrooms. Fry 5 minutes in butter. Cool.

Roll out a large square of pastry ¼ inch thick. Put a rectangular layer of semolina in the centre of the pastry. Cover with a boned salmon steak and over this put a layer of mushrooms. Sprinkle with salt and pepper and continue alternations until all the filling is used. Moisten the edges and lap them over the filling. Brush the pie with melted butter and egg yolk. Make a hole for the steam to escape. Cook 3 hours in 375°F. oven. Let the pie stand one or two days before using. It is eaten cold.

M

Macaroni, Noodles Ravioli and Rice

IT SHOULD be remembered that Tante Marie is French and not Italian. The recipes that follow may not be truly Italian but are, none the less, delicious. [C. T.]

378. Italian Macaroni   *Macaroni à l'italienne*

1 lb. macaroni	4 ozs. grated Parmesan cheese
6 ozs. butter	Italian Tomato Sauce (22)
salt and pepper	

The macaroni may be served without the sauce, but if the sauce is to be served, it should be started well in advance of the macaroni. Boil a large quantity of water in a big saucepan. Add 1 tablespoon salt. Cook the macaroni in the uncovered saucepan for 15 to 17 minutes or until the macaroni is tender but still firm. Drain well and reheat with butter. Add cheese, salt, and pepper. Serve with a bowl of Parmesan cheese and a bowl of sauce, or pour the sauce over the macaroni before serving.

379. Baked Macaroni   *Macaroni au gratin*

Follow the directions in the preceding recipe for cooking macaroni. When the macaroni is well drained and seasoned, place in ovenproof dish, cover with the grated cheese, and dot with butter. Cover and place in hot oven 15 minutes.

380. Macaroni and Sweetbreads   *Macaroni à la financière*

1 lb. macaroni   Sweetbreads Financière (280)

Study recipe 280 in order to judge the time for cooking the macaroni (379). Arrange the well-drained and seasoned macaroni in a ring on a heated dish. Fill the centre with the sweetbread sauce.

381. Home-made Noodles   *Pâte à nouilles*

10 ozs. flour   1 teaspoon salt
6 egg yolks   ½ gill water
2 egg whites

Mix the ingredients together, working them with your hand until a thick dough is formed. Let the dough rest 15 minutes and then roll out on a floured board until paper-thin. Let the sheet of paste dry for 2 hours. Cut in narrow strips and store in a warm place. These noodles are richer than shop noodles.

To cook noodles: Boil 12 minutes in a large amount of boiling salted water. Drain well and season with butter, salt, and freshly ground black pepper.

382. Milanaise Timbale   *Timbale milanaise*

Pie Pastry (553)   6 ozs. grated Parmesan cheese
½ lb. spaghetti   ½ cooked sweetbread (optional)
2 ozs. butter   ½ cup Italian Tomato Sauce (22)
salt and black pepper   ½ lb. mushrooms

Choose a smooth round mould and follow recipe 371 for lining
it with pastry. Prick the bottom of the mould with a fork and
line the pastry with brown paper. Fill the mould with dried
peas or beans, or with flour. This will keep the crust in shape.
Cut out a round of pastry for the top and place over the mould.
Paint the top with egg yolk mixed with a little water. Bake 15
to 20 minutes in 450°F. oven or until the crust is light brown.

Meanwhile plunge spaghetti in briskly boiling salted water
and cook 12 minutes. Drain well. Add the remaining ingredients
and season with salt and pepper. Reheat. Remove the paper and
dried peas from the mould and slip the shell onto a heated dish.
Fill with spaghetti mixture and replace the cover. This is a good
way to serve left-over spaghetti and tomato sauce.

383. Russian Macaroni Pie
                          Timbale de macaroni à la Bekendorf

1 lb. macaroni   ½ lb. smoked salmon
¼ lb. butter   Italian Tomato Sauce (22)
salt and pepper   grated Parmesan cheese
bread crumbs

Cook the macaroni (378). Drain and season with butter, salt,
pepper, and grated cheese. Butter a deep, smooth mould. Sprinkle
with fine bread crumbs so that both the bottom and sides are
covered. Put in half the macaroni. Dip slices of salmon in tomato

sauce and place on the macaroni. Cover with the rest of the macaroni. Cover and bake 20 minutes in 400°F. oven. Serve in the mould, or unmould and serve with tomato sauce and grated cheese.

384. Caneloni

1 lb. flour	2 egg yolks
5 eggs	salt and pepper
1 teaspoon salt	dash of nutmeg
3 or 4 tablespoons warm water	2 tablespoons grated Parmesan
½ lb. left-over poultry or meat,	cheese
finely chopped	2 egg whites, stiffly beaten
1 clove garlic, finely chopped	Italian Tomato Sauce (22)

If you prepare the following paste a day ahead, it will roll out much more easily. Place the flour on a pastry board or in a deep bowl. Make a depression in the centre and put in the salt and unbeaten eggs. With the tips of the fingers work the flour into the eggs, adding a little water from time to time as the paste becomes too dry. Work as quickly as possible and as soon as the paste is a smooth mass, place it in the refrigerator. This can be used after 2 hours, but the longer it stands the better it is.

Make the stuffing by combining the meat, garlic, egg yolks, salt, pepper, nutmeg and grated cheese. Any meat or combination of meats will do. When the mixture has been combined into a smooth paste, fold in the egg whites. If the mixture is too stiff add a little milk.

Roll the paste out very thinly and cut into 3-inch squares. Poach the squares in salted boiling water for 8 minutes. Remove from the water with a skimmer and drain on a towel. Spread a thin layer of the stuffing on each square. Roll them up and place in a buttered oven-proof dish. Sprinkle with Parmesan cheese, with tomato sauce, and heat 15 minutes in a moderate oven.

385. Ravioli

2 small eggs	1 raw egg yolk
8 to 10 ozs. flour	1 hard-boiled egg
1 teaspoon salt	salt and pepper
¼ lb. minced beef	dash of nutmeg
½ lb. chopped cooked spinach	2 ozs. grated Parmesan cheese
2 ozs. butter	Italian Tomato Sauce (22)

Beat the eggs until the whites and yolks are blended. Add salt and gradually work in the flour, using the finger tips. The amount of flour used depends on the size of the eggs. As soon as the mixture no longer sticks to the fingers, it is ready. Set in the refrigerator for at least 15 minutes. Longer resting makes the paste easier to handle.

Fry the beef lightly in butter. Add the spinach, egg yolk, chopped boiled egg, salt, pepper, nutmeg, and cheese. Combine to make a smooth mixture.

Place the ravioli paste on a floured board and roll out as thinly as possible. Cut into as many 3 x 1½-inch strips as possible. Moisten half of the strips with water. On the moistened strips, place two dabs of the beef and spinach mixture. This may be done with a pastry tube or from the end of a teaspoon. Place the dry strips over these and press along the edges so that the top and bottom stick together. The squares may be outlined with the pastry wheel. Let these rest 15 minutes. Boil salted water in a large shallow pan. Poach the strips 10 minutes, drain on a dish towel, and place in an oven-proof dish. Cover with tomato sauce and Parmesan cheese and reheat in the oven.

Mauvais ouvrier n'a jamais bons outils.

386. Milanaise Rice   *Risotto à la milanaise*

1 onion, finely chopped	large pinch of saffron
3 ozs. butter	salt and pepper
3 pints stock, preferably chicken	2 ozs. grated Parmesan cheese
¾ lb. rice	

Fry the onion in butter until it is yellow. Add the rice and stir gently until the rice is transparent. Gradually add the liquid, about ½ pint at a time, and as the rice absorbs the stock, add more. Add the saffron along with the first amount of liquid. The rice should be cooked in 30 to 35 minutes. It should not be too soft, but it should not be completely dry. Add more liquid if necessary. Sprinkle with cheese, season with salt and pepper, and serve very hot.

387. Boiled Rice   *Riz à la créole*

Wash 1 lb. of rice thoroughly. Drain and place in 3 pints boiling salted water. Boil 17 minutes, drain and pour over it 2 pints of warm water. This will wash away the excess starch. Place in a moderate oven for 20 to 30 minutes. Each grain of rice will be separate and of just the right degree of softness.

VEGETABLES are often served in France as a separate course, and, if they are properly prepared, they should frequently receive such attention. Particular care should be given to the washing of the vegetables. If the vegetables are thoroughly clean it is often unnecessary to peel them; flavour as well as nutritive value is increased when they are cooked 'in their jackets.'

388. Artichokes, Hollandaise Sauce

Artichauts à la hollandaise

Select medium-sized, firm artichokes. If they are too large or the outer leaves are spiny, they will be tough. Cut off the stem and the top. Remove the very hard outer leaves. Plunge them, stem-end down, into rapidly boiling salted water and boil uncovered 25 to 30 minutes or until the outer leaves can be easily detached. Drain well. Turn upside down and press out the water. Serve hot with Hollandaise Sauce (10).

389. Artichoke Bottoms   *Fonds d'artichauts*

Tinned artichokes are very satisfactory and often more economical unless one is fortunate enough to live in a large town where artichokes are sold. With fresh artichokes, the leaves and choke are removed from the boiled and drained artichoke, leaving just the bottoms. These are dipped in cold water to which a little vinegar has been added. The bottoms are then dried and fried in butter or olive oil. They are usually used as a garnish for a roast.

390. Braised Artichokes   *Artichauts au jus*

4 to 6 artichokes	½ pint stock
2 ozs. butter	salt and pepper
3 strips lean bacon, diced	*bouquet garni* (42)
2 tablespoons flour	

Remove the stems and cut off the tops of the artichokes. Spread open the centre leaves and cut out the chokes. Divide the artichokes in quarters and boil in salted water 15 minutes. Drain. Melt the butter in a large saucepan. Fry the bacon in the butter. and remove when it is brown. Add flour and brown. Stir in stock and when the sauce is smooth, add salt, pepper, and *bouquet garni*. Put the artichokes and bacon in the sauce. Cover and simmer 45 minutes. Place the artichoke quarters in a crown around the dish and fill the centre with the sauce which has been strained.

Il n'y a pas de petites économies.

391. Stuffed Artichokes   *Artichauts à la barigoule*

4 medium-sized artichokes	¼ lb. mushrooms
¼ lb. sausage meat	2 ozs. butter
½ lb. fine bread crumbs	1 tablespoon flour
1 gill stock	1 tablespoon oil
2 tablespoons chopped parsley	salt and pepper
1 small onion, finely chopped	lemon slices

Boil the artichokes (388). Drain well and cut out the choke. Moisten the bread crumbs with stock or water. combine with sausage meat, parsley, onion, and mushrooms which have been washed and finely chopped. Fry the mixture in butter until it is light brown. Sprinkle with flour and blend. This will thicken the stuffing. Fill the centres with the stuffing and replace top on artichoke. Brush the inside of a heated casserole with oil. Put in the artichokes and bake 30 minutes in a 350°F. oven. Serve each artichoke with a slice of lemon.

392. Fried Artichokes   *Artichauts frits*

Remove the stems and all the very hard leaves from 2 small artichokes. Cut each one lengthwise in 8 or 10 pieces. Remove the pieces of choke. Boil in salted water 15 minutes. Drain dry, dip in frying batter (40), and fry in deep fat (370°F.). Sprinkle with salt and serve immediately.

393. Artichokes with French Dressing
                              Artichauts à la vinaigrette

Boil artichokes (388). Serve hot or cold with French Dressing (31).

394. Asparagus in White Sauce

Asperges à la sauce blanche

Wash 2 lbs. of asparagus. Cut off the hard ends and make 6 to 8 small bunches. Tie with kitchen string. Boil gently in salted water. Drain and arrange the bunches on a heated dish. Serve with a bowl of White Sauce (3).

395. Asparagus in French Dressing   *Asperges à l'huile*

Prepare asparagus as in the preceding recipe. Cool but do not chill. Serve with French Dressing (31).

396. Chopped Asparagus   *Asperges en petits pois*

1-lb. bunch of asparagus	1 teaspoon cornflour
2 ozs. butter	1 egg yolk, beaten with 1 table-
1 tablespoon sugar	spoon water
gill water	

Wash the asparagus and cut off the hard ends. Cut the green part into tiny pieces, the size of a pea. Cook 5 minutes in boiling, salted water. Drain. Melt better and add sugar and water. Add the asparagus. Cover and simmer 20 minutes. Stir in the cornflour. Remove from the flame and add the egg yolk. Do not let the sauce boil again. Serve hot.

La vérité comme l'huile vient au dessus.

397. Asparagus with Parmesan Cheese

Asperges à la parmesane

Wash 2 bunches of asparagus and cut off the hard ends. Boil 15 minutes in salted water. Drain and cut in 1-inch pieces. Place a layer of the pieces in a well-buttered casserole. Sprinkle with salt, pepper, and Parmesan cheese and dot with butter. Repeat the process until all the asparagus has been used. Brown in a moderate oven.

398. Green Beans, Maître d'hôtel

Haricots verts à la maître d'hôtel

1½ to 2 lbs. green French beans
3 ozs. butter

1 tablespoon chopped parsley
salt and pepper

Try to obtain dark green beans that are quite small. These will have the highest flavour. If they are large, slice them lengthwise. Do not cut them in small pieces. Remove the ends and wash them. Boil in salted water 15 to 20 minutes. Do not cover them. This preserves the colour. When they are tender, drain. Melt butter and reheat the beans in the butter. Add parsley, salt and pepper.

399. Green Beans à la Poulette   *Haricots verts à la poulette*

Follow the preceding recipe for preparing and boiling the beans. Serve in a Poulette Sauce (8).

400. Green Beans in French Dressing   *Haricots verts en salade*

Follow recipe 398 for preparing and boiling the beans. Cool and
cover with French Dressing (31). Hot green beans as well as cold
may be served in this way.

401. Haricot Beans à la Bretonne   *Haricots blancs à la bretonne*

1 lb. dried haricot beans	1 tablespoon flour
2 ozs. butter	salt and pepper
1 large onion, thinly sliced	

Soak the beans in cool water overnight. Start cooking the beans
in cold water and simmer 2 hours. When they are tender, drain.
Fry slices of onion in butter until they are yellow. Add flour
and let it brown. Put in the beans and $\frac{1}{2}$ cup of the water in which
the beans have been cooked. Season with salt and pepper, cover
and simmer 15 minutes.

402. Haricot Beans, Maître d'hôtel
Haricots blancs à la maître d'hôtel

1 lb. dried haricot beans	2 tablespoons chopped parsley
3 ozs. butter	salt and pepper

Soak the beans overnight and cook as in the preceding recipe.
Drain, reheat in melted butter. Add parsley, salt and pepper.

403. Haricot Beans in French Dressing
Haricots blancs à la l'huile

Soak and cook 1 lb. of haricot beans as in recipe 401. Drain well
and serve either hot or cold in French Dressing (310).

404. Purée of Haricot Beans   *Haricots blancs en purée*

1 lb. haricot beans   salt and freshly ground black
3 ozs. butter   pepper

Soak and cook the beans as in recipe 401. When they are soft,
force them through a food mill. Moisten with the water in which
they have been cooked. The purée should be thicker than soup
but not as thick as mashed potatoes. Reheat with butter, salt,
and pepper. Serve very hot.

405. Kidney Beans   *Haricots rouges*

Any of the recipes for Haricot Beans may be applied to Kidney
Beans.

406. Beetroot   *Betteraves*

French Beetroot is usually baked for hours in sweet butter. It
is also boiled and eaten cold in French Dressing (31) or combined with other vegetables or lettuce to make a salad. Beetroot
should be washed and boiled in salted water 35 to to 60 minutes,
depending on the size and age. They may be peeled after they
are cooked.

407. Broccoli   *Brocolis*

Wash the broccoli and examine for tiny green worms. Remove
the large leaves and the thickest part of the stems. The smaller

leaves and stems are edible and delicious. Many of the recipes
for cauliflower may be applied to broccoli. Boil 15 to 20 minutes
in salted water. It may be served hot: Creamed (417), Buttered
(418),in Tomato Sauce (419), Au Gratin (420), Fried (421), or
cold, with French Dressing (422).

408. Buttered Brussels Sprouts   *Choux de Bruxelles au beurre*

2 lbs. Brussels sprouts	1 tablespoon chopped parsley
3 ozs. butter	salt and pepper

Wash the sprouts. Remove the stems and outer leaves if they are
not perfect. Cook in briskly boiling, salted water for 10 to 15
minutes. Do not cover the pan. Drain and reheat in butter. Add
parsley, salt, and pepper.

409. Braised Brussels Sprouts   *Choux de Bruxelles au jus*

Follow the preceding recipe for preparing the sprouts. While they
are being reheated, add 4 tablespoons of juice from a roast or
1 tablespoon of beef jelly mixed with 3 tablespoons water.

410. Creamed Cabbage   *Choux à la crème*

Remove the outer leaves of the cabbage. Cut in quarters and
remove the hard core. Boil 20 minutes in salted water. Do not
cover the pan. Place in a warm vegetable dish and pour over it
a well-seasoned Béchamel Sauce (1).

411. Stuffed Cabbage   *Chou farci*

1 large, firm cabbage	1 pint stock or water
½ lb. chopped beef or veal	1 onion, thinly sliced
½ lb. sausage meat	1 carrot, cut in rounds
salt and pepper	soup bone or veal knuckle sawn
2 ozs. butter	in 2 or 3 pieces
2 tablespoons flour	

Remove the outer leaves and cut out the centre core without breaking the cabbage. Pour boiling water over the cabbage. Drain well and put between each leaf a little of the stuffing made by combining the chopped meat, sausage, salt, and pepper. Tie the cabbage with string. In a pan large enough to hold the cabbage, melt butter and stir in flour. Let it brown and then add liquid. Stir until the sauce is smooth. Place cabbage in the saucepan and add onion, carrot, and soup bone or knuckle. Cover tightly and simmer 3 hours. Add more liquid if necessary. Place the cabbage on a deep dish. Remove the string and pour the strained sauce over it.

412. Red Cabbage with Apples   *Chou rouge aux pommes*

1 medium-sized red cabbage	3 cloves
5 large crab-apples	2 tablespoons red currant jelly
2 ozs. butter	1 teaspoon cornflour
salt and pepper	1 tablespoon cider or vinegar

After removing the outer leaves, wash the cabbage and cover with water. Peel and core the apples. Add the apples, butter, salt, pepper, and cloves to the cabbage. Cover and simmer 2½ hours. Bind the sauce with the currant jelly, mixed with cornflour and vinegar. Serve very hot. This is a Flemish dish.

413. Carrots, Burgundian Style*

Carottes à la bourguignonne

12 large carrots	2 tablespoons flour
2 ozs. butter	½ pint stock or water
2 onions, sliced	salt and pepper

Scrub the carrots and, if necessary, scrape them. Boil in salted water until tender. Fry the onions in butter until they are yellow. Sprinkle with flour and stir in stock. When the sauce is smooth, season with salt and pepper and put in the carrots, cut in small pieces. Cover and simmer 15 minutes.

414. Buttered Carrots*   *Carottes au beurre*

10 carrots	2 tablespoons chopped parsley
½ oz. butter	2 tablespoons chopped chives
salted water	salt and pepper
2 ozs. butter	

Scrub and, if necessary, scrape 10 carrots. Cut in 1-inch pieces. cook in rapidly boiling salted water to which ½ oz. butter has been added. Cook until tender—approximately 20 minutes. Drain. Melt 2 ozs. butter in a saucepan. Add parsley, chives, salt and pepper, and carrots. Cover and simmer 5 minutes. Small new carrots may be left whole and prepared in the same manner.

* Recipes 413–15 may be prepared more quickly by using a pressure cooker for the first part of the process.

N

415. Carrots à la Poulette   *Carottes à la poulette*

Wash and scrape 10 to 12 carrots or 2 bunches of small carrots.
If small carrots are used, leave them whole. Otherwise, cut in
1-inch pieces. Boil in salted water until they are tender. Drain,
place in a heated vegetable dish, and cover with a Poulette
Sauce (8).

416. Carrots Vichy   *Carottes Vichy*

8 to 10 carrots	1 teaspoon sugar
¼ lb. butter	½ teaspoon salt
1 tablespoon water	

Scrub and, if necessary, scrape the carrots. Cut in long, very
thin strips. Melt butter in heavy saucepan. Put in the carrots
with water and butter. Cover tightly and cook over slow flame
1 hour. Stir occasionally and very gently. The carrots must not
fry, but they must not be mashed by too vigorous stirring. Just
before serving, sprinkle with sugar and salt. Carrots are at their
very best served this way.

417. Creamed Cauliflower   *Choux-fleurs à la sauce blanche*

Remove the green leaves from a good, white cauliflower. Wash
and carefully inspect for little green worms. Leave whole or
divide into flowerets. Boil in salted water. If left whole, cook
25 to 30 minutes; if divided, 10 to 15 minutes. Drain well.
Place in warm vegetable dish and cover with Cream Sauce (2).

418. Buttered Cauliflower   *Choux-fleurs au beurre*

1 cauliflower	1 tablespoon chopped parsley
2 ozs. butter	salt and pepper

Prepare and cook the cauliflower as in the preceding recipe. Melt butter. Add parsley, salt, and pepper. Heat until the butter bubbles. Place well-drained cauliflower in heated vegetable dish and pour the butter sauce over it.

419. Cauliflower in Tomato Sauce

Choux-fleurs à la sauce tomate

Prepare and cook cauliflower as in recipe 417. Drain and place in warm vegetable dish. Cover with Tomato Sauce (21).

420. Cauliflower au Gratin *Choux-fleurs au gratin*

1 cauliflower	2 ozs. grated Parmesan cheese
Cream Sauce (2)	fine bread crumbs
¼ lb. grated Swiss cheese	

Prepare and cook the cauliflower as in recipe 417. Divide the cauliflower into flowerets. Add the cheese to the cream sauce and combine the cauliflower with the sauce. Place in a well-buttered casserole. Cover with bread crumbs. Dot with butter and brown in 375°F. oven.

421. Fried Cauliflower *Choux-fleurs frits*

Prepare the cauliflower as in recipe 417. Divide into bouquets of 2 or 3 flowerets. Boil in salted water 8 minutes. Drain thoroughly. Soak in ½ gill white wine vinegar, seasoned with salt and pepper. Prepare a thick frying batter (40). Dip the flowerets in the batter and fry in deep fat (375°F.) 3 minutes. See recipe 41.

422. Cauliflower in French Dressing   *Choux-fleurs à l'huile*

Follow recipe 417 for preparing and cooking cauliflower. Drain
and cool. Cover with French Dressing (31). This makes a
delicious hors-d'œuvre or salad.

423. Celery Rémoulade   *Céleri en salade*

Wash a large bunch of celery. Remove the leaves and cut into
thin strips, 2 inches long. Mix with a Rémoulade Sauce (23).
This makes a good hors-d'œuvre.

424. Braised Celery   *Céleri au jus*

2 bunches of celery	½ teaspoon beef extract
2 ozs. butter	1 teaspoon brandy
1 tablespoon flour	salt and pepper
½ pint consommé	

Wash the celery and remove the leaves. Cut off the tops, leaving
the bunch 7 inches long. Cut each bunch lengthwise into 4
pieces. Boil in salted water 20 minutes. Drain. Melt butter and
brown the flour in it. Stir in consommé and, when the sauce
is smooth, add extract, brandy, salt, and pepper. Simmer the
celery in the sauce 15 minutes. The sauce should be quite
thick.

425. Celery au Gratin.   *Céleri au gratin*

Follow directions in the preceding recipe, but place the boiled
celery in a flat, oven-proof dish. Pour the sauce over the celery.
Chopped mushrooms or thinly sliced truffles make a good addition to the sauce. Cover with bread crumbs and a layer of
grated Swiss cheese. Dot with butter and brown in 375°F. oven.

426. Celeriac Salad   *Céleri-rave rémoulade*

See recipe 55.

427. Celeriac au Gratin   *Céleri-rave au gratin*

Peel the celeriac roots. Slice in $\frac{1}{8}$-inch thick pieces. Boil 40 to 60 minutes in salted water. It is then prepared like Celery au Gratin (425).

428. Chestnut Purée   *Marrons en purée*

1 lb. chestnuts	1 oz. butter
$\frac{1}{4}$ pint hot milk	salt and pepper

Cut an X on the flat side of each chestnut. Place the nuts in a pan of cold water and bring to the boil. Boil 30 minutes. Remove the outer and inner skins. This is easier to do while the chestnuts are hot. Force the chestnuts through a food mill. Season with milk, butter, salt, and pepper. Reheat, taking care that the chestnuts do not burn. Serve in place of potato with pork or turkey.

429. Braised Chicory   *Chicorée au jus*

2 large heads of chicory	$\frac{1}{4}$ pint stock or consommé
2 ozs. butter	salt and pepper
1 tablespoon flour	croutons

After removing the tough outer leaves, wash the chicory well and boil in salted water for 30 minutes. Drain thoroughly and chop rather coarsely. Melt butter and stir in flour. Add liquid, salt, and pepper. When the sauce is smooth, add chicory and reheat. Serve very hot with croutons.

430. Cucumber Salad   *Concombres en salade*

See recipe 54.

431. Cooked Cucumbers   *Concombres à diverses sauces*

Select large green cucumbers. Peel and quarter them. Boil 10
minutes in salted water to which ½ gill vinegar has been added.
Drain and serve with Béchamel Sauce (1), Poulette Sauce (8),
or Maître d'hôtel Sauce (9).

432. Dandelion Leaves   *Pissenlit*

Use fresh small dandelion leaves and cook like Braised Chicory
(429).

433. Stuffed Aubergines   *Aubergines farcies*

2 small aubergines	1 clove garlic, chopped
2 tablespoons oil	¼ lb. mushrooms, chopped
1 tablespoon chopped parsley	salt and pepper
2 spring onions, finely chopped	fine bread crumbs

Wash the aubergines and split. Remove the centres and chop
rather coarsely. Heat 1 tablespoon of oil in a small pan. Add
parsley, spring onion, garlic, mushrooms, and chopped auber-
gine centres, and heat thoroughly. Fill the aubergines with this
mixture and place in a flat oven-proof dish. Sprinkle with bread
crumbs and moisten with the rest of the oil. Bake 30 minutes in
a 375°F. oven.

434. Fried Aubergines   *Aubergines frites*

2 small aubergines   Frying Batter (40)

Wash and peel the aubergines. Slice ½ inch thick. Dip the slices
in the frying batter and fry in deep fat (370°F.) 3 to 5 minutes
or until golden brown. Sprinkle with salt and serve immediately.

435. Braised Endive   *Endives glacées au jus*

12 small, white French endive	¼ pint stock or consommé
salt and pepper	1 teaspoon cornflour mixed with
dash of nutmeg	½ gill consommé
1 teaspoon sugar	

Wash and trim the endive. If only very large ones are obtainable
they should be blanched in boiling salted water 5 minutes. The
small ones do not need this. Arrange the endive in a heavy, well-
buttered saucepan. Sprinkle with salt, pepper, nutmeg, and sugar
and moisten with liquid. Cut out a piece of brown paper that
will fit the saucepan, butter it, and place on the endive. Cover
with a tight cover and cook as slowly as possible for 1 hour. Turn
the endive once at the end of 30 minutes. Place the endive on a
heated dish. Thicken the sauce with the cornflour and pour the
sauce over the endive.

436. French Endive in Béchamel Sauce   *Endives à la béchamel*

Wash and trim 12 French endives. Cook in boiling salted water
15 minutes. Drain and place in a heated vegetable dish. Cover
with a well-seasoned Béchamel Sauce (1).

Jerusalem Artichokes   *Topinambours*

Jerusalem artichokes are becoming more common but are still
foreign to many. They taste somewhat like hearts of artichokes
but are a little sweeter. They look like and are cooked like potatoes.

437. Jerusalem Artichokes, Maître d'hôtel
                              Topinambours à la maître d'hôtel

Follow recipe for Potatoes, Maître d'hôtel. (464).

438. Creamed Jerusalem Artichokes   *Topinambours au lait*

Follow recipe for Creamed Potatoes (467).

439. Fried Jerusalem Artichokes   *Topinambours frits*

Wash and boil 1 lb. of Jerusalem artichokes in salted water.
Peel and slice $\frac{1}{8}$ inch thick. Dip the slices in frying batter (40)
and fry in deep fat (370°F.) 2 to 3 minutes or until golden
brown.

440. Leeks au Gratin   *Poireaux au gratin*

Remove the green tops and roots of a large bunch of leeks.
Cut each leek in quarters lengthwise. Boil in salted water for
20 to 25 minutes. Cover with Béchamel Sauce (1), sprinkle
generously with grated Gruyère cheese, and dot with butter.
Brown in a 350°F. oven.

441. Lentils   *Lentilles*

Lentils are prepared like dried haricot beans. See recipes 401–4.
They are particularly delicious served cold with French Dressing
(31).

442. Braised Lettuce   *Laitue au jus*

4 firm heads of lettuce	½ teaspoon beef extract
2 ozs. butter	salt and pepper
1½ tablespoons flour	*bouquet garni* (42)
¼ pint stock	

Remove the outer imperfect leaves and wash the heads carefully. Boil in salted water 10 minutes. Remove and plunge the
heads into cold water. Drain and dry on a cloth. Melt butter in
a heavy saucepan, stir in flour, and allow it to brown. Add stock,
salt, pepper, beef extract, and *bouquet garni* and stir until the
sauce is smooth. Add lettuce. Cover and simmer 45 minutes.
Baste the lettuce often with the sauce. Place the lettuce in a deep
serving dish, remove the *bouquet garni*, and pour the sauce over
the lettuce.

Mushrooms   *Champignons*

Unless one is an expert, the only safe mushrooms to use are
the cultivated ones available in the markets. There are, however, six common wild mushrooms with which it is worthwhile
to become acquainted. These include the *field mushroom*, the
chanterelle, the *shaggy cap*, the *morel*, and the *puff ball*. Mushrooms should always be carefully washed. Unless they are very
large and tough they do not need to be peeled. Any peelings and
stems that are not used should be saved for flavouring sauces
and soups.

443. Mushroom Canapé   *Croûte aux champignons*

1 lb. mushrooms	1 teaspoon lemon juice
Béchamel Sauce (1)	4 large slices of bread, fried in
1 egg yolk	3 ozs. butter

Stem and wash the mushrooms. Boil the mushrooms 5 minutes
in just enough water to cover them. Drain and save the liquid
to replace some of the milk in the sauce. Thicken the sauce with
an egg yolk and add lemon juice just before pouring the mushrooms over the fried bread. Serve very hot.

444. Mushrooms with Herbs

Champignons sautés aux fines herbes

1 lb. mushrooms	2 tablespoons chopped parsley
1 tablespoon vinegar	1 tablespoon chopped chives
2 ozs. butter or 2 tablespoons olive	1 clove garlic, finely chopped
oil	1 teaspoon lemon juice
salt and black pepper	

Boil the mushrooms in just enough salted water to cover them.
Drain and reheat with butter or oil, salt, pepper, and herbs.
When thoroughly hot, add lemon juice and serve immediately.

445. Stuffed Mushrooms   *Champignons farcis*

12 extra-large mushrooms	½ clove garlic, finely chopped
4 tablespoons olive oil	salt and pepper
2 tablespoons chopped parsley	fine bread crumbs
2 tablespoons chopped onion	

Wash and peel the mushrooms. Remove the stems. Place the
caps upside down in a pan greased with 2 tablespoons olive oil
and fry gently until they are light brown. Meanwhile, put the
rest of the oil in a saucepan with the herbs and the stems of the

mushrooms, finely chopped. Cook 2 minutes. Season with salt and pepper and add enough bread crumbs to make a thick stuffing. Fill each cap with the stuffing, sprinkle with bread crumbs, and bake in 375°F. oven for 20 minutes.

446. Mushrooms à la Provençale

Champignons à la provençale

1 lb. mushrooms	1 large clove garlic
2 tablespoons olive oil	1½ tablespoons flour
salt and pepper	½ gill dry white wine
2 tablespoons chopped parsley	2 tablespoons water

Wash the mushrooms. If they are large, cut in pieces. If small, leave whole. Heat the oil in a frying pan. Add mushrooms, salt, pepper, parsley, and garlic and fry gently for 10 minutes, stirring occasionally. Sprinkle with flour and stir in gently. Add water and wine and stir until well blended. Simmer 10 minutes and serve very hot.

447. Mushrooms in Scallop Shells   *Champignons en coquilles*

Follow the recipe for Mushroom Canapé (443). Place in large scallop shells or ramekins. Sprinkle with fine bread crumbs, dot with butter, and brown in hot oven (375°F.).

448. Morels   *Morilles*

Dried morels can often be purchased in Italian markets. Soak them several hours before using. They can then be prepared like ordinary mushrooms except that they cannot be stuffed. They are delicious fried in butter, chopped, and added to an omelette.

449. Mushrooms in Sour Cream   *Champignons à la russe*

1 lb. mushrooms
2 ozs. butter
a bouquet of parsley, green onion
    tops, and fennel leaves
salt and pepper

dash of nutmeg
4 tablespoons thick Béchame
    Sauce (1)
2 tablespoons sour cream
1 teaspoon chopped fennel

Wash the mushrooms. Cut in 2 or 4 pieces, depending on the
size. Place in a heavy saucepan with butter, bouquet, salt, pepper,
and nutmeg. Cook gently 15 minutes. Remove the bouquet, add
the sauce and sour cream. Bring to the boil, add chopped fennel,
and serve very hot.

450. Mushroom and Rice Croquettes

Croquettes de riz aux champignons

½ lb. rice
½ lb. mushrooms
salt and pepper
fine bread crumbs

1 egg, beaten slightly
oil
sprigs of parsley

Wash and boil the rice in salted water 20 minutes. At the same
time, wash the mushrooms and cook in just enough salted water
to cover them for 15 minutes. Drain and slice them. Add to the
rice. Cook 5 minutes more or until the rice is tender. The water
should be completely absorbed. Season with salt and pepper
and chill. Form little balls of the mixture, roll in bread crumbs,
dip in beaten egg, roll again in bread crumbs, and fry in deep
fat (370°F.) for 2 to 3 minutes. Arrange the balls in a pyramid
on a heated dish and garnish with sprigs of parsley.

451. Glazed Onions   *Oignons glacés*

12 very small onions	2 tablespoons sugar
3 ozs. butter	1 gill consommé

Select small onions of uniform size and peel them. Melt butter and add sugar. Brown the onions in the butter, stirring gently from time to time. Add the consommé and boil over a high flame so that the liquid will quickly be reduced. Keep spooning the liquid over the onions until a thick syrup is formed. The onions must not be overcooked. These are usually used as a garnish.

452. Stuffed Onions   *Oignons farcis*

4 to 6 large Spanish onions	2 tablespoons flour
¼ lb. sausage meat	½ pint consommé
¼ lb. chopped beef	1 teaspoon brandy
2 ozs. butter	salt and pepper

Peel the onions and scoop out the centres. Mix the sausage and beef and fill the centres with the mixture. Slice the centres of the onion very thinly and brown in butter. Sprinkle with flour, add consommé, brandy, salt, and pepper. When the sauce is smooth, pour into a casserole. Place the onions in the casserole and bake 1½ hours in a moderate oven. Spoon the sauce over the onions several times during the cooking.

Marchand d'oignons se connaît en ciboules.

453. French Peas   *Petits pois au sucre*

4 lbs. fresh green peas	1 head green cabbage lettuce
2 ozs. butter	2 teaspoons sugar
6 small white onions	salt
bouquet garni (42)	2 tablespoons water

Shell the peas, peel the onions, and wash the lettuce carefully, keeping the head whole. Put all the ingredients in a heavy saucepan with a tight-fitting cover. Bury the lettuce and onions in the peas. Cover and cook over a very slow flame for 1 hour. Remove the *bouquet garni* and serve. The sauce may be thickened with the yolk of an egg (page 3).

454. Green Peas with Salt Pork   *Petit pois au lard*

4 lbs. green peas	2 cups water
¼ lb. lean salt pork, diced	salt and pepper
2 ozs. butter	*bouquet garni* (42)
2 tablespoons flour	3 small onions

Fry the salt pork in butter and when it is browned remove it. Stir in flour and water. When the sauce is smooth add salt, pepper, *bouquet garni*, onions, and peas. Cover tightly and cook 1½ hours over a very slow flame. Remove *bouquet garni* and serve very hot.

455. Purée of Peas   *Purée de pois*

1 pint large peas, too hard for ordinary use (or 1 pint dried peas), soaked
    in water several hours

Boil the peas until they are tender. Drain and force through a food mill or strainer. Moisten with the water in which they

have been cooked. Season with butter, salt, and pepper. Reheat
but take care that the purée does not burn. It should be thicker
than soup but thinner than mashed potatoes.

456. Buttered Green Peas   *Petits pois à l'anglaise*

4 lb. green peas	salt and pepper
2 ozs. butter	

Shell the peas as soon after they are gathered as possible. Boil
in salted water 20 minutes or until tender. Drain and season
with butter, salt, and pepper. Serve very hot.

457. Boiled New Potatoes   *Pommes de terre en robe de chambre*

Scrub small new potatoes with a stiff brush. Boil 30 to 40 minutes
in salted water. Serve them in their skins and eat with fresh
butter.

458. Baked Potatoes   *Pommes de terre cuites au four*

Scrub large potatoes with a stiff brush. Prick with a fork and
bake in 450°F. oven for 1 hour.

459. Steamed Potatoes   *Pommes de terre cuites à la vapeur*

Wash medium-sized or small potatoes carefully. Put them in a
heavy saucepan with $\frac{1}{2}$ pint of water and $\frac{1}{2}$ teaspoon salt. Lay
over the pan a double thickness of cheesecloth. Cover the pan
and steam 40 minutes or until tender. Be careful that the potatoes do not burn and have hot water ready to add if necessary.
Special steamer saucepans are very common and may be used
without the cloth. The potatoes may be peeled before bringing
them to the table or may be served in their jackets.

460. Fried Potatoes   *Pommes de terre sautées*

Wash medium potatoes and boil them in salted water until
tender. Drain and peel them. Slice them ¼ inch thick. Melt
¼ lb. butter in frying pan and, when it is sizzling, fry the potatoes
until they are golden. They should not brown. Sprinkle with salt
and serve.

461. French Fried Potatoes   *Pommes de terre frites*

Peel 6 large potatoes, wash and wipe dry. Cut lengthwise in
strips approximately ½ inch thick. Heat fat to 370°F. Fry small
batches of the potatoes 2 to 3 minutes, keeping the temperature
as near constant as possible (41). Drain on absorbent paper and
keep in warm place. When all the potatoes have been fried,
increase the temperature to 385°F. Return the potatoes in larger
batches to the fat and fry 2 minutes more or until golden brown.
Drain and sprinkle with salt.

462. Tiny New Potatoes, Sautéed in Butter
                                    Petites pommes de terre frites

Select very small new potatoes. Scrub with a stiff brush. Rinse
and dry. Melt ¼ lb. of butter in a frying pan and fry the potatoes
in the butter slowly for 30 to 40 minutes. Turn them fairly often.
The potatoes should be golden brown all over. Do not let the
butter burn.

463. Souffléed Potatoes   *Pommes de terre soufflées*

Wash, peel, and slice medium-sized potatoes ⅛ inch thick. Dry
thoroughly. Have 2 pans of deep fat. The first pan should be

heated to a temperature of 370°F. and the second to 390°F. Fry a handful of the potatoes slices in the first pan and as soon as they begin to brown, remove from the first pan and place in the second. If the temperatures are exact the second frying will make the slices swell. Do not try to fry too many at one time. It takes practice to master souffléed potatoes but it is worth the effort. Sprinkle generously with salt before serving. Potatoes, fried this way, cannot wait.

464. Potatoes, Maître d'hôtel

Pommes de terre à la maître d'hôtel

Scrub the required number of potatoes and boil in salted water until tender. Drain, peel, and slice them ⅛ inch thick. Melt 3 ozs. butter. Add 2 tablespoons chopped parsley, salt, and freshly ground black pepper. Put the potatoes in this sauce and stir gently so that the butter covers all the slices. Serve very hot.

465. Potatoes à la Parisienne

Pommes de terre à la parisienne

8 medium-sized potatoes	*bouquet garni* (42)
2 tablespoons butter, oil, or fat	salt
1 large onion, thinly sliced	freshly ground black pepper
1 pint water	

Fry the onion lightly in the butter, oil, or fat until it is a pale yellow. Add potatoes, peeled and thinly sliced, water, *bouquet garni*, salt, and pepper. Cover and simmer until the potatoes are tender—approximately 30 minutes. Remove the *bouquet garni* and serve. This is frequently served as a separate course.

o

466. Potato Ragout   *Pommes de terre en ragoût*

8 medium potatoes	1 pint water
2 tablespoons butter or oil	*bouquet garni* (42)
1 tablespoon flour	salt and pepper

Wash, peel, and slice the potatoes in 1-inch pieces. Melt butter and stir in flour, allowing it to brown. Add water gradually and stir until smooth. Add salt, pepper, and *bouquet garni*. Add the potatoes, cover, and simmer until the potatoes are tender. Take care that they do not burn. Remove *bouquet garni* and serve.

467. Creamed Potatoes   *Pommes de terre au lait*

6 medium potatoes	¾ pint warm milk
2 ozs. butter	salt and black pepper
1 tablespoon flour	dash of nutmeg (optional)

Wash, peel, and halve the potatoes. Boil in salted water until tender. Meanwhile melt the butter and stir in flour. Do not let the flour colour. Stir in milk and, when the sauce is smooth, season with salt, pepper, and nutmeg. Drain the potatoes, slice them or not as you will, and add to the sauce. Serve very hot.

468. Potatoes with Bacon   *Pommes de terre au lard*

6 medium-sized potatoes	2 tablespoons flour
2 ozs. butter	½ pint stock or water
¼ lb. lean, lightly cured bacon	salt and pepper
	bouquet garni (42)

Wash, peel, and quarter the potatoes. Melt butter in a heavy saucepan. Dice the bacon and fry lightly in the butter until

golden brown. Stir in flour and when it begins to darken, add
stock and *bouquet garni*. Add potatoes. Cover and simmer 1 hour.

469. Potatoes in Wine and Herbs

Pommes de terre en matelote

8 medium-sized potatoes	½ pint red wine
2 ozs. butter	salt and pepper
2 tablespoons flour	*bouquet garni* (42)
½ pint hot water	8 small onions

Wash, peel, and quarter potatoes. Melt butter in a heavy saucepan. Stir in flour and when it is lightly browned add water,
wine, salt, pepper and *bouquet garni*. Stir the sauce until it is
smooth. Add the small peeled onions and the potatoes. Cover
and simmer 1 hour.

470. Stuffed Potatoes   *Pommes de terre farcies*

4 to 6 large potatoes	2 tablespoons chopped parsley
¼ lb. sausage meat	salt
1 oz. butter	freshly ground black pepper
1 small onion, finely chopped	

Wash, peel, and cut the potatoes in half lengthwise. Scoop out
a large hole in each half. Cook the scooped-out centres in boiling
salted water until tender. Mash them, add butter, sausage meat,
onion, parsley, salt and pepper. Fill the holes in the raw potatoes
with this mixture. Place in a buttered oven-proof dish and
bake in a 350°F. oven for 1 hour. This makes a good luncheon
dish.

471. Potato Purée   *Purée de pommes de terre*

6 medium-sized potatoes   ½ pint milk
2 ozs. butter   salt and pepper

Wash, peel, and boil potatoes in salted water until soft. Heat
butter and milk together until the butter is melted. Force the
potatoes through a food mill or strainer or beat with an electric
beater. Stir in the milk and butter and continue stirring vigorously until the potato purée is very light. French puréed
potatoes are not as thick as our mashed potatoes. More milk may
be needed to give the desired consistency. Season with salt and
pepper and reheat before serving.

472. Potato Soufflé   *Pommes de terre en soufflé*

Prepare the potato purée of the preceding recipe. Add the well-
beaten yolks of 2 large or 3 medium-sized eggs. Beat the egg
whites stiff and fold into the potatoes. Place in a well-buttered
oven-proof dish and bake in a 375°F. oven until the potatoes
are golden brown—approximately 20 minutes.

473. Cheese Potatoes   *Pommes de terre au fromage*

8 potatoes   butter
1 cup grated Gruyère cheese   salt and pepper

Wash, peel, and boil potatoes. Mash them thoroughly. Butter
a casserole and place a layer of potato on the bottom. Cover
with a layer of cheese. Sprinkle with a very little salt and a
generous dash of freshly ground black pepper. Dot with butter.
Cover with another layer of potato. Continue the process until
cheese and potatoes are used. Finish with a layer of cheese and

pour a little melted butter on the top. Place in 400°F. oven and
bake until the top is golden brown.

474. Potato Croquettes   *Croquettes de pommes de terre*

6 potatoes	1 egg
½ lb. finely chopped cold roast beef	salt and pepper
2 tablespoons chopped parsley	1 egg white
1 onion, finely chopped	

Purée the potatoes (471). Keep the purée quite thick. Combine
with beef, parsley, onion, egg, salt, and pepper. Chill the mixture.
Make small balls of the mixture, dip in egg white and fry in
deep fat (375°F.) until golden brown.

475. Duchess Potatoes   *Pommes de terre duchesse*

6 to 8 potatoes	1 oz. butter
1 egg	salt and pepper
1 tablespoon chopped parsley	

Wash, peel, and boil potatoes in salted water until tender. Force
through a food mill or mash very thoroughly. Stir the potatoes
over a slow flame for several moments in order to dry them
completely. Add unbeaten egg, parsley, salt, and pepper. Stir
quickly and remove from fire. Let the potatoes cool and make
little patties ¼ inch thick. Fry in ¼ inch of sizzling hot butter
until they are golden brown on both sides. Salt and serve hot,
garnished with sprigs of fried parsley. These may also be browned
in the oven.

Duchess potatoes may be forced through a pastry tube to
form spiral-shaped patties or arranged in a ring around a dish.

476. Potato Salad   *Pommes de terre en salade*

Marinate 4 cups cold, sliced, boiled potatoes in French Dressing
(31) several hours before serving. Drain and arrange on a bed
of lettuce. Garnish with rounds of gherkins, fillets of anchovies,
and sliced hard-boiled eggs. Serve with a bowl of Mayonnaise
(17), if desired.

477. Green Salad   *Salade*

1 large head green lettuce	4 tablespoons olive oil
1 tablespoon chopped parsley	salt
1 teaspoon chopped tarragon	freshly ground black pepper
1 tablespoon wine vinegar	

Any of the salads—chicory, endive, cabbage lettuce, cos lettuce,
small dandelion leaves, watercress, or a combination of these—
may be used. The important thing is that the salad is fresh and
bright-coloured. Use only perfect leaves. Wash thoroughly and
dry before placing the leaves in a wooden bowl. Add the seasonings just before serving. Toss well.

478. Salad with Cream Dressing   *Salade à la crème*

Substitute 4 tablespoons of thick cream for the oil used in the
preceding recipe.

479. Vegetable Salad   *Salade jardinière*

Cook as large a variety of vegetables as possible in salted water.
Drain and cool. Marinate them in French Dressing (31) for
1 hour. Drain and arrange on lettuce leaves. Garnish with hard-
boiled eggs and serve with Mayonnaise (17).

480. Creamed Salsify   *Salsifis à la sauce blanche*

Trim the tops, wash and scrape 1 bunch of salsify. Soak in fresh water to which a little vinegar has been added. This will keep them from discolouring. Cook in boiling salted water for 20 minutes. Drain well, place in a warm vegetable dish, and cover with Cream Sauce (2).

481. Buttered Salsify   *Salsifis au beurre*

Follow recipe 414.

482. Salsify à la Poulette   *Salsifis à la poulette*

Follow recipe 415.

483. Fried Salsify   *Salsifis frits*

Prepare and boil the salsify as in recipe 480. Drain. Dip in a thick frying batter (40) and put them, one after another, in deep hot fat (370°F.). When they are golden brown, sprinkle with salt and serve on a heated dish, garnished with parsley.

484. Sauerkraut   *Choucroute*

Sauerkraut may be bought tinned or by the pound in most
delicatessen shops. For those who prefer to prepare it at home,
Tante Marie gives the following recipe:

Be sure that the cabbages are firm and white. Remove the
imperfect outer leaves. Quarter the heads and remove the hard
core. Shred the cabbage. Line the bottom of a keg or crock with
salt. Put in a layer of shredded cabbage, a few juniper berries
(if possible), and whole peppercorns. Press the cabbage down
without breaking it and continue alternating layers of cabbage
with peppercorns and salt until the vessel is ¾ full. 12 cabbages
require 2 lbs. of salt. Cover with several layers of cheesecloth.
Place a board or plate that will fit over the cabbage in the crock.
Place a heavy weight on this. When fermentation starts, the
cover will go down and the brine will come over the cover.
Some of this should be removed but some should be left on the
cover. The sauerkraut may be used at the end of a month. As
the sauerkraut is taken out of the crock, wash the cover and cloth
before putting it back and place a little fresh water on the cover.
The fermentation has an unpleasant odour but it disappears when
the sauerkraut is washed.

485. Sauerkraut and Sausage   *Choucroute garnie*

2 lbs. sauerkraut   4 frankfurters
8 slices fat bacon   ½ bottle white wine
salt and pepper   1 pint stock
½ lb. pork sausages

Put 3 slices of bacon in the bottom of a heavy saucepan. Place
a layer of sauerkraut, which has been washed in several waters
and thoroughly drained, over the bacon. Sprinkle with salt and

pepper. Lay half the pork sausages, 2 slices of bacon, and 2 frankfurters on the sauerkraut. Cover with a layer of sauerkraut and repeat the process. Pour wine and water over it all. Cover tightly and simmer 5 hours. Skim off the fat before serving. This recipe may be doubled or tripled.

486. Garden Sorrel   *Purée d'oseille*

4 or 5 handfuls of sorrel	1 egg yolk, mixed with 4 table-
2 ozs. butter	spoons cold milk
	salt and pepper

Wash the sorrel well and remove the hard stems. Place in a heavy saucepan. Cover and wilt over a slow flame 10 minutes. Add butter and heat 5 minutes longer. Stir in the egg yolk and milk. Season with salt and pepper. If the sorrel is large and bitter, blanch it 5 minutes in salted water, drain, and then add the butter, etc. This is usually served with hard-boiled eggs, sausage, or ham.

487. French Spinach   *Epinards au jus*

2 lbs. spinach	salt, black pepper
2 ozs. butter	2 hard-boiled eggs, sliced
2 tablespoons flour	croutons
¼ pint stock or spinach broth	

Remove all the hard stems from the spinach and wash in several waters. Plunge into boiling salted water and cook 5 minutes. Drain and press out the water. Chop finely and place in saucepan with butter. When the butter has melted, add flour. When this has blended add the liquid and stir until smooth. Season with salt and pepper and, if desired, a dash of nutmeg. Serve on a heated dish. Garnish with slices of hard-boiled egg and croutons.

488. Creamed Spinach   *Epinards à la béchamel*

Follow the preceding recipe, substituting 1 cup of milk for the
stock or spinach broth.

489. Sweet Spinach   *Epinards au sucre*

2 lbs. spinach	1 egg yolk, mixed with
1 tablespoon sugar	½ gill cold milk
2 ozs. butter	salt, black pepper
1 tablespoon flour	croutons

Follow recipe 487 for cooking spinach but instead of adding the
liquid, add sugar and thicken with egg yolk and milk. Do not
let the spinach boil after adding the egg.

490. Tomatoes au Gratin   *Tomates au gratin*

6 large ripe tomatoes	1 spring onion, finely chopped
2 tablespoons olive oil	fine bread crumbs
1 tablespoon chopped parsley	salt and pepper
1 clove garlic, finely chopped	

Choose the tomatoes with care. They should be uniform in size
and should be ripe but very firm. Cut the tomatoes horizontally
in half. Heat 1 tablespoon olive oil with the herbs. Spread the
mixture on the bottom of a casserole. Place the tomato halves
on top. Sprinkle with salt and pepper and cover with bread
crumbs. Brush with the remaining olive oil and cook ¾ hour in
a 350°F. oven.

Plus on se presse, moins on arrive.

491. Stuffed Tomatoes   *Tomates farcies*

6 large, firm, ripe tomatoes	¼ lb. mushrooms, chopped
4 tablespoons olive oil	salt and pepper
2 tablespoons chopped parsley	fine bread crumbs
2 tablespoons chopped spring onions	4 tablespoons grated Gruyère cheese
1 clove garlic, finely chopped	

Wash the tomatoes and hollow out a large cavity in the centre of each one. Heat 2 tablespoons oil with the herbs and mushrooms and cook 3 minutes. Season with salt and pepper and add enough bread crumbs to make a thick stuffing. Place the tomatoes in a large well-oiled casserole. Fill with the stuffing. Sprinkle with cheese and brush with the remaining oil. Bake 45 minutes in 350°F. oven, basting from time to time with juice that comes from the tomatoes.

492. Sweet Turnips   *Navets au sucre*

2 bunches small turnips	½ pint stock or water
2 ozs. butter	salt
1 tablespoon sugar	1 tablespoon sugar
1 tablespoon flour	

Wash and peel the turnips. Melt butter in a saucepan and add 1 tablespoon sugar. Fry the turnips gently until they are yellow. Stir in flour carefully and add liquid, salt, and 1 more tablespoon sugar. Cover the pan tightly and simmer 1 hour.

493. Braised Turnips   *Navets au jus*

2 bunches small turnips	salt and pepper
2 ozs. butter	*bouquet garni* (42)
1 tablespoon flour	½ pint stock or consommé

Follow the preceding recipe but do not add sugar. Add the *bouquet garni*. This is removed just before serving.

494. Mashed Turnips   *Navets en purée*

2 bunches small turnips   salt and pepper
2 ozs. butter

Wash and peel the turnips. Boil in salted water until they are
tender—approximately 40 minutes. Force through a food mill
or strainer. Season with butter, salt, and pepper and reheat
before serving.

495. Truffles in Wine   *Truffes au vin*

Truffles, those highly prized nuggets usually found by inquisi-
tive pigs at the base of French oak trees, are rarely obtainable
in Great Britain excepting in tins. For the record we include
Tante Marie's instructions for cleaning them. They should be
washed and scrubbed in several waters, using a stiff wire brush.
They are then peeled and sliced or left whole, as the recipe
requires. The peelings should always be saved for sauces. Truffles
may be bought in tins. The peelings and chopped truffles are
cheaper. The whole truffles must be saved for very special
occasions. The flavour lost in the canning process can be partly
revived by frying the truffles gently in butter [C. T.]

2 large tins whole truffles   *bouquet garni* (42)
2 ozs. salt pork, diced   salt and pepper
½ bottle dry white wine

Drain the tinned truffles. Combine with the remaining ingredients and simmer in a covered saucepan for ¾ hour. Place
in a heated vegetable dish and pour the strained sauce over
them.

496. Sweet Omelette *Omelette au sucre*

6 eggs	¼ teaspoon salt
2 tablespoons sugar	2 ozs. butter

Separate the yolks and whites of eggs. Beat the yolks until they are lemon-coloured. Beat the whites stiff but not dry. Add 1 tablespoon sugar and the salt to the egg yolks and fold in egg whites. Follow recipe 125 for cooking the omelette. When it is cooked, sprinkle generously with sugar and, if possible, press with a red-hot poker. Serve immediately.

497. Rum Omelette *Omelette au rhum*

Follow the preceding recipe for making Sweet Omelette. Place it on a heated metal dish. Pour on 2 tablespoons of hot brandy and touch a match to it as you carry the dish to the table.

498. Jelly Omelette   *Omelette aux confitures*

Follow recipe 496 for making Sweet Omelette. Make sure that
the omelette is thoroughly cooked and that the centre is not
runny. Before folding the omelette put a layer of jelly or jam on
one half. Serve immediately.

499. Omelette Soufflé   *Omelette soufflée*

4 eggs   1 teaspoon grated lemon rind
4 teaspoons castor sugar

Beat the egg yolks until lemon-coloured. Add sugar and grated
lemon. Fold in stiffly beaten egg whites. Place in a deep buttered
oven-proof dish and bake 10 minutes in 450°F. oven. Sprinkle
with sugar before serving.

500. Snow Pudding   *Œufs à la neige*

4 eggs   ½ teaspoon vanilla extract
1 pint milk   6 ozs. sugar

Separate the yolks from the whites. Beat the egg whites very
stiffly. Add sugar and vanilla to the milk and bring to the boil.
Poach the egg whites in the milk in the following manner:
Take a generous tablespoonful of egg whites and place in the
simmering milk. When the whites swell turn them and cook for
a moment longer. Remove carefully and put on a dish. Three
tablespoonsful can be done at once. Continue this until all the
egg whites have been used. Beat the yolks and add to the milk,
taking care that the milk is cool enough not to curdle the yolks.
Strain into the top of a double boiler and cook, stirring constantly,

until the sauce begins to thicken. Remove and cool. When cool, pour the sauce around the islands of egg white. This makes an attractive dessert.

501. White Lady   *Dame blanche*

4 eggs	6 ozs. sugar
1 pint milk	½ teaspoon vanilla extract

Separate the yolks from the whites. Beat the whites very stiffly and place in a buttered mould or casserole. The dish should be only half full. Cover and bake 15 to 20 minutes in a 350°F. oven. If the whites rise too high, remove the cover. Meanwhile beat yolks until lemon-coloured and combine with milk and sugar. Cook in the top of a double boiler until the sauce begins to thicken. When the egg whites are cooked, turn the mould upside down on a dish. Surround with the sauce. Serve cold. The mould may be caramelized before putting in the egg whites (538) but in this case it becomes *Gâteau d'œufs à la neige* and not the traditional *Dame blanche*.

502. Chocolate Mousse   *Mousse au chocolat*

4 1-oz. squares bitter chocolate	5 eggs
½ gill water	1 tablespoon cognac
6 ozs. sugar (caster)	

Melt the chocolate in the top of a double boiler. Add water and sugar and stir until the sugar is dissolved. Separate the yolks from the whites. Add the yolks, one by one, beating vigorously. Remove from the heat and add cognac. Beat egg whites stiff and fold into the chocolate mixture. Pour into individual moulds or a glass bowl and place in the refrigerator. Let it stand for at least 12 hours. The longer it stands the better it is. It will keep well for several days.

503. French Applesauce   *Marmelade de pommes*

8 cooking apples   ½ teaspoon vanilla extract or ½ tea-
2 ozs. butter   spoon grated lemon rind
4 ozs. sugar   3 tablespoons water
                            candied fruits

Peel, core, and quarter the apples. Place in a heavy saucepan
with butter, sugar, water, and flavouring. Cook over low flame
until the apples are tender. Stir often to prevent burning. Strain
the apples and serve hot in a deep dessert dish. Sprinkle with
caster sugar. Decorate with candied fruits. This sauce may be
served cold. If so, heat half a glass of apricot or currant jelly with
a little water and pour over the sauce.

504. Apple Charlotte   *Charlotte de pommes*

several slices white bread   ½ jar apricot jam
4 tablespoons melted butter 1 tablespoon rum
French Applesauce (503)

Remove the crusts from the bread. Cut 12 long triangles. Fry
gently in melted butter. Line the bottom of a smooth mould
with these triangles, with the points meeting in the centre. Line
the sides with rectangles which have been cut the height of the
mould and lightly fried. Fill the mould with the applesauce.
Bake 30 minutes in 375°F. oven. Turn upside down on a dish
and serve with a sauce made by heating apricot jam with a little
water and flavouring it with rum.

505. Apple Charlotte Meringue

Charlotte de pommes meringuées

Fill a buttered casserole with hot French Applesauce (503). Beat 1 egg white very stiff and add 1 generous tablespoonful of caster sugar. Spread this mixture over the sauce. Sprinkle with granulated sugar and cook in 375°F. oven until the egg whites have risen and are golden brown—approximately 20 minutes.

506. Apple Supreme *Pommes au riz*

¼ lb. rice	4 ozs. sugar
1 pint milk	½ teaspoon vanilla extract
4 ozs. sugar	1 egg yolk
8 cooking apples	red currant jelly
1 pint water, mixed with	candied fruits

Wash the rice carefully and cook in boiling milk until the rice is soft. The milk should be entirely absorbed. Sweeten with sugar and set aside to cool. Peel and core 4 apples and simmer in syrup until a fork will easily enter the apples. Do not overcook. Remove them carefully with a skimmer. Core, peel, and cut the rest of the apples in small pieces and cook in the same syrup until they have the consistency of apple sauce. Add vanilla. Mix with the cooked rice and let it stand 15 minutes. Add slightly beaten egg yolk and pour into a baking dish. Bury the 4 whole apples in the rice so that only the top halves are visible. Place under the grill a few moments to colour the apples. Just before serving fill the centres of the apples with red currant jelly and decorate the rice with candied fruits.

P

507. Buttered Apples   *Pommes au beurre*

4 to 6 medium-sized baking apples   4 ozs. sugar
4 to 6 thin slices white bread   4 ozs. butter

Core and peel apples. Place the bread in a buttered baking dish
and put an apple on each slice. Fill half of each centre with
butter and the rest with sugar. Bake 45 to 60 minutes, depending
on size, in 350°F. oven. Melt the remaining butter and combine
with remaining sugar. Spoon a little of this over the apples from
time to time. Serve hot with the juice from the bottom of the pan
poured over the apples. If the centres are filled with red currant
jelly just before serving, they become *Pommes portugaises*.

508. Flaming Apples   *Pommes flambantes*

12 small, tart apples $\frac{1}{4}$ teaspoon cinnamon
1 pint water $\frac{1}{2}$ gill hot rum
8 ozs. sugar

Bring water, cinnamon, and sugar to the boil. Wash the apples
and poach them in the syrup until they are tender. Do not overcook or they will not keep their shape. Remove from the syrup,
one by one, and arrange in a pyramid on a heated dish. Quickly
reduce the syrup by boiling until it is quite thick. Pour over the
apples and sprinkle with sugar. Just before carrying the dish to
the table, pour the rum over the pyramid and touch with a
flame.

509. Buttered Peaches   *Pêches au beurre*

Follow recipe 507, substituting $\frac{1}{2}$ large peach for each apple.
The peach should be placed cavity side up on the bread, in order
to hold the butter and sugar.

510. Apple Fritters   *Beignets de pommes*

10 ozs. flour   ½ pint milk
2 egg yolks   2 egg whites
1 teaspoon brandy   4 cooking apples
½ teaspoon salt

Put the flour in a bowl and make a well in the centre. Place the
egg yolks, brandy, and salt in the well and work them in the flour
until it is thoroughly mixed. Add the milk gradually until the
batter is smooth. Beat the egg whites stiff and fold into the batter.
Peel and core the apples and cut them in ⅛-in. rounds. Dip each
piece into the batter and fry 3 to 5 minutes in 375°F. deep fat.
Sprinkle with caster sugar and serve.

511. Apricot Fritters   *Beignets d'abricots*

Choose apricots that are not quite ripe. Split them but do not
peel them. Follow the preceding recipe.

512. Peach Fritters   *Beignets de pêches*

Choose peaches that are not quite ripe. Peel them and cut in
two. Follow recipe 510.

513. Strawberry Fritters   *Beignets de fraises*

Choose large strawberries that are not quite ripe. Leave them
whole. Follow recipe 510.

514. Sweet Almond Fritters   *Beignets sucrés aux amandes*

10 ozs. flour
¼ lb. almonds, blanched and peeled
5 ozs. caster sugar

4 ozs. butter
½ teaspoon grated lemon rind
2 eggs

Blanche almonds by dropping them into boiling water and then removing the skins. Force almonds through a food chopper, using the finest blade. Beat eggs slightly. Add flour, sugar, almonds, butter that has been softened but not melted, and lemon rind. Work the dough with your hands until it is smooth. Roll out quite thinly. Cut the dough into whatever shapes you desire and fry in deep fat (370°F.) 2 to 3 minutes.

515. Cream Fritters   *Crème frite*

5 ozs. flour
¼ pint cold water
1 pint milk
6 tablespoons sugar
¼ teaspoon salt

½ teaspoon grated lemon or orange
   rind
1 egg yolk
1 egg yolk, beaten with
2 tablespoons sugar
fine bread crumbs

Mix the flour with the water until it is a smooth paste. Bring the milk to the boil and add the flour-and-water paste, stirring until it is well blended. Add sugar, salt, and lemon rind and continue cooking very slowly 15 minutes. Remove from the heat and when it has cooled a little, stir in the egg yolk, slightly beaten. Pour into a buttered cake tin and chill thoroughly. Cut into rounds or strips, dip in the sweetened egg yolk, roll in bread crumbs, and fry 2 to 3 minutes in 370°F. deep fat.

516. Puff Paste Fritters   *Beignets soufflés dits pets de nonne*

½ pint water   1 oz. butter
1 teaspoon sugar   5 ozs. flour
¼ teaspoon salt   4 eggs
1 tablespoon grated lemon rind   granulated sugar

Bring water, sugar, salt, lemon rind, and butter to a boil. Add flour and stir vigorously until all the flour is mixed in. Continue stirring this mixture over the flame until it is thick and dry. Remove from the flame and add the unbeaten eggs, one at a time, stirring hard after each addition. The dough will become smooth and when it drops slowly from the spoon it is the right consistency. Drop teaspoons of the mixture into deep fat (370°F.) and fry until golden brown. Sprinkle with caster sugar. Serve hot or cold; they are delicious tea cakes.

517. Crêpes   *Crêpes*

10 ozs. flour   1 teaspoon salt
1 pint milk   1 tablespoon salad oil
½ pint water   1 tablespoon brandy
2 eggs

Add the milk and water to the flour gradually, beating constantly so that the batter becomes very smooth. Add eggs, salt, oil, and brandy. Beat the batter until smooth and set aside to rest for an hour or two. Heat a large frying pan and grease very slightly. Pour a serving spoonful of the batter into the frying pan and move the pan around until its entire surface is covered. Both the batter and the resulting crêpe should be thin. When it is brown, turn with a large spatula and cook a moment on the other side. Continue this process until all the batter is used. Keep the crêpes in a warm place. Fold each in quarters or roll it. Sprinkle with sugar. Apricot jam flavoured with cognac may be placed on each crêpe before folding it.

518. Crêpes Suzette   *Crêpes Suzette*

4 ozs. butter
5 tablespoons sugar
grated rind of 2 oranges
2 teaspoons curaçao or cointreau

Sauce:
  juice of 2 oranges
  2 tablespoons sugar
  2 tablespoons curaçao (or 2
     tablespoons cointreau)

Prepare the crêpes as in the preceding recipe. Cream the butter and sugar. Add the rind and liqueur. Spread each crêpe with this mixture and keep in a warm place. Boil the orange juice and sugar for a few moments and add the liqueur. Pour this hot sauce over the crêpes and touch with a flame as the dish is carried to the table. Brandy may be substituted for the orange liqueur.

519. Rice Cake   *Gâteau de riz*

¼ lb. rice
1½ pints milk
4 eggs
¼ lb. butter

¼ lb. almonds, finely ground
3 tablespoons sugar
½ teaspoon vanilla extract

Wash and cook the rice in the boiling milk. When the rice is tender, add vanilla and set aside to cool. Soften the butter by working it with a wooden spoon. Separate the yolks from the whites and add the yolks one by one to the butter, beating vigorously after each addition. This can be done with an electric beater set at a low speed. If done by hand it should be beaten 15 minutes in order to get the right consistency. Add sugar and almonds and gradually add the rice, beating all the time. Fold in stiffly beaten egg whites and pour into a buttered mould. Set the mould in a pan of hot water and bake in 350°F. oven 45 minutes. Unmould and serve plain or with a Custard Sauce (533). Raisins may be substituted for the almonds.

520. Chocolate Soufflé   *Soufflé au chocolat*

2 ozs. butter	2 tablespoons water
2 tablespoons flour	6 tablespoons caster sugar
1½ gills milk, warmed	3 eggs
¼ lb. bitter chocolate	½ teaspoon vanilla extract

Melt butter and stir in flour. Add warm milk and stir until well blended. Melt the chocolate in the top of a double boiler. Add sugar and water and stir until smooth. Combine the mixtures. Separate the yolks from the whites of eggs and beat the yolks thoroughly. Add them to the chocolate mixture. Add vanilla. Beat the egg whites stiff and fold in carefully. Bake in a buttered casserole 20 minutes in 350°F. oven. The casserole should be set in a pan of hot water. A French soufflé should not be dry, but if a drier soufflé is preferred, bake 5 to 10 minutes longer. Powder with caster sugar and serve plain or with whipped cream. It cannot wait. This sweet can easily be made even if the hostess is the cook. Prepare the soufflé ahead of time except for beating the egg whites. Just before dinner is served add the stiffly beaten egg whites and bake during dinner.

521. Quickly Done   *Tôt-fait*

3 eggs	5 ozs. caster sugar
6 ozs. flour	½ teaspoon vanilla extract
½ pint milk	

Preheat the oven to 400°F. Beat the egg yolks until lemon-coloured. Stir in flour and when well blended add milk, sugar, and vanilla. Fold in stiffly beaten egg whites. Bake 20 minutes in hot oven and sprinkle with caster sugar before serving.

522. Vanilla Cream   *Fromage à la vanille*

½ pint milk	1 quart whipping cream
4 ozs. sugar	2 tablespoons gelatine
½ teaspoon vanilla	4 ozs. caster sugar
5 egg yolks	4 ozs. candied fruit peel

Scald the milk. Add sugar and vanilla and cool to lukewarm.
Add well-beaten egg yolks and cook in the top of a double
boiler, stirring constantly with a wooden spoon until the sauce
is thick but still runny. Pour into a bowl and cool. Dissolve the
gelatine in a little water in the top of a double boiler. When it has
dissolved, let it cool but not thicken before adding it to the
cream, which has been beaten to the thickness of custard. Add
sugar and most of the candied fruit peel. Combine the mixtures
and when thoroughly blended pour into a mould and place in
ice or in the coldest part of the refrigerator for at least 4 hours.
Just before serving, place the mould for a moment in hot water
and then reverse it onto a glass dish. Garnish with candied peel.

523. Sweet Whipped Cream   *Fromage à la Chantilly*

Beat 1 pint of heavy cream until it is thick but not stiff and dry.
Stir in 4 to 6 ozs. of caster sugar and store in refrigerator until
ready for use. It may be flavoured with vanilla, coffee essence,
or the juices of crushed fruits, and served as a sweet, or it may
be used as a garnish for many sweets. If the cream is to be kept
a long time, dissolve 1 tablespoon of gelatine in a little water and
stir in the top of a double boiler until it is completely dissolved.
Cool but do not let it thicken before adding to the cream.

524. Coffee Bavarian Cream   *Bavaroise au café*

1 pint thick cream	4 egg yolks
6 tablespoons caster sugar	4 tablespoons coffee essence or
2 pints milk	½ cup strong boiled coffee
10 ozs. sugar	2 tablespoons gelatine

Prepare the whipped cream as in the preceding recipe. Chill
in refrigerator. Scald the milk. Add sugar and coffee extract.
Cool until lukewarm. Add well-beaten egg yolks and cook in a
double boiler until the sauce thickens. Stir in gelatine, which
has been dissolved in ½ gill water. Pour the sauce into a bowl and
cool. Combine with cream and chill in a buttered mould for at
least 4 hours. Unmould and serve.

525. Charlotte Russe

Sponge Fingers (596)   variations: chopped walnuts, pe-
Sweet Whipped Cream (523)   cans, almonds, candied fruits
                                 or maraschino cherries

Line the sides and bottom of a lightly buttered, smooth mould
with sponge fingers. Cut some in half and make the ends meet
in the centre of the bottom. Line the sides with the whole sponge
fingers pressing close together so that the mould will be completely lined. Trim the ends off the top of the mould. Fill the
centre with the cream, to which any of the suggested variations
may have been added. Chill several hours. Unmould and serve.
If the cream is mixed with chopped almonds and decorated with
cherries and whipped cream, it becomes *Charlotte Malakoff*.

526. Diplomat Rum Pudding   *Diplomate au rhum*

Sponge Fingers (596)   *Rum Syrup;*
Apricot or Peach Jam (624–5)   ½ pint water
6 ozs. seedless raisins   8 ozs. sugar
1 oz. finely cut citron   1 gill rum
1½ ozs. chopped candied orange
   peel

Spread each sponge finger with jam. Place a layer of the sponge
fingers in the bottom of a deep, buttered, oven-proof dish.
Pour a little rum syrup—made by heating sugar, water, and rum
until the sugar is dissolved—over the fingers. Sprinkle raisins,
citron, and orange peel over this. Continue this process until the
dish is three-quarters filled. Finish with a layer of sponge fingers.
Place the dish in a pan of hot water and bake 1½ hours in 350°F.
oven.

527. Diplomat Cream Pudding   *Diplomate à la crème*

Sponge Fingers (596)   *Sauce:*
Apricot or Peach Jam (624–5)   1 pint milk
6 ozs. seedless raisins   ½ teaspoon vanilla extract
1 oz. finely cut citron   6 ozs. sugar
1½ ozs. candied orange peel   4 egg yolks

Follow the preceding recipe for preparing the pudding but,
instead of moistening the sponge fingers with rum syrup, prepare
the following sauce: Scald the milk and add sugar and vanilla.
Cool to lukewarm and add well-beaten egg yolks. Pour half
of the sauce over the pudding. Place the dish in a pan of hot
water and bake 1 hour in 350°F. oven. Thicken the rest of the

sauce by stirring in the top of a double boiler until it thickens a little. Pour into a bowl and chill. Turn the pudding out into a glass bowl. Garnish with candied fruits and pour the sauce around the pudding.

528. Plum Pudding   *Plum-Pudding*

¼ lb. suet
2 ozs. fine bread crumbs
3 ozs. flour
1 gill milk
2 eggs
1 teaspoon salt
¼ teaspoon ginger
¼ teaspoon nutmeg
½ teaspoon cinnamon

4 ozs. combined candied orange and lemon peel, citron, and angelica
¼ lb. seeded raisins, cut in small pieces
¼ lb. seedless raisins
½ gill rum or cognac
juice of ½ lemon
2 ozs. sugar

Finely chop the suet. Add bread crumbs, flour, and milk. Mix well. Beat the eggs until lemon-coloured. Add ginger, nutmeg, cinnamon, and salt and combine the mixtures. Add sugar, lemon juice, and rum to the fruit and mix thoroughly. Add to the pudding, and let it stand overnight. Butter a mould or large basin. Fill the basin with the pudding. Wrap the mould in a large dish cloth or cheesecloth. Bring water to a boil in a large saucepan. Tie the ends of the cloth to the handle of the saucepan so that the mould will be suspended in the water. Boil the pudding 4 hours. Replace the water as it boils away. Before serving, plunge the mould in cold water for a few moments. Turn on to a heated dish. Cover the pudding with hot cognac or rum and ignite just before bringing it to the table.

529. Bread Pudding with Rum Sauce

Pudding au pain, sauce au rhum

8 slices white bread
¼ pint milk
1 teaspoon cinnamon
1 teaspoon salt
1 tablespoon flour
3 eggs
6 ozs. seeded raisins
6 ozs. seedless raisins

2 ozs. butter
Sauce:
  4 ozs. butter
  1 tablespoon flour
  3 tablespoons water
  3 tablespoons rum
  3 ozs. sugar
  ¼ teaspoon salt

Soak the bread in milk for 10 minutes. Add salt, cinnamon, flour, unbeaten eggs, raisins, and butter that has been softened but not melted. Mix all this with your hands or with a heavy spoon until the dough is thick and smooth. Dip a large dish cloth or double thickness of cheesecloth in boiling water. Spread flat on a table and sprinkle with flour. Place the mixture, formed into a large ball, in the middle of the cloth and tie the ends together. Suspend the pudding in boiling water. Tie the ends of the cloth to the handle so that the pudding cannot touch the bottom of the saucepan. Boil 2½ hours, taking care to replace the water as it boils away. Remove from the water and let it stand 20 minutes before taking the pudding out of the cloth.

To make sauce: Melt butter and stir in flour. Add water, rum, sugar, and salt. Simmer 10 minutes, stirring constantly. This sauce can be made ahead of time and kept warm in a covered double boiler over hot—not boiling—water. Pour the sauce over the hot pudding.

Pain dérobé réveille appétit.

530. Russian Mousse   *Mousse à la russe*

5 egg whites   granulated sugar
1 cup French Applesauce (503)   Sweet Whipped Cream (523)

Beat the egg whites very stiff. Fold in cold applesauce. Shape
this in an oven-proof dish into a pyramid. Smooth the sides
with the blade of a knife. Sprinkle with granulated sugar and
bake in 300°F. oven 40 minutes. Serve with a bowl of cream,
whipped thick but not stiff.

531. Chestnut Pudding   *Gâteau de marrons*

1 lb. chestnuts   3 egg whites
1 pint milk   3 tablespoons sugar
8 ozs. sugar   1 tablespoon water
1 teaspoon vanilla extract

With a sharp, pointed knife make an X on the flat side of each
chestnut. Plunge the chestnuts into rapidly boiling water and
boil 10 minutes. Remove from the water and, while they are
still hot, remove the shell. Scald the milk. Add sugar and cook
the chestnuts in the milk 40 minutes. Force through a food
mill or strainer. Add vanilla and cool. Put 3 tablespoons of sugar
in a mould large enough to hold the pudding. Decorative moulds
may be used. Melt the sugar and let it turn brown. Add the
water and move the mould around until the caramel has reached
every part of the interior. Use more sugar for a large mould.
Fold in stiffly beaten egg whites with the chestnuts. Pour into
mould. Place the mould in a pan of hot water and cook 40 minutes
in 325°F. oven. Turn mould upside down on to a dish. Serve
plain or with Sweet Whipped Cream (523).

532. Mont Blanc

Follow the preceding recipe for preparing and cooking the chestnuts. When the chestnuts have been forced through the food mill or strainer, heap them on a dish in the shape of a pyramid. Smooth the sides with the moistened blade of a knife and decorate with sweetened whipped cream forced through a pastry tube. Serve warm or cold.

533. Custard Sauce   *Crème à la vanille*

1 pint milk	3 egg yolks
4 ozs. sugar	1 teaspoon vanilla extract

Scald the milk and cool to lukewarm. Beat the egg yolks and add sugar. Add the milk gradually, stirring constantly. Place in the top of a double boiler and stir over simmering water until the sauce thickens to the consistency of heavy cream. Remove from the fire and add vanilla.

534. Baked Custard   *Pots de crème à la vanille*

2 pints milk	3 egg yolks
4 ozs. sugar	1 egg white
1 teaspoon vanilla extract	

Scald the milk and cool to lukewarm. Beat the yolks and egg white together. Add sugar and vanilla. Stir into the milk gradually. Pour into individual custard cups or in one large mould. Place in a pan of hot water and bake 30 to 40 minutes in 325°F. oven, or until set. This can be tested by inserting a silver knife in the custard. If it comes out clean the custard is set. Serve warm or chilled.

535. Coffee Custard   *Crème au café*

Follow the preceding recipe but add 2 tablespoons of powdered
coffee or 2 tablespoons of coffee essence to the egg mixture.

536. Chocolate Custard   *Crème au chocolat*

Follow recipe 534 but add $\frac{1}{4}$ lb. of cooking chocolate, melted
over hot water, to the egg mixture.

537. Caramel Custard   *Crème au caramel*

Heat 2 oz. sugar and 3 tablespoons water in a heavy pan until
it is dark-brown liquid. Cool this to lukewarm before adding to
the lukewarm milk. Follow recipe 534 for making custard.

538. Caramelized Custard   *Crème renversèe*

1 pint milk	4 eggs
4 ozs. sugar	3 tablespoons sugar
1 teaspoon vanilla extract	1 tablespoon water

Scald the milk with the sugar and cool to lukewarm. Add vanilla.
Beat eggs and gradually add the milk to eggs. Place 3 tablespoons
of sugar in the mould and place over a direct flame. Heat until
it is dark brown. Add water and turn the mould around in your
hands until the liquid caramel has reached every part of the
mould. Pour the custard into the mould and place the mould in
a pan of hot water and bake 40 to 45 minutes or until the custard
is set. Chill before unmoulding it on a dish. It is safer to place
the dish on top of the mould before turning it upside down.

539. Zabaglione   *Crème Sambaglione*

6 eggs	¼ pint Marsala wine or Madeira
3 ozs. sugar	

Separate the yolks from the whites. Beat egg whites almost—
but not quite—stiff. Beat the yolks slightly with the sugar and
wine. Place in a double boiler over simmering water and stir
constantly and smoothly until the yolks thicken. Remove from
the flame. Stir in the egg whites quickly. Serve warm in custard
cups or small goblets. This sweet cannot wait.

540. Blancmange   *Blanc-manger*

½ lb. almonds, blanched and peeled	¼ pint milk
½ pint cold water	1 teaspoon orange water
8 ozs. sugar	1 tablespoon gelatine

Blanch almonds by dropping them into boiling water and then
removing the skins. Force them through the food chopper,
using the finest blade. With a mortar and pestle or a heavy potato
masher, pound the almonds, gradually adding water. Put this
almond milk in a dish towel and squeeze out the excess water.
Dissolve gelatine in the top of a double boiler with ½ gill water.
Add this and the sugar, milk, and orange water to the almond
milk. Mix all the ingredients well until the sugar is dissolved.
Pour into a mould or glass bowl and chill several hours before
serving.

541. Bacchus' Delight   *Crème bachique*

1 pint Sauterne wine	¼ teaspoon cinnamon
4 ozs. sugar	6 egg yolks

Bring wine, sugar, and cinnamon to the boil. Beat egg yolks
well and gradually add the wine. Pour into individual custard

cups and place in a pan of hot water. Bake in 325°F. oven for 30 to 40 minutes or until the custard is firm.

542. Kirsch Jelly   *Gelée au kirsch*

½ pint boiling water
1 tablespoon gelatine, softened in
½ gill water
6 ozs. sugar

1 tablespoon lemon juice
¼ teaspoon salt
¼ pint kirsch
red colouring

Add the softened gelatine to boiling water and stir until the gelatine is dissolved. Add sugar, lemon juice, salt, kirsch and colouring. Stir until the sugar is dissolved and pour into a decorative mould. Chill. Just before serving, place the mould upside down on a dish. Place a hot dish cloth around the mould for a moment to loosen the jelly. Surround the jelly with whipped cream, sweetened and flavoured with kirsch.

543. Rum Jelly   *Gelée au rhum*

Follow preceding recipe substituting rum for kirsch.

544. Lemon Jelly   *Gelée au citron*

1 pint boiling water
1½ tablespoons gelatine soaked in
½ gill cold water

6 ozs. sugar
juice of 3 lemons
¼ teaspoon salt

Put the dissolved gelatine in boiling water. Stir in sugar and salt. When the sugar is dissolved add lemon juice. Pour the jelly into a mould and chill for several hours. Unmould and serve with sweetened whipped cream flavoured with a little curaçao or cointreau.

Q

545. Fruit Jelly   *Gelée aux fruits*

1 pint strawberries, raspberries,
    red currants, or a combination
    of these
1 tablespoon water
6 ozs. sugar
¼ teaspoon salt

1½ tablespoons gelatine soaked in
    ½ gill water
1 tablespoon lemon juice
1 pint boiling water
Sweet Whipped Cream (523)

Crush the fruit in a saucepan and bring to the boil with 1 table-spoon of water. This will extract the juice. Dissolve the gelatine in the boiling water. Add sugar, salt, and lemon juice, and when the sugar has dissolved, combine with the juice, which has been strained. Pour into a decorative large mould or into individual moulds and chill for several hours. Unmould and serve with cream.

546. Vanilla Ice Cream 1   *Glace à la vanille*
    (*to be frozen in ice-cream freezer*)

1 pint milk
4 egg yolks
¼ teaspoon salt

6 ozs. sugar
1 tablespoon vanilla essence
½ pint thick cream

Scald the milk. Add sugar and salt and stir until sugar is dissolved. Cool to lukewarm and add to slightly beaten yolks. Cook in a double boiler, stirring constantly until the mixture thickens. Cool and add to cream. Pour into the freezing container, cover, and place in freezer. Surround with 1 part salt to 4 parts chopped ice. Turn slowly until ice begins to melt and then turn rapidly until the crank is difficult to turn. Remove the cover, scrape off the dasher, plug up the hole, and replace the cover. Let the ice cream stand 4 hours.

547. Vanilla Ice Cream II   *Glace à la vanille*
      (*for mechanical refrigerator*)

2 eggs
2 tablespoons brandy (or 1 table-
    spoon vanilla essence)

4 ozs. sugar
½ pint milk, scalded
½ pint thick cream

Beat the egg yolks until they are thick and lemon-coloured.
Add hot milk and sugar gradually, beating constantly. Add
brandy or vanilla and chill. Fold in stiffly beaten egg whites
and cream whipped until it is thick but not stiff. Freeze until
firm. This may be frozen in a mould. If so, unmould just before
serving and add sweetened fresh or preserved fruits. This makes
a festive sweet.

548. Strawberry Ice Cream I   *Glace à la fraise*
      (*to be frozen in ice-cream freezer*)

1 quart strawberries, hulled and
    crushed

8 ozs. sugar
2 pints thick cream

Combine strawberries and sugar and chill for 30 minutes. Mix
with thick cream and pour into ice-cream container. Place in
the freezer and surround with 1 part salt to 4 parts chopped
ice. Turn the crank until it turns with difficulty. Let it stand at
least 4 hours in the ice before serving.

Plus on a, plus on veut avoir.

549. Strawberry Ice Cream II   *Glace à la fraise*
         (*for mechanical refrigerator*)

1 pint strawberries	2 egg whites, beaten stiff
1 tablespoon water	dash of salt
8 ozs. sugar	1 pint thick cream
2 tablespoons lemon juice	

Wash, hull, and crush the strawberries in the bottom of a saucepan. Add sugar and water and bring to the boil. Set aside to cool. Add salt to the egg whites and beat stiff. Whip cream until very thick but not stiff. Add lemon juice to the strawberries and combine all the mixtures. Place in ice trays and freeze, or freeze in a mould.

350. Kirsch or Rum Sorbet I   *Sorbet au kirsch ou au rhum*
         (*for ice-cream freezer*)

1 pint water	juice of 1 lemon
8 ozs. sugar	¼ pint kirsch or rum

Boil water and sugar for 5 minutes. Add lemon juice. Strain and cool. Pour into container and place in ice-cream freezer. Surround with 1 part salt to 4 parts chopped ice. Turn for 8 minutes. Remove cover and pour in kirsch or rum. Continue turning the crank until the ice is stiff. Keep in freezer until ready to serve.

Contentement passe richesse.

551. Kirsch or Rum Sorbet II   *Sorbet au kirsch ou au rhum*
(*for mechanical refrigerator*)

2 teaspoons gelatine soaked in	juice of 2 lemons
½ gill cold water	2 egg whites
8 ozs. sugar	⅛ teaspoon salt
1 pint water	¼ pint Kirsch

Boil sugar and water 10 minutes. Add softened gelatine and when it has dissolved, remove from the fire. Add lemon juice and kirsch or rum. Freeze 1 hour in an ice tray. Remove to a chilled bowl and beat with a rotary beater until frothy. Add salt to egg whites. Beat stiff and fold into the other mixture. Return to ice tray and freeze until firm.

552. Bombe Glacée   *Bombe glacée*

1 lb. sugar	*various flavours:*
½ pint water	1 tablespoon vanilla essence, or
6 egg yolks	1 tablespoon powdered coffee, or
1 quart thick cream	2 tablespoons cocoa, or
	1½ tablespoons curaçao

Dissolve sugar in water. Beat egg yolks and combine mixtures. Cook in the top of a double boiler until the eggs thicken. Stir constantly. Remove and beat with a rotary beater 15 minutes. Fold in cream, beaten thick but not stiff, and add flavouring. Pour into a chilled mould and place in ice until frozen. It may be served this way or, if preferred, a large scoop may be taken from the centre and refilled with sorbet. The extra cream may be spread on the top of the mould. This must then be refrozen until firm. Unmould on dish just before serving.

It is good for the lady of the household to know how to make good pastry—or, at least, to be able to teach others how to make it. In England, almost every young girl knows how to make cakes, and in France, the privilege of making tarts and cakes is specially reserved for the young ladies of the household. These young ladies are well aware of the good effect it makes when it is announced that the beautiful cake appearing on the table has been prepared by them. It indicates an interest in domestic life.

TANTE MARIE

GOOD PASTRY-MAKING is an art that can be acquired with practice. French pastry, famous for flavour and texture, uses only the best materials. This means good bread flour and sweet butter. But sweet butter is comparatively rare and expensive, so that substitutes are often necessary. Salted butter may be washed and used with good results, or vegetable fats with butter may be used. The necessary utensils are a large smooth rolling pin, a smooth surface—preferably a marble or wooden slab—a pastry wheel, and a variety of tart plates, and flan rings, and a baking sheet. The following 5 recipes are basic in the art of French pastry making.

236

553. Pie Pastry   *Pâte brisée*

1 lb. flour   ½ teaspoon salt
½ lb. butter   7 tablespoons cold water

Place the flour in a bowl or in a heap on a pastry board. Make a depression in the middle of the flour. Wash the butter by holding it under running water or in a large bowl of water and squeezing it between the hands for 3 to 4 minutes. Place the butter, water, and salt in the centre and, without disturbing the flour, blend these ingredients by working them with the finger tips. Gradually work in the flour until it is all one smooth mass of dough. Knead the dough 30 to 60 seconds. Better pastry is achieved if it is not handled too much. Set aside to rest for at least 15 minutes. Roll out to the desired thickness.

554. Sweet Pastry   *Pâte à tarte*

½ lb. flour   3 ozs. sugar
4 ozs. butter   ½ teaspoon baking powder
1 unbeaten egg   1 gill cold milk

Place flour in a mixing bowl. Wash the butter as in the preceding recipe. Place in the centre of the flour and work in with finger tips until the flour and butter are blended. Add egg, sugar, baking power, and milk. Work the dough quickly with your hands. As soon as the dough detaches itself from the sides of the bowl, stop working it and let it stand at least 15 minutes before rolling out.

555. Puff Paste   *Pâte feuilletée*

1 lb. flour   just under ½ pint cold water
1 teaspoon salt   11 ozs. washed butter

Place flour in a bowl or in a heap on a pastry board. Make a depression in the centre. Place the salt and some of the water in the depression and work the dough with the ends of your fingers. Gradually add water, working the dough as quickly as possible. As soon as the dough is a soft ball, place it on a floured board and flatten it slightly with the palm of the hand. Let it stand 10 minutes. Wash the butter so that the excess salt and buttermilk is removed (see recipe 553). The butter should be soft and workable before combining it with the dough. Shape the butter so that it is approximately the same shape but half the circumference of the dough. Place it in the centre of the dough. Flour the rolling pin and roll the dough into a strip three times as long as it is wide. It should be about 8 inches wide and ¼ in. thick in order to handle it easily. Use quick, deft strokes with the rolling pin and never roll over the edge of the pastry. Fold the strip in thirds, starting with the nearer end and folding it toward the centre. Lap the further end over this so that a square is formed. Set the dough aside for 15 minutes. Turn the square around so that the square will be rolled transversally. Repeat the process of making a long strip and folding it in thirds and then letting it rest 15 minutes. This process should be repeated 3 to 5 times, alternating the direction of rolling every time. The more times it is rolled out the flakier the pastry. If possible, the pastry should be used immediately after the last rolling. Otherwise chill in the refrigerator until ready for use.

556. Pastry Custard   *Frangipane*

3 tablespoons flour
3 eggs
1 pint milk
5 ozs. sugar

1 teaspoon vanilla
¼ lb. finely ground almonds (optional)

Add flour to slightly beaten eggs. Stir in milk gradually. Add
sugar and cook over simmering water in a double boiler, stirring
constantly. When the custard thickens, remove from the stove
and add vanilla. If the almonds are added, this becomes Almond
Pastry Custard or *Frangipane aux amandes*.

557. Pies and Flan Cases

Two-crust pies: Cut the pastry dough in two, with one piece
a little larger than the other. Roll out the larger half to ⅛-in.
thickness. Use quick, deft strokes, rolling from the centre out
and taking care not to roll over the edges. Cut a circle 1½ inches
larger than the pie plate. Line the plate with the pastry and trim
even with the edge. Moisten the edge with cold water. Roll out
and cut the top crust 1 inch larger than the circumference of the
pie-plate rim. When the pie has been filled, place the top
crust over the plate. Press the edges together firmly with a fork.
Trim the edges or fold the margin under the bottom crust.

One-crust pie or tart: Roll out the pastry to ⅛-inch thickness
and cut 1½ inches larger than the pie plate. Line the plate with the
pastry. Fold the extra margin under so that the pastry is ½ inch
above the rim. Flute the edges with thumb and forefinger.
Prick the bottom with a fork. If a juicy filling is to be used, paint
the crust with unbeaten egg white. There are various methods of

keeping the crust in shape if it is to be baked before filling. A second pie plate may be placed over the first during the baking, or the crust may be lined with brown paper or heavy stationery paper and then filled with dried peas or beans or with flour. Bake the case 15 to 20 minutes in 450°F. oven or until light brown.

Crust for tarts: French tarts have one crust with narrow, straight sides, measuring ½ to ¾ inch. They are served without benefit of pie plate. They are baked with a pie ring or square, which is placed on a moistened baking tray. Roll the crust out ⅛ inch thick. Cut 1 inch larger than the ring or square. Lay the pastry over the rim. Press the sides to the ring allowing ½-inch margin above the rim. The edges may be fluted or left plain. Prick the pastry with a fork. The tart is then ready to be filled. If it is to be baked before filling, follow directions in the preceding paragraph.

To glaze tarts: French fruit tarts always glisten. This is achieved by painting the fruit, while it is still hot, with a fruit syrup. Heat ¼ lb. apricot jam or red current jelly with 1 tablespoon of water. As soon as the tart is baked, brush the top of the fruit with this hot syrup. These two preserves are best for glazing, because of their texture and because their flavour blends well with other fruits.

Pies and Tarts

558. Apple Tart I *Tarte aux pommes* I

Pie Pastry (553)   French Applesauce (503)

Prepare the pastry and line a pie plate or a ring with the crust
(see recipe 557). Fill the unbaked crust with the sauce and
bake in 375°F. oven 45 minutes. Little strips of pastry may
be placed on the sauce in decorative shapes. These should be
moistened before the tart is baked.

559. Apple Tart II *Tarte aux pommes* II

Pie Pastry (553)   4 to 6 tart apples
French Applesauce (503)   apricot jam

Roll out the pastry ⅛ inch thick. Line a pie ring or square with
the pastry (557). Fill the tart half full with the sauce. Peel and
core the apples and slice very thinly. Arrange the pieces of apple
in a spiral on top of the sauce. Make a little rosette of apple in
the centre. Sprinkle with sugar and bake in 375°F. oven for 45
minutes. When the tart is baked, glaze with apricot jam (557).
Let the tart stand in the ring until it is cool.

560. English Apple Pie   *Pudding aux pommes*

Pie Pastry (553) (for 8-inch pie)   ¼ teaspoon powdered cloves
6 to 8 tart apples   ¼ teaspoon nutmeg
8 ozs. sugar   1 teaspoon grated lemon rind
1 teaspoon cinnamon   2 ozs. butter

Prepare the pastry. Line pie plate with pastry, following directions in recipe 557 for two-crust pies. Peel, core, and slice the
apples very thinly. Place the apples in the pie plate. Sprinkle
with sugar, cinnamon, cloves, nutmeg, and lemon rind and dot
with butter. Roll out the top crust and place over the apples,
making sure that the edges are firmly pressed together. The
pie should be hermetically sealed. Place the pie near the bottom
of a 450°F. oven. Reduce the oven to 350°F. at the end of 10
minutes and move the pie to the middle of the oven and continue
cooking 40 minutes. Serve hot. The left-over pie may be reheated
with a sauce consisting of 3 tablespoons water, 1 tablespoon rum,
and 2 ozs. sugar.

561. Apricot Tart   *Tarte aux abricots*

Line a pie ring or plate with Pie Pastry (553). See recipe 557
for baking unfilled crust. When the case is cool, remove from
the ring or plate and fill with Apricot Compote (610).

562. Peach Tart   *Tarte aux pêches*

Follow the preceding recipe substituting Peach Compote (613)
for the filling.

563. Plum Tart   *Tarte aux prunes*

Prepare Pie Pastry (553) and line a pie ring or circle (557). Fill
the tart with a single closely packed layer of plums. If Victoria
plums are used, stone and halve them and place in tart, cavity
side down. If greengages are used, stone them but do not halve
them. Sprinkle with 6 to 8 ozs. sugar. Bake 45 minutes in 375°F.
oven. Immediately on taking the tart from the oven, glaze the
plums with red currant jelly (557).

564. Cherry Tart I   *Tarte aux cerises* I

Prepare Pie Pastry (553). Line a pie ring or plate with the pastry
(557). Prick the crust with a fork. Fill the crust with a Cherry
Compote (612) or with tinned cherries. Before the cherry syrup
is poured over the cherries it should be reduced to a thick syrup
by boiling. Bake the tart 45 minutes in 375°F. oven.

565. Cherry Tart II   *Tarte aux cerises* II

Prepare Pie Pastry (553). Line pie square or ring or pie plate
with the pastry (557). Prick the bottom with a fork. Stone 1 lb.
of cherries. Line the cherries in rows, one tightly pressed against
the other, in the pastry case. The cut side of the cherry should
be hidden. Sprinkle with 6 ozs. sugar and bake 45 minutes in
375°F. oven. As soon as the tart is baked, glaze with red currant
jelly (557).

566. Pear Tart   *Tarte aux poires*

Prepare Pie Pastry (553). Line pie ring or plate. Prepare a Pear
Compote (608) or use tinned pears. Place the pears, cavity side
down, in the case. Reduce the pear syrup until it is quite thick.
Spread over the pears and bake the tart 45 minutes in 375°F.
oven. As soon as the tart is taken from the oven, glaze with apricot
jam (557).

567. Strawberry Tart   *Tarte aux fraises*

Prepare Pie Pastry (553). Line a pie ring or square or a pie
plate to make a case. Follow directions in recipe 557 for baking
the case. When the case is baked and cooled, fill with a closely
packed layer of strawberries. Glaze with red currant jelly (557).
Serve cold.

568. Alsatian Tart   *Tarte alsacienne*

Sweet Pastry (554)
fruit (sliced apples, strawberries,
    peaches, or apricots)

1 teaspoon cinnamon
4 ozs. sugar
1 gill thick cream
1 egg

Prepare the pastry and line a pie circle or pie plate (557). Fill
with a layer of fruit not too closely packed. Sprinkle with sugar
and cinnamon. Bake 30 minutes in 375°F. oven. Beat the egg
slightly and add cream. Pour over the fruit. Bake 10 minutes
longer.

A merle soûl cerises sont amères.

569. Custard Tart   *Tarte à la frangipane*

Line a pie circle or pie plate with Pie Pastry (553) or Sweet
Pastry (554). Prick with a fork and fill with cooled Pastry Custard
(556). Bake 20 to 25 minutes in 375°F. oven.

570. Rhubarb Tart   *Tarte à la rhubarbe*

Pie Pastry (553)   10 ozs. sugar
1½ pints unpeeled rhubarb cut in   1 teaspoon grated lemon rind
    2-inch pieces

Line a pie ring or square or pie plate with pastry (557). Prick
the bottom and cover with a layer of closely packed pieces of
rhubarb. Sprinkle with sugar and grated lemon rind. Bake 45
minutes in 375°F. oven.

571. Apple Tarts   *Dartois aux pommes*

Puff Paste (555)   red currant jelly or apricot jam
French Applesauce (503)   caster sugar
egg yolk mixed with 1 tablespoon
    water

Prepare the flaky pastry. Roll the pastry as thinly as possible.
Cut the pastry into rectangles 3 by 4 inches. Divide the number
of rectangles and on half of them spread a layer of applesauce,
leaving a margin on all sides. Cover with 1 teaspoonful of red
currant jelly or apricot jam. Moisten the margins with water
and place the remaining rectangles on the filled ones. Press the
edges together firmly. Paint each tart with the egg yolk. Make
several small slashes in the top layer, sprinkle with caster sugar,
and bake in 400°F. oven 30 minutes. The tarts may be eaten
hot or cold. They are particularly delicious hot.

572. Cheese Tart   *Tarte au fromage*

Puff Paste (555)
1 tablespoon flour
4 tablespoons grated Gruyère cheese
½ pint thick cream

½ teaspoon salt
½ teaspoon sugar
4 ozs. butter
¼ teaspoon nutmeg
4 egg whites

Prepare the pastry and roll out to ⅛ inch thickness. Line a buttered pie plate with pastry and follow recipe 557 for baking an unfilled crust. Remove from the oven and cool before filling. Mix flour, cheese, and cream. Add salt, sugar, butter, and nutmeg and stir over a low flame until the butter is melted. Cool and fold in stiffly beaten egg whites. Fill pastry shell and bake 15 minutes in 400°F. oven. Serve immediately.

573. Cinnamon Tart   *Tarte à la cannelle*

1 egg
8 ozs. sugar
¼ teaspoon salt
12 ozs. flour

2 teaspoons cinnamon
6 ozs. butter
1½ cups French Applesauce (503)

Heap flour on a pastry board. Make a depression in the centre and place in it the egg, sugar, salt, cinnamon, and butter that has been softened but not melted. Work the flour in gradually with your fingers and knead until the dough is smooth. Chill 1 hour. Roll out ⅛ inch thick and line a buttered pie plate. Trim the edge with a sharp knife. There should be an ⅛-inch margin. Fill with the applesauce. Cut the remaining dough into long strips and cross them over the sauce to form a crust. The ends should be pressed to the lower crust. Bake 30 minutes in 400°F. oven.

574. Four-Part Cake   *Quartre-quarts*

This cake is so named because the traditional method of making it is to weigh the eggs and use equal weights of flour, butter, and sugar.

4 large eggs
12 ozs. sugar
12 ozs. softened butter
1 tablespoon lemon juice

12 ozs. flour
2 ozs. finely chopped almonds (optional)

Separate the yolks from the whites. Beat the yolks slightly and add sugar and butter, beating constantly until the mixture is smooth. Add lemon juice and flour and continue stirring until well blended. Fold in stiffly beaten egg whites. Pour into large round, buttered cake tin, filling it only half full because the cake will rise very high. Bake 1 hour in 350°F. oven.

If desired, blanch 2 ozs. of almonds by dropping them into boiling water and then removing the skins, chop finely, and sprinkle over the cake before baking.

575. Cream-Puff Pastry   *Pâte aux choux*

½ pint water
3 ozs. butter
5 ozs. flour

1 teaspoon sugar
¼ teaspoon salt
4 eggs

Bring water and butter to the boil. Add flour, mixed with sugar and salt. Stir vigorously until the mixture is quite dry—approximately 3 minutes. Remove from the flame and add unbeaten eggs, one by one, beating hard after each addition. The resulting paste should be smooth.

576. Tea Puffs   *Choux sans crème*

Follow the preceding recipe for making Cream-Puff Pastry. Drop small balls of the mixture from the end of a teaspoon or from a pastry tube on a buttered and lightly floured baking tray, leaving ½ inch between each ball. Brush with egg yolk mixed with a little water. Let them stand 20 minutes. Bake 30 minutes in 375°F. oven or until they are a delicate brown. Sprinkle with caster sugar and finely chopped almonds and put back in the oven until the sugar has melted.

577. Cream Puffs   *Choux à la crème*

Drop small or large balls of Cream-Puff Pastry (575) on a buttered and lightly floured baking tray. Bake 30 to 45 minutes in 375°F. oven until a delicate brown and until there is no moisture on the outside of the puffs. Remove from the oven and cool. Make a small hole in the bottom of each puff and force Sweet Whipped Cream (523) through a pastry tube into the puff. This leaves the top unblemished. The small puffs make an attractive tea cake. The larger ones are used for a sweet.

578. Profiteroles with Chocolate Sauce

Profiteroles au chocolat

Prepare small cream puffs according to directions in the preceding recipe. The little cream puffs may be filled with Sweet Whipped Cream (523) or with Pastry Custard (556). Pile the cream puffs in a pyramid on a dish and cover with the following Chocolate Sauce:

10 ozs. sugar
2 ozs. butter
4 1-oz. squares of cooking chocolate

½ pint thick cream
1 teaspoon vanilla (or 2 teaspoons cognac)

Combine sugar, butter, and chocolate in the top of a double boiler. When the chocolate is melted, add cream and flavouring. Serve hot.

Qui veut bien se porter demeure sur son appétit.

579 Saint-Honoré Birthday Cake   *Gâteau Saint-Honoré*

double recipe Cream-Puff Pastry   1 gill water
   (575)   Sweet Whipped Cream (523)
12 ozs. sugar   candied fruits

Butter and lightly flour 2 large baking trays. Fill a large pastry
tube, fitted with a wide-mouthed dispenser, with the pastry.
Describe a large circle—the size of a large saucepan cover— on
one baking tray by forcing the pastry through the tube. The
circle should be approximately 1 inch thick. Using the same
pastry tube, drop about 20 small balls on the other baking tray.
Place both trays in 375°F. oven and bake until both the circle
and small puffs are a delicate brown and free of any moisture
on the outside. The circle should take 5 to 10 minutes longer than
the small puffs. Meanwhile, boil the sugar and water until the
syrup reaches a temperature of 238°F. or until it will form a soft
ball when put in cold water. When the puffs are baked, dip each
one in the syrup and place on a lightly oiled surface to cool.
When the puffs and ring are cool, attach the puffs to the ring
using a little hot syrup to make them stick. Fill the centre of the
ring with the cream and decorate with candied fruits. Place a
birthday candle in each small puff.

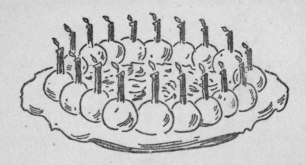

580. Brioche   *Brioche*

The famous French brioche requires time and patience. It should be started the day before it is to be used. It cannot be hurried.

4 ozs. flour	3 large eggs
1 oz. yeast dissolved in	½ lb. softened butter
½ gill water	1 teapoon salt
12 ozs. flour	1 tablespoon sugar

Dissolve the yeast in warm water and mix with 4 ozs. flour. Make a gash in the top of the mass and place in a bowl of warm water to make a sponge. This will double in size. Meanwhile work the unbeaten eggs into the rest of the flour. Add a little warm water if it is too dry to beat. It should be beaten 10 minutes. Hands are the best tool for this operation. Add butter, salt, and sugar and beat 5 minutes longer. Remove the yeast from the water and combine the mixtures, but do not mix it any longer than necessary. Cover and let it rise 3 to 4 hours or until doubled. Knead it down and place in a cool place overnight. It is ready for baking the next morning. The brioche dough should then be broken down gently so that it will remain light. It may be baked in a loaf, on a buttered baking tray, or in a buttered ring mould. Let the brioche rest in the tin 30 minutes before baking. Bake 30 to 35 minutes in 450°F. oven. Cover with buttered unglazed paper if the brioche browns too much. Test by inserting a needle in the cake. If it comes out dry, the cake is baked.

On ne peut manier le beurre qu'on ne se graisse les doigts.

581. Large Brioche   *Brioche à tête*

Follow the preceding recipe for making Brioche. Butter a fluted
mould carefully. Take ¾ of the dough and form into a large ball
which is placed in the mould. Make a smaller ball of the remaining dough and place on the larger one. Let it rest 30 minutes.
Brush with egg yolk mixed with a little water. Bake 30 minutes
in 450°F. oven.

582. Small Brioches   *Les petites brioches*

Place small pats of brioche dough in well-buttered, fluted or
plain muffin tins. Place a tiny ball of the dough on each pat. Let
it rest 30 minutes. Brush with egg yolk mixed with a little water.
Bake 10 to 15 minutes in 450°F. oven.

583. Brioche Tarts in Madeira   *Croûtes au Madère*

Brioche (580)   1 jar Apricot Marmalade (627)

This is a good recipe for left-over brioche dough and it is really
worthwhile saving a little of the dough expressly for this sweet.

Roll out the brioche dough to ⅛-inch thickness. Cut into small
diamond-shaped tarts. Melt 4 ozs. good butter and, when it is
sizzling hot, fry the tarts until golden brown. Cover each tart
with a thin layer of Apricot Marmalade (627). Place these tarts
in a ring around the edge of an oven-proof dish. Make a sauce
by adding ½ gill of water and ½ gill Madeira wine to the rest of
the jar of marmalade and heating. Stir until the sauce is smooth.
Pour in the centre and place the dish in the oven for a few
moments before serving.

584. Croissants   *Croissants*

This recipe does not appear in the original TANTE MARIE since croissants are almost never baked at home in France. It is quite possible to make these rolls at home, however.

½ pint scalded skimmed milk	½ gill warm water
1 oz. butter	1 lb. flour
1 teaspoon salt	½ lb. butter
1½ tablespoons sugar	1 egg yolk, mixed with
1 oz. yeast dissolved in	2 tablespoons milk

Place butter, salt, and sugar in a bowl. Pour the scalded milk over it and cool to lukewarm. Add the dissolved yeast cake and stir a moment. Care must be taken that the milk is comfortable to touch but not cool. Add the flour and knead thoroughly. The dough should be smooth and elastic. Cover the bowl and let the dough rise in a warm place until doubled in size. Knead it a moment and chill several hours in the refrigerator. Wash the butter (553). Roll out the chilled dough into a strip 3 times as long as its width. Spread the butter over the dough and fold the ends of the strip in toward the centre to form a three-tiered quare. Turn the square side for end and roll it out transversally. Fold in the ends to form a three-tiered square and place in the refrigerator for 30 minutes. Repeat this process at intervals of 30 minutes twice more, and the final time, keep the dough in the refrigerator 1 hour. It is then ready for shaping.

Roll the dough out to ¼-inch thickness. Cut into 4-inch squares. Divide each square into 2 triangles. Beginning with the wide base, roll each triangle toward the point so that the pointed end will be in the centre. Shape into crescents and place on unbuttered baking tray. Brush with egg yolk and bake 15 minutes in 375°F. oven. If the croissants are not to be baked immediately, return to the refrigerator.

585. Rum Baba   *Baba au rhum*

6 ozs. flour	2 ozs. raisins
½ oz. yeast	2 ozs. chopped lemon peel
6 tablespoons warm milk	2 ozs. currants
2 eggs	small pinch of saffron
1 teaspoon sugar	*syrup:*
¼ teaspoon salt	4 ozs. sugar
2 ozs. butter	4 tablespoons water
3 ozs. sugar	2 tablespoons rum

Dissolve ½ oz. yeast in milk and add to the flour. Add unbeaten
eggs and beat the dough 3 minutes. Hands are the best tools
for this operation. Cover and let the dough rise until doubled.
Add sugar, salt, and butter which has been softened but not
melted. Beat vigorously for 5 minutes. Mix in the remaining
ingredients, place the dough in a buttered cake tin, and cover
with a cloth. Let the dough rise until doubled. Bake 1 hour in
375°F. oven.

If the baba does not come out of the pan easily, wrap the pan
completely in kitchen towels so that no steam may escape. At
the end of 6 to 8 minutes the cake will slip out easily. Meanwhile
prepare the syrup by boiling the sugar and water gently for 10
minutes and then adding the rum. Cool a little before pouring
carefully over the baba and letting it permeate the cake. Serve
hot or cold.

586. Small Rum Babas   *Les petits babas au rhum*

Follow the preceding recipe for making the baba dough. Fill
small buttered muffin or brioche tins half full with the dough.
Let them rise until doubled and bake 10 to 12 minutes in 400°F.
oven. Dip in rum syrup. Serve hot or cold. These may be

garnished with Sweet Whipped Cream (523) flavoured with a little rum.

587. Savarin Cake   *Savarin*

6 ozs. flour	2 ozs. finely chopped almonds
½ oz. yeast dissolved in	2 ozs. sugar
6 tablespoons warm milk	2 tablespoons water
2 eggs	1 tablespoon rum
1 teaspoon sugar	whole almonds and glazed cherries
½ teaspoon salt	
2 ozs. butter	

Warm the mixing bowl for a moment in the oven before using. Sift the flour into the bowl and make a well in the centre of it. Add ½ oz. yeast dissolved in warm milk and the unbeaten eggs and beat with your hands for 3 minutes. Cover the bowl and let the dough rise ¾ hour or until doubled in size. Knead down and add the sugar, salt, and butter that has been softened but not melted. Beat this mixture for 4 to 5 minutes. Butter a cake tin or a ring mould, dust with the finely chopped almonds, which have been blanched (514), and fill a little less than half full with the dough. Cover and let it rise until it reaches the top of the pan. Bake 20 minutes in 450°F. oven. Cover with a piece of buttered paper if it gets too brown. Meanwhile boil sugar and water for 10 minutes. Add rum and cool to lukewarm. As soon as the cake is baked, run a sharp knife around the sides and unmould. Spoon the syrup over the cake and decorate with almonds and candied cherries.

Il faut casser le noyau pour avoir l'amande.

588. Galette (Household Pastry Cake)   *Galette de ménage*

12 ozs. flour   ½ teaspoon salt
6 ozs. butter   1 egg yolk mixed with
1 gill warm milk   1 tablespoon water
1 tablespoon sugar

Heap the flour on a pastry board. Make a well in the centre
and place in it the sugar, salt, milk, and butter that has been
softened but not melted. Work the flour into the liquid with
the finger tips until a smooth ball has been formed. Let it rest
45 minutes before rolling it out to ½-inch thickness. With a sharp,
pointed knife, trace vertical and horizontal lines over the cake
so that it is covered with a pattern of squares or rectangles.
Do not cut through the pastry. Place on a buttered and floured
baking tray and brush with egg yolk. Bake 30 minutes in 450°F.
oven.

589. Tea Tarts   *Petites galettes pour le thé*

Follow the preceding recipe. When the pastry has been rolled,
cut out little tarts with a round biscuit cutter. Brush each tart
with the egg yolk mixture and place on greased and floured
baking tray. Bake 20 minutes in 450°F. oven.

590. Cheese Sticks   *Allumettes au fromage*

12 ozs. flour   1 teaspoon salt
½ lb. grated gruyère cheese   1 oz. grated gruyère
6 ozs. butter   1 egg yolk mixed with
1 gill cold water   1 tablespoon water

Combine flour, cheese, butter, water, and salt to make a smooth
mass. The butter should be soft and workable before adding to
the flour. Roll into a strip 3 times as long as its width. Lap the

ends over each other toward the centre to form a three-tiered
square. Turn the square side for end and roll out transversally.
Sprinkle with cheese, fold into a square, and let it rest 15 minutes.
Repeat this process twice at 15-minute intervals. After a final
15-minute rest, roll out the pastry ⅛ inch thick. Cut into strips
3 inches long and ¾ inch wide. Brush with egg yolk and sprinkle
with grated cheese. Bake 6 to 8 minutes in 450°F. oven.

591. Plain Tea Cakes   *Gâteaux secs*

12 ozs. flour	4 ozs. butter, cut in little pieces
6 ozs. sugar	1 gill milk

Combine the ingredients and knead until a smooth ball of
dough has been formed. Roll out very thin on a floured board.
Cut out little circles with a biscuit cutter or small glass. Place
on buttered baking tray and bake 15 minutes in 350°F. oven.

592. Madeleines   *Gâteaux de madeleine*

These traditional tea cakes are cooked in special tins shaped like
small scallop shells.

Follow recipe 574 for Four-Part Cake, only add the egg whites
without beating them. (One half of the recipe will make 24
cakes.) Fill well-buttered madeleine tins with the batter and
cook in 325°F. oven 25 minutes.

Chacun le sien n'est pas trop.

593. Strasbourg Galette   *Galette strasbourgeoise*

12 ozs. flour   2 ozs. seeded raisins
½ pint milk   ½ oz. yeast dissolved in
2 ozs. butter   ½ gill warm milk
2 ozs. sugar

Heat the milk and butter until the butter is melted. Combine
with flour and, when it is well mixed, add sugar, raisins, and
dissolved yeast. Beat the mixture with your hands for several
minutes. The dough should be quite liquid. Place in a deep,
buttered cake tin and let it rise 2 hours. Cook ½ hour in 450°F.
oven.

594. Almond Tea Cakes   *Gâteaux nantais*

1½ lbs. flour   grated rind of ½ lemon
10 ozs. castor sugar   4 eggs, unbeaten
4 ozs. butter   2 ozs. almonds
6 ozs. almonds

Blanch 6 ozs. almonds by dropping them into boiling water and
then removing the skins. Force them through a food chopper,
using the finest blade. Combine with flour, sugar, butter which
has been softened but not melted, lemon rind, and eggs. Mix
well until a stiff dough has been formed. Roll out to ⅛-inch
thickness and cut into rounds with a small biscuit cutter. Sprinkle
with granulated sugar and chopped or shredded almonds. Bake
in 350°F. oven until pale brown—approximately 10 minutes.

595. Sponge Cake   *Biscuit de Savoie*

4 eggs   grated rind of ½ lemon
8 ozs. sugar   9 ozs. flour

Separate the yolks from the whites. Beat the yolks until lemon-coloured and gradually add sugar. Add lemon rind and continue beating until the mixture is foamy and very pale. Stir in flour and, when thoroughly blended, fold in stiffly beaten egg whites. Butter a plain or tubular cake tin and sprinkle with sugar. Place in the oven a moment before filling half full with the mixture. Bake 1 hour in 325°F. oven. The cake will double in size. When the cake is golden brown and firm to the touch, it is baked. Remove and let it cool before removing from the pan.

596. Sponge Fingers   *Biscuits à la cuiller*

Follow the preceding recipe. Put the mixture in a large pastry bag fitted with a large, plain pastry tube. Force the mixture through the tube onto a buttered and floured baking tray or one lined with buttered, unglazed paper, forming strips 3 inches long and $\frac{1}{4}$ inch wide. Sprinkle evenly with caster sugar and bake 15 minutes in 325°F. oven.

597. Rum Cake   *Gâteau au rhum*

Sponge Cake (595)
Apricot Marmalade (627)
$\frac{1}{2}$ pint water
12 ozs. sugar

$\frac{1}{2}$ gill rum
2 teaspoons cornflour dissolved in a little cold water
candied fruits

Cut the cake horizontally to make 3 layers. Spread the 2 bottom layers with marmalade. Boil water and sugar together for 10 minutes and add rum. Cool to lukewarm. Spoon the syrup over the 3 layers so that the cake is well permeated. Place one layer on top of the other. Add cornflour to the remaining syrup and spread over the cake. When this has cooled, decorate with candied fruits.

260 TANTE MARIE'S FRENCH KITCHEN

598. Pithiviers Cake   *Gâteau de Pithiviers*

Puff Pastry (555)
Pastry Custard (556)

1 egg yolk mixed with
1 tablespoon water

Prepare the pastry and divide in 2 parts. Roll out each part to ¼-inch thickness. Using a saucepan cover as a form, cut out 2 equal circles and moisten them both with water. Spread one circle with the custard, which has been prepared in advance. Leave a small margin. Place the other circle, moistened side down, on the first circle, and press the edges together firmly. Make several decorative incisions in the top circle and place on a moistened baking tray. Bake 45 minutes in 350°F. oven.

599. Marzipan Cakes   *Massepains*

½ lb. almonds
2 egg whites

grated rind of ½ lemon
18 ozs. caster sugar

Soak almonds in hot water for 15 minutes. After removing the skins, chop finely or force through a meat chopper, using the finest blade. Place the almonds in a mortar or, lacking that, in a wooden bowl. With a pestle or potato masher grind the almonds, adding the unbeaten egg whites very gradually. When the egg whites have been absorbed, mix in the lemon rind and sugar. Roll tiny balls of this dough between your hands and place on oiled, unglazed paper. Flatten each ball with a moistened finger. Let them stand 5 hours before baking. Place the paper on a baking tray and bake 15 minutes in 250°F. oven.

600. Tea Kisses   *Petits fours au blanc d'œuf*

2 egg whites
4 ozs. sugar

grated rind of ½ lemon

Beat egg whites very stiff. Add sugar and lemon rind gradually and continue beating until the mixture is quite stiff. Drop the mixture from the end of a teaspoon on a baking tray lined with oiled, unglazed paper. Bake 50 minutes in 250°F. oven. The mixture may be forced through a pastry bag fitted with a decorative tube. This makes a more attractive *petit four* and can be kept well in a tightly covered container.

601. Nougat Tart   *Nougat*

½ lb. almonds   Sweet Whipped Cream (523)
8 ozs. sugar

Blanch (594), peel, and chop the almonds. Place in a moderate oven so they will be hot before adding to the sugar. Melt sugar in a heavy frying pan. When the sugar has melted, add nuts and remove from the stove. Have a well-oiled cake tin ready. Place some of the mixture in the tin. Press it out with a lemon. The mixture is so sticky that a knife or spatula is not satisfactory. It is necessary to work quickly because the nougat becomes brittle. If it becomes too brittle it may be reheated. Line the sides of the cake tin with a thin layer. When it is cold, remove from the mould and fill with cream.

602. Meringues   *Meringues*

4 egg whites   Sweet Whipped Cream (523)
8 ozs. caster sugar

Beat the egg whites until very stiff. Sift the sugar and add gradually, beating continually. Drop from the end of a teaspoon onto a baking tray, lined with unglazed paper. Sprinkle with sugar and bake 50 minutes in 250°F. oven. When they are cool, stick the bottoms of 2 meringues together with the cream.

603. Russian Rhubarb Cake   *Crakinoskis à la rhubarbe*

4 large eggs
12 ozs. softened butter
12 ozs. sugar
12 ozs. cake flour
1 tablespoon lemon juice

½ teaspoon cinnamon
dash of nutmeg
1 pint diced rhubarb
sugar

Mix all the ingredients except the rhubarb and beat vigorously until smooth. Roll out the dough on a floured board to ⅛-inch thickness. Cut with a large, round biscuit cutter. Line individual moulds or large muffin tins with the dough. Fill with diced rhubarb and sprinkle generously with sugar. Bake 45 minutes in 400°F. oven.

604. Plum Cake   *Plum-cake*

6 ozs. caster sugar
6 ozs. softened butter
6 ozs. seeded raisins, chopped
2 ozs. currants
2 ozs. mixed candied peel, chopped

4 eggs
12 ozs. flour
2 teaspoons baking powder
2 tablespoons rum

Cream sugar and butter and beat with a wooden spoon until the mixture is very smooth. Add the fruit and add the eggs one by one, beating vigorously after each addition. Combine flour and baking powder and fold into the batter. Add rum. Beat the dough 20 minutes. Line a cake or bread tin with wax paper. Fill ¾ full with the mixture and bake 45 to 50 minutes in 375°F. oven.

Dans les petits sacs sont les fines épices.

605. Steam Cake   *Dampfnoudel*

4 ozs. butter
1½ gills milk
1 oz. yeast dissolved in
½ gill warm milk
3 tablespoons sugar
1 teaspoon salt

4 egg yolks
1 lb. flou.
¾ pint milk
2 ozs. sugar
cinnamon and sugar

Melt butter in warm milk and, when it is cooled to lukewarm, add 1 oz. yeast dissolved in milk. Add sugar, salt, and egg yolks. Stir until the sugar is dissolved. Add flour and stir until the dough is smooth. Shape into a long roll. Cut in ¾-inch slices and place in a large buttered baking tin. Cover and let them rise until doubled. Bake 20 minutes in 350°F. oven. Meanwhile scald milk and dissolve sugar in the milk. As soon as the cake is light brown, pour the hot milk over it. The milk will be quickly absorbed and the cake will rise very high. Sprinkle with sugar and cinnamon and serve.

606. Sand Tarts   *Pâte sablée*

½ lb. flour
1 egg
4 ozs. sugar
¼ teaspoon salt

½ teaspoon cinnamon
4 ozs. butter

Heap the flour on a pastry board and make a depression in the centre. Place the egg, sugar, salt, cinnamon, and softened butter in the centre and work in the flour. Knead the dough until it is very smooth. Chill the dough 1 hour. Roll out very thinly and cut into various shapes with biscuit cutters. Place the tarts on a buttered baking tray and bake 10 to 12 minutes in 350°F. oven.

s

607. Apple Compote   *Compote de pommes*

8 or 10 cooking apples   ½ teaspoon grated lemon rind
5 ozs. sugar   red currant jelly (optional)
½ pint water

Peel, core, and quarter the apples. Heat sugar and water until
the sugar is dissolved and place the apples and lemon rind in
the syrup. Simmer until the fruit is soft. It is important not to
overcook the fruit, which should keep its form. Place the apples
in a bowl. Increase the heat and reduce the syrup until it has a
thick consistency. Pour the syrup over the fruit and cool. Little
dots of red currant jelly may be used as a garnish.

608. Pear Compote   *Compote de poires*

7 or 8 medium-sized pears   ½ pint water
5 ozs. sugar   juice of ½ lemon

Peel the pears but leave the stems on. As soon as the pears are
peeled, place them in cold water so that they will not turn
brown. Heat sugar and water until the sugar is dissolved. Add
lemon juice. Allow the fruit to simmer until it is tender. Do
not let it get too soft. Stand the pears upright in a dessert bowl;
if necessary, slice a little off the bottom so that they will stand
erect. Boil the syrup down until it is thick, and pour it over the
pears.

609. Pears in Red Wine   *Compote de poires au vin rouge*

Follow recipe 608. Just before removing the pears from the
syrup, add 1 gill red wine. Substitute ½ teaspoon of cinnamon
for the lemon juice.

610. Apricot Compote   *Compote d'abricots*

12 apricots   ½ pint water
5 ozs. sugar

Wash and stone the apricots. The apricots may be left whole
or split in two. Heat the sugar and water until the sugar has
dissolved, then simmer the apricots in the syrup 15 minutes.
Remove the apricots and place in a bowl. Boil the syrup down
until quite thick. Pour over the apricots and cool.

611. Plum Compote   *Compote de prunes*

1 lb. Victoria plums or greengages   ½ pint water
5 ozs. sugar

Boil sugar and water for 30 seconds. Simmer the plums, which
have been carefully washed, 8 to 10 minutes. Remove the plums
and reduce the syrup until thick. Pour over the plums and
cool.

612. Cherry Compote   *Compote de cerises*

Follow the preceding recipe, but allow the cherries to simmer 5 minutes only.

613. Peach Compote   *Compote de pêches*

Follow directions in recipe 610.

614. Red Currant Jelly   *Gelée de groseilles*

4 lbs. red currants   1 gill water
sugar

Wash and drain the currants. It is best to have at least $\frac{1}{3}$ of the currants white. Mash a few in the bottom of a heavy saucepan. Add the water and place over a moderate flame. Continue to add the currants, mashing them as they are added. When the currants have all turned white, drain them through a strainer and then allow the juice to drip through a jelly bag or double thickness of cheesecloth. To ensure clear jelly, do not squeeze the bag. Measure the juice and bring it to the boil. Add 1 lb. sugar to each pint of juice. Stir over low heat until the sugar is completely dissolved and boil 30 minutes. Pour into clean, hot jelly jars and cool. Cover with paraffin wax and store in a cool, dry place.

615. Apple Jelly   *Gelée de pommes*

Crabapples or any tart apples make excellent jelly. Wash the apples thoroughly. Remove the stems and blossom ends. Cut in quarters and remove the core. Place in a large saucepan and add enough water so that the apples are just floating. Boil until the apples are soft. Place a coarse sieve over an earthenware bowl and mash the apples through it. Do not press the apples too hard, because that will make the jelly cloudy. Place the sieved apples in a jelly bag or in a double thickness of cheesecloth. Let the juice drip into a bowl. Do not try to hurry it by squeezing the bag. Measure the juice and allow $\frac{3}{4}$ lb. sugar for every pint of juice. Boil the sugar and juice until it forms a coating on a spoon. Stir every few minutes. Place a sliver of lemon rind in the bottom of clean, hot jelly jars. Pour the jelly into the jars and let it stand 2 days before covering with paraffin wax. Store in a cool, dry place.

616. Quince Jelly   *Gelée de coings*

Follow the preceding recipe, substituting quinces for the apples. Instead of putting lemon peel in the glasses, add a little vanilla along with the sugar.

617. Currant and Raspberry Jelly

Gelée de framboises et de groseilles

Follow recipe 614, using half currants and half raspberries.

618. Household Jam   *Confiture de ménage*

plums   apricots
peaches   sugar

Wash the fruit and remove the stones. Weigh the fruit and add half its weight in sugar. Bring slowly to the boil. Stir frequently. Continue boiling gently until the fruit falls in a lump from the spoon and is brilliant in colour. This will take approximately 45 minutes. Pour into hot, clean jars and let it stand 2 days before covering with paraffin wax. Store in a cool dry place.

619. Barberry Jelly   *Gelée d'épine-vinette*

Pick the berries over very carefully so that no leaves or thorns
are mixed in. Place in a saucepan and add enough water so
that the berries are floating. Boil slowly 30 minutes. Remove
from the fire. Crush the berries with a wooden spoon and drain
through a strainer. Measure the juice and add 1 lb. of sugar to
each pint of juice. Boil gently until it becomes frothy. Skim
and pour into hot clean jars and let it stand 2 days before covering with paraffin wax. Store in a cool, dry place.

620. Cherry Jam   *Confitures de cerises*

2 lbs. red currants	sugar
4 lbs. cherries	

Extract the juice from the currants (614). Remove the stems
and stones from the cherries. Measure the juice and cherries
together. For every pint of combined juice and cherries add
1 lb. sugar. Boil the sugar and fruit 30 minutes. Skim and pour
into clean, hot jars. Let it stand 2 days before covering with
paraffin wax. Store in cool, dry place.

621. Four-Fruit Jelly   *Gelée de quatre-fruits*

1 lb. raspberries	1 lb. strawberries
1 lb. cherries	sugar
1 lb. red currants	

Wash the fruit. Remove the stones from the cherries. Pick over
the currants and raspberries and hull the strawberries. Crush
the fruit in the bottom of a heavy saucepan. Heat over a low
flame until the juice is extracted. Be careful not to let the fruit
stick to the pan. Place the fruit in a jelly bag or in a double

thickness of cheesecloth and allow the juice to drip into an earthenware bowl. For every pint of juice measure 1 lb. of sugar. Boil sugar and juice 30 minutes. Pour into clean, hot glasses and let it stand 2 days before covering with paraffin wax.

622. Strawberry Jam   *Confitures de fraises*

strawberries   water
sugar

Wash and hull the strawberries. Weigh the berries. Weigh an equal amount of sugar. For every pound of sugar allow ½ pint of water. Bring water and sugar to a full boil. Add the strawberries and boil 2 minutes. Remove the strawberries with a skimmer and place in clean, hot jars. Each jar should be half filled. Boil down the syrup until quite thick and pour over the fruit, filling the jar almost to the top. Let it stand 2 days before covering with paraffin wax.

623. Grape Jam   *Confitures de raisins*

grapes   water
sugar

Remove the stems and seeds from very ripe grapes. Tante Marie suggests a goose feather to remove the seeds; a toothpick will do. Weigh the grapes. Measure half the weight in sugar. Add ½ pint water for every pound of sugar. Boil the sugar and water. Add the grapes and boil 2 minutes. Remove the grapes with a skimmer and place in hot, clean jars, filling them half full. Boil down the syrup until thick and pour over the fruit. Fill the jars almost to the top. Let the jars stand uncovered for 2 days before covering them with paraffin wax.

624. Apricot Jam   *Confitures d'abricots*

apricots   water
sugar

Wash the apricots and cut in two. Remove the stones but do
not throw them away. Weigh the apricots and weigh an equal
amount of sugar. Add ½ pint of water to every pound of sugar.
Bring the sugar and water to the boil and add apricots. Boil
30 minutes. Remove the apricots with a skimmer and place in
clean, hot jars. Boil down the syrup until thick and pour over
the fruit. Break the shells of the stones and extract the nuts.
Soak them in hot water to remove the skins. Divide each nut
in half and place 4 or 5 halves in each jar. Let them stand uncovered for 2 days before covering with paraffin wax.

625. Peach Jam   *Confitures de pêches*

peaches   water
sugar

Place the peaches in boiling water for 30 seconds and then in
cold water. This will make it easy to remove the skin. Halve and
stone the peaches. Proceed as in recipe 624.

626. Apple Marmalade   *Marmelade de pommes*

Follow directions for French Applesauce (503). Pour the hot
sauce into clean, hot jars and cool before covering with paraffin
wax.

627. Apricot Marmalade   *Marmelade d'abricots*

apricots   sugar

Peel and stone the apricots. Measure the fruit. For every pound
of fruit use 1 lb. of sugar. Let the apricots and sugar stand

in an earthenware bowl for 24 hours. Cook gently until the
fruit becomes brilliant. Test by placing a little on a cold plate.
If it jells in a moment or two, it is ready. Stir often to prevent
burning. The marmalade should be cooked in 30 or 40 minutes.
Pour into hot, clean jars. Use the stones as in Apricot Jam (624).
Let it stand until cooled. Cover with paraffin wax.

628. Greengage Marmalade

Marmelade de prunes de reine-Claude

greengage plums   water
sugar

This marmalade is made like Apricot Marmalade (627). Do not
peel the plums and do not use the stones.

629. Plum Marmalade   *Marmelade de prunes*

plums   sugar

This marmalade is made like Apricot Marmalade (627). Do not
peel the plums and do not use the stones.

630. Bar-le-Duc   *Confitures de groseilles de Bar*

Wash the currants. Remove the seeds carefully with a toothpick or goose feather. Do not break the skin of the berry. Weigh
the fruit. For every pound of fruit measure 1½ lbs. of sugar.
For every pound of sugar allow ½ pint of water. Boil the sugar
and water until it registers 250°F. or until it reaches the *hard-
ball stage* (see recipe 635). Skim the syrup and add the currants.
Boil 2 minutes and pour into clean, hot, porcelain jars. Keep
forcing the berries down into the syrup until they no longer
float on top. Do not try to make too much of this at one time.
It takes care to make it, but the result is delicious.

631. Melon Rind Jam   *Confitures d'écorce de melon*

Peel thick slices of melon rind and cut into 1-inch pieces. Weigh equal amounts of sugar and melon rind. Add enough water to keep the sugar from scorching and heat in a heavy saucepan. Stir until the sugar is dissolved. Add 1 teaspoon of lemon rind for every pound of sugar. Cook 2 hours over low flame. Place in clean, hot jars and let it stand 2 days before covering with paraffin wax.

632. Burgundy Jam   *Raisiné de Burgogne*

dark blue or black grapes   pears

Wash and stem the grapes. Heat the grapes over a low flame to extract the juice. Just before it reaches the boiling point, remove from the heat and strain the juice through a strainer or cheese-cloth. Boil the juice down to half its original quantity. Stir often. Peel, quarter, and core the pears. Simmer in the grape juice until tender. Take care not to let the jam burn. Pour into clean, hot jars and let it stand 2 days before covering with paraffin wax.

633. Candied Quince Paste   *Pâte de coings*

Peel, quarter, and core ripe quinces. As the quinces are prepared, place in cold water so that they will not darken. Cover with cold water and boil until they are soft. Put in a strainer placed over a bowl. Use the juice to make Quince Jelly (616). Weigh the drained quince and weigh an equal amount of caster sugar. Pound the sugar and fruit together with a pestle or potato masher. Line the bottom of pie plates with this mixture $\frac{1}{8}$ inch thick. Let it stand 4 or 5 days before cutting into narrow strips.

The strips may be stored in a covered jar and used as a candy or garnish. It will remain good for a year.

634. Candied Apricot Paste   *Pâte d'abricots*

Follow the directions in the preceding recipe substituting apricots for the quinces. Spread the paste $\frac{1}{4}$ inch thick. When it is dry cut into narrow strips. Each layer should be separated by a piece of wax paper and it should be stored in a dry place.

635. Sugar Testing

A thermometer is very useful in sweet making. However, sugar can be tested by putting a little of the hot sugar syrup into cold water and testing the sugar between the thumb and finger. Sweet and syrup recipes call for different stages of consistency. The following table is helpful in determining these stages.

238°F.	thread stage	*le filet*
240°F.	soft ball	*petit boulet*
244°F.–250°F.	medium ball	*boulet*
270°F.–290°F.	hard ball	*grand boulet*
290°F.–310°F.	brittle	*grand cassé*

636. Fondant

1½ lbs. sugar   ½ pint water

Boil the sugar and water to the soft-ball stage or approximately 240°F. Wash down the sides of the pan with a wet pastry brush to prevent the sugar from sticking. When the sugar has reached the proper stage, pour on to a well-oiled enamel table top or marble slab. Let the syrup cool. Work the syrup with a broad spatula, turning in the edges towards the centre. The syrup will become creamy and white. The fondant may be flavoured with almond or peppermint oil. It may be used as a coating for strawberries or cherries or may be coloured and shaped into little sweets. It may also be placed in a covered jar and stored until needed.

637. Pralines

1½ lbs. sugar
1 gill water

1 lb. almonds, hazel nuts, or pistachio nuts

Blanch the nuts in boiling water for 2 minutes. Place in cool water and peel. Boil sugar and water until it registers between 244°F. and 250°F.—the medium-ball stage. Add nuts and cook 3 minutes. Pour on well-oiled marble slab or enamel top table. Cool before breaking into pieces.

638. Caramels   *Bonbons au caramel*

10 ozs. sugar   ½ pint thick cream

Boil the ingredients in a heavy pan. Stir often and wash down the sides of the pan with a wet pastry brush to prevent crystallizing. Boil to the medium-ball stage (244°F.–50°F.). Pour into a well-oiled, square cake tin and cool. Cut into small squares with a sharp knife.

639. Chocolate Caramels   *Caramels mous au chocolat*

10 ozs. sugar
½ pint cream

¼ lb. grated chocolate

Combine ingredients and follow instructions in preceding recipe.

640. Nougat   *Nougat*

½ lb. almonds   8 ozs. sugar

Blanch almonds by dropping them into boiling water and then
removing the skins. Melt sugar in a heavy frying pan. Add the
almonds, which have been coarsely chopped. Stir for a moment
and pour on a well-oiled marble slab or enamel-top table. Cool
before breaking into pieces.

641. Chocolate Truffles   *Truffes au chocolat*

6 ozs. chocolate   1 teaspoon vanilla
6 ozs. butter   cocoa
8 ozs. caster sugar

Melt the chocolate and butter in the top of a double boiler. Add
sugar and stir until the sugar is well blended. Add vanilla and
if the mixture is too dry add a little cream. It should be firm
and moist enough to form into small balls. Roll the little balls
in cocoa and place in individual sweet papers.

642. Tea   *Thé*

The secret of making good tea lies not only in the choice of tea but in the brewing of it. Allow 1 teaspoon of choice tea leaves for 3 teacups of water. Fill the teapot with hot water before making the tea. Pour out the water and put in the tea leaves. Pour fresh boiling water over the leaves. Serve with milk or thin cream, lemon, or rum.

643. Coffee   *Café*

Allow 1 generous tablespoon of freshly ground coffee for every coffee cup of water. Tante Marie recommends the 'drip method.' Pour $1\frac{1}{2}$ cups boiling water through the coffee and when it has filtered through, add the rest of the water. Coffee should be made just before serving.

644. Café au lait   *Café au lait*

Café au lait is made with coffee extract. It is not, as is generally supposed, ordinary coffee mixed with milk. To make the extract allow 2 tablespoons powdered coffee and 1 teaspoon chicory to ½ pint of water. Filter it as in making 'drip' coffee. The extract may be made in quantity and kept in a covered jar or bottle. Use 1 to 2 tablespoons of the hot extract with ½ pint of hot milk.

645. Hot Chocolate   *Chocolat*

3 1-oz. squares of cooking choco-   3 pints milk
    late   6 to 8 tablespoons sugar

Melt the sugar and chocolate in the top of a double boiler. Add 1 pint of the milk and stir until the mixture is smooth. Add the rest of the milk and beat with a rotary beater until frothy. Serve very hot. Serve a bowl of Sweet Whipped Cream (523) with the chocolate.

646. Hot Rum Punch   *Punch pour soirée*

3 teaspoons tea   1 lemon, sliced, peeled, and seeded
boiling water   1 lb. sugar
grated rind of 1 lemon   1 quart of rum

Place the tea leaves in a mixing bowl. Add lemon rind, the slices of lemon, and sugar. Pour 2 pints of boiling water over the tea leaves. Cover and let it stand 30 minutes. Strain and add the rum. Reheat but do not let it boil. Serve in large, stemmed wine glasses.

Qui a bu n'a point de secrets.

647. Hot Wine   *Vin chaud*

1 quart red wine (Bordeaux type)   1 small piece of cinnamon stick
10 ozs. sugar   lemon slices

Heat the wine, sugar, and cinnamon stick to boiling point. Just
before the wine reaches the boiling point remove the cinnamon
stick and pour into stemmed wine glasses. Place a slice of lemon
in each glass.

648. Lemonade and Orangeade   *Limonade et Orangeade*

lemons or oranges   cold water
sugar

Allow ½ lemon or 1 orange (or both) and 2 ozs. sugar to each
glass of water. Slice the lemon or orange quite thinly and remove
the seeds. Place in a large bowl and add sugar and water. Let
this stand 2 hours before serving. Serve with cracked ice.

649. Cold Grog   *Grog froid*

1 lemon   2 teaspoons brandy
2 ozs. sugar   1 glass ice water

Press the juice from the lemon and mix with sugar and brandy.
Add to ice water. This makes a good summer drink.

650. Hot Grog   *Grog chaud*

Place a slice of lemon in a thick glass. Add 1 teaspoon sugar.
Fill ¾ full with boiling water. Add a measure of brandy or rum.
Serve very hot.

T

651. Russian Punch   *Punch à la russe*

2 bottles of champagne   1 lb. sugar
1 large fresh pineapple, peeled and   ½ pint kirsch, rum, or cognac
    cut in pieces

Combine the ingredients in a large silver punch bowl. Touch
with a lighted match. Let it burn until the punch is hot—a matter
of a few moments—and pour into punch glasses. There should
be a piece of pineapple in each glass.

652. American Punch   *Punch à l'américaine*

Combine the ingredients of the preceding recipe. Stir until the
sugar has dissolved and add a large quantity of cracked ice.
Serve very cold.

There is a real economy in making liqueurs at home. They will not be as good as commercial liqueurs but they will be very good and will serve the same purpose as those bought from the wine dealer.

Liqueurs should be brilliantly clear. This is achieved by very careful filtering. It is best to use filter paper instead of cheesecloth since the liqueur is apt to take on a taste of cloth.

TANTE MARIE

(Note:—Where pure alcohol is not available, gin may be used in its place.)

653. Black Currant Liqueur   *Cassis*

1 lb. black currants
2 quarts of pure alcohol

6 ozs. sugar

Wash and stem the currants. Crush them a little and place in a heavy crock. Add the alcohol and cover tightly. If half the recipe is made, a 2-quart preserving jar may be used. Cover and let it stand in a cool dark place for 2 months. Filter the juice and add the sugar. Put back into clean crock and let it stand 3 days before bottling.

654. Curaçao   *Curaçao*

6 tangerines	1 gill water
1 quart cooking brandy	4 teaspoons sugar
1 lb. sugar	

Peel the tangerines and let the skin dry until almost brittle. Place the skins in a wide-mouthed jar and cover with brandy. Cover the jar. Let it stand 2 or 3 months. When it is time, filter the liqueur. Combine water and sugar and boil for 2 minutes. Skim and cool. Caramelize 4 teaspoons sugar by heating it in a heavy frying pan until dark brown. Add both sugars to the filtered liqueur. Mix well and bottle.

655. Gin   *Genièvre*

2 ozs. juniper berries	1 lb. sugar
2 quarts pure alcohol	1 gill water

Pour alcohol over very ripe juniper berries. Let it stand in a covered crock for 6 weeks. Filter the liqueur. Heat sugar and water until the sugar is completely dissolved. Skim the syrup and add to the liqueur. Mix well and cool thoroughly before bottling.

656. Orange Blossom Liqueur   *Liqueur de fleurs d'oranger*

¼ lb. orange blossom petals	4 lbs. sugar
2 quarts of pure alcohol	½ pint water

Cover the orange blossom petals with alcohol and let the mixture stand in a covered crock for 6 weeks. Filter the liqueur. Combine sugar and water and bring to a full rolling boil. Skim the syrup and add to the liqueur. Cool thoroughly before bottling.

657. Apricot Brandy *Noyau*

apricot stones	10 ozs. sugar
1 quart pure alcohol	½ gill water

Fill a jar half full of cracked apricot stones. Fill the jar with alcohol and cover. Let it stand 6 weeks. Shake the jar once a week. Boil the sugar and water 2 minutes. Skim and mix with the liqueur after it has been filtered. Cool thoroughly before bottling.

658. Brandied Fruits *Fruits à l'eau-de-vie*

4 lbs. raspberries	sugar
2 lbs. strawberries	domestic brandy
2 lbs. cherries	

Wash and pick over the fruit. The cherry stems should be clipped if they are very long and the strawberries should be hulled. Weigh the fruit and weigh an equal amount of sugar. Place a layer of cherries in the bottom of a wide-mouthed jar or crock. Cover with sugar and place a layer of strawberries on the sugar. Cover this with sugar and place a layer of raspberries on the sugar. Continue this process until the crock is ¾ full. Cover the fruit with brandy and seal tightly. Let this stand for 1 month. This makes an excellent sweet in itself or may be used as a sauce for ice cream.

659. Brandied Candied Fruits *Fruits confits à l'eau-de-vie*

2 lbs. candied fruits (plums, apricots, peaches, or pears)	cooking brandy

Place the fruit in a crock or jar. Cover with brandy. Seal and keep in a cool dry place for at least 2 weeks before using.

660. Brandied Cherries   *Cerises à l'eau-de-vie*

cherries   cooking brandy
sugar

Choose perfect cherries that are not too ripe. Clip the stems
of the cherries if they are very long. Place the cherries in a
jar or crock. Cover with brandy and seal the jar or crock tightly.
Let this stand 3 weeks before adding sugar. Allow 1 lb. sugar
for every quart of brandy. Mix well and cover again. It is important that the jar be hermetically sealed. Let the cherries stand
2 months before using.

English Index

(*For* French index, *see page* 303.)

French Index

TABLE des MATIERES